# THE MANY FACES OF
# SANDINISTA DEMOCRACY

This series of publications on Africa, Latin America, and Southeast Asia is designed to present significant research, translation, and opinion to area specialists and to a wide community of persons interested in world affairs. The editor seeks manuscripts of quality on any subject and can generally make a decision regarding publication within three months of receipt of the original work. Production methods generally permit a work to appear within one year of acceptance. The editor works closely with authors to produce a high quality book. The series appears in a paperback format and is distributed worldwide. For more information, contact the executive editor at Ohio University Press, Scott Quadrangle, University Terrace, Athens, Ohio 45701.

Executive editor: Gillian Berchowitz
AREA CONSULTANTS
Africa: Diane Ciekawy
Latin America: Thomas Walker
Southeast Asia: James L. Cobban

The Monographs in International Studies series is published for the Center for International Studies by the Ohio University Press. The views expressed in individual monographs are those of the authors and should not be considered to represent the policies or beliefs of the Center for International Studies, the Ohio University Press, or Ohio University.

# THE MANY FACES OF
# SANDINISTA DEMOCRACY

*Katherine Hoyt*

*Ohio University Center for International Studies*
*Monographs in International Studies*
*Latin American Series, Number 27*
*Athens*

© 1997 by the Center for International Studies, Ohio University
Printed in the United States of America
All rights reserved
02 01 00 99 98 97   5 4 3 2 1

The books in the Center for International Studies Monograph Series
are printed on acid-free paper

*Library of Congress Cataloging-in-Publication Data*

Hoyt, Katherine.
    The many faces of Sandinista democracy / by Katherine Hoyt.
        p.   cm. — (Papers in international studies. Latin America
    series : 27)
    Includes bibliographical references and index.
    ISBN 0-89680-197-7 (alk. paper)
        1. Nicaragua—Politics and government—1979–1990. 2. Nicaragua—
    Politics and government—1990–  3. Democracy—Nicaragua—History.
    4. Political participation—Nicaragua—History. I. Title.
    II. Series.
    F1528.H69  1997
    320.97285—dc20                                                    96-43208
                                                                                    CIP

*Cover photographs by Cliff McCarthy.*
*Large photo:* Rural mother with her children,
near Matagalpa 1995
*Inset photo:* Liberation Day Celebration, Jinotepe
Sunday, July 3, 1988

*Cover and text designed by Chiquita Babb*

# Contents

# Preface

I first went to Nicaragua in 1966 as a clinic secretary and interpreter on the SS *Hope Hospital Ship*. I ended up marrying a Nicaraguan pediatrician and living there for sixteen years. (We also lived for two years in Santiago, Chile, from 1968 to 1970.) I had three children, taught English, did volunteer work, and, during the revolutionary struggle from 1977 to 1979, was active in the Red Cross and in human rights work. After the revolutionaries took power in 1979, I worked for the Sandinista government, first as a social worker in a day care center and later as the translator for the legislature. Since returning to the United States in late 1983, I have worked for organizations involved in Central America solidarity activities and received my doctorate in political science from Rutgers University. I am presently co-director of the Nicaragua Network Education Fund in Washington, D.C. (In early 1996, I wrote a short series of articles for the *Nicaragua Monitor* called "Thirty Years of Memories" to commemorate these past three decades of involvement with the people of Nicaragua. Folks who read it began to pressure me to write my "memoirs." Perhaps that will be my second book!)

The decision to write a political theory book about Nicaraguan thought on democracy was a natural result of a love of political philosophy combined with a continuing concern for Nicaragua and a strong commitment to democracy. It also rose from the conviction that there is significant political theory being produced in the Third World that is ignored in academic circles in the United States. Once my decision was made, the enjoyment I have derived from working on the project has not diminished.

I spent several months in the early part of 1994 interviewing in depth more than two dozen leading Sandinista figures. These interviews I taped, transcribed, and translated for use in this book. I tried to obtain as wide a variety of political opinions as possible. In addition, my research included the examination of previously published speeches, interviews, articles, and books by Sandinista figures that present their views on the aspects of democracy I wanted to cover in the study. My goal was to give the Nicaraguans their voice as thinkers on the subject of democracy. This is therefore a work on political thought, not on comparative politics.

I am indebted to many people who helped me with my research in Nicaragua, including the personnel at the Centro Regional de Investigacion y Estudios Sociales (CRIES), especially Barbara Stewart; Carlos Pacheco at the Centro de Estudios Internacionales; Octavio Corea and Carolina Espinoza at FUNDECI; Coleen Littlejohn at CAPRI: Sonia Cano at the Sandino Foundation; Dr. Ricardo Zambrana of the staff of Sergio Ramírez; Ricardo Zambrana Jr. at IPADE; and José González for arranging the interview with Orlando Núñez Soto. I would like to thank all the Nicaraguans who agreed to be interviewed and who, in several cases, spent some hours answering my questions. Victoria Morales has provided me with many valuable books on Nicaragua throughout the years. Thanks are due to the staff of the Nicaragua Network Education Fund in Washington for the use of its library and for its encouragement and support. Heartfelt thanks for their encouragement and constructive comments go to Stephen Eric Bronner, Robert Kaufman, and Pedro Caban at Rutgers University, Arthur McGovern, S.J., at the University of Detroit-Mercy, and David Close of the Memorial University of Newfoundland. The suggestions of my daughter, Victoria Gonzalez, a budding scholar of Latin American women's history, were especially useful. Many thanks also to Thomas Walker and Mary Gillis, and Gillian Berchowitz at Ohio University Press.

My husband, Benjamin Rigberg, not only provided the "year of grace" in which this work was researched and written, but came out of retirement as a college professor himself to read every word and offer invaluable editorial advice. No words of thanks are enough. My parents, Paul and Charlotte Hoyt, have supported me in so many ways through the years and have my heartfelt thanks. And my children, Victoria, Bayardo, and Paula Gonzalez, make me very happy when they tell me how proud they are that their mom has finished her Ph.D. I thank them as well. It is to all these family members that this work is dedicated.

THE MANY FACES OF
SANDINISTA DEMOCRACY

# Introduction

The Sandinista Revolution in Nicaragua attempted to combine in a creative fashion three essential aspects of democracy:

1. political, or representative, democracy—that is, a republican form of government which is based on periodic elections with universal suffrage;

2. participatory, or mass, democracy—a regime which incorporates citizen participation in popular organizations in civil society; and

3. economic democracy—under which there is an equalization in the ownership of wealth and the people exercise control over the use of the resources of the nation as well as over the type of economic system under which they live.

These can be called the three legs of the stool of Nicaraguan revolutionary democracy. They are not the only aspects of democracy that could be examined but they have been the most important in the Nicaraguan case. In the formation of the theoretical and practical project for each leg, there have been conflicts, differences of opinion, and changing evolution in policy and thought. The development of the democratic project in Nicaragua has been analyzed in books and articles by many scholars[1] but there has been little study of the theories behind the practice—that is, of the thought of Sandinista party members, government officials, writers, intellectuals, researchers, and teachers on these significant issues. Undoubtedly this has been due to the fact that the Nicaraguans were too busy carrying out their revolution to write about it and probably also in part due to the limited public discussion of differences among Sandinistas before the electoral defeat of 1990.

But now that the Sandinistas are democratizing their party (rather a long time after they democratized the nation), discussion among party members is occurring everywhere: from radio commentaries to op-ed pieces in the newspapers to journal articles and books. To these can be added the always available, though rather sanitized, speeches and interviews which, taken together, now make possible an analysis of the Sandinista revolutionaries as democratic theorists.

The Sandinista experiment has been important because it has addressed one of the most perplexing and difficult questions around democracy and socialism since Lenin's time: What is the role of political or representative democracy in a society where the working class is not in the majority? Marx, assuming that workers *would* soon be in the majority (although in truth they never were, even in the industrialized countries), emphasizes winning "the battle for democracy." A republican form of government was seen as a necessary first step toward socialism, which is democracy extended into the economic sphere as well as the political. Lenin's model for countries without large industrial working classes is to place power not in the hands of a democratically elected workers' government but in those of a vanguard party in control of the state bureaucracy. Competing organizations, trade unions, and peasant associations are either eliminated or brought under control by the state. Because Third World revolutionaries saw that their countries more closely approximated prerevolutionary Russia than they did Germany or Britain, they took up Lenin's model of the vanguard party, and along with it, the Soviet concepts of limited elections and mass organizations subordinate to the party, along with an emphasis on economic equality. Most Third World "vanguardist-statist movements" (as Nicaraguan Orlando Núñez Soto calls them) rejected the forms of what they call "bourgeois democracy," maintaining that such forms were sterile and easily manipulated by powerful capitalists and outside imperialist forces in order to preserve their interests. But even before *perestroika* and Gorbachev's call for "democracy and more democracy," the Nicaraguan Sandinistas were able to retrieve democracy for the Third World socialist movement. They produced a unique and, in the end, possibly untenable combination of democratic and vanguard principles. The examination of this combination of ideas and how it arose will be the concern of this work.

Other scholars have approached the ideology of the Sandinista revolution from different directions. Much has been written about the influence on the Sandinistas of José Carlos Mariátegui of Peru and Antonio Gramsci of Italy, about their respect for national traditions while emphasizing the importance of internationalism. Giulio Girardi, Donald Hodges and others affirm that the thought of Sandino, Marxism, and the theories embedded in the Christian theology of liberation are the three most important aspects of Sandinista thought. The Sandinista National Liberation Front (FSLN) described its policies while in power as having been based throughout on political pluralism, mixed economy, and international nonalignment while at the same time speaking of the transition to socialism.

While all this is interesting and true, probably the major contribution of the Sandinista revolution for Latin America and the Third World was to bring together *in practice and in theory* representative, participatory and economic aspects of democracy. In the present work, each of these aspects will be examined in turn. The forms that each was to take in Nicaragua were worked out painfully over time. Orlando Núñez Soto said in 987:

> [W]e can say that the Sandinista revolution symbolizes the real possibility that the flag of democracy can be torn from the hands of the right and flown in a revolutionary fashion by the left; that political pluralism strengthens the participatory democracy of the workers and of the popular majorities of a society; that not only does it not impede

the tasks of the revolution but that it strengthens that work; [and] that a mixed economy does not impede the defense of the interests of the workers or of popular hegemony in the economic sphere.[2]

While each of the three aspects of democracy to be examined here will be scrutinized from the point of view of political theory, there has been more theoretical writing about participatory democracy and economic democracy than about political democracy. As a result, there is more in-depth discussion of the ideas of individual thinkers in the chapters that treat the former. The paucity of thoughtful writing on formal democracy is due to the fact that, during their underground period and in the early years of their period in government, the Sandinistas regarded "bourgeois democracy" with its periodic elections as an unnecessary and, in the case of Nicaragua at least, probably dangerous practice. Ironically, what many in Nicaragua regard as the major achievement of the Sandinista revolution, the formation of democratic institutions and the laying down of the custom of one party turning over power to another after democratic elections, has been examined least by Nicaraguan writers and thinkers. Therefore the chapter on political democracy will weave the story of Sandinista practice and theory together in one single narrative, while in the chapters on participatory and economic democracy a historical background will be presented before an examination in detail of several theorists. As research proceeded on this work, it began to seem desirable and even necessary to add a chapter on the evolution toward democracy of the FSLN Party itself, although this was not part of the original plan. It is in this final chapter also that the impact on Nicaragua of recent developments in Eastern Europe will be appraised.

# 1

## The Setting

### HISTORICAL SURVEY

The indigenous peoples of the Pacific side of Pre-Columbian Nicaragua[1] were sedentary and farmed the land while those on the Caribbean side were hunting and gathering peoples. The former spoke a language similar to Nahuatl of the Aztecs of Mexico and were related to other groups of meso-American Indians. On the Caribbean side of Nicaragua, the indigenous peoples were related to the Chibcha and Arawak of Colombia and the islands of the West Indies. Columbus, on his last voyage in 1502, landed in Nicaragua at the mouth of the Matagalpa River on the Caribbean coast. The country was conquered by Francisco de Córdoba, who founded, in 1524, the colonial cities of León and Granada. Nicaragua remained under the Spanish crown as part of the Captaincy General of Guatemala under the Viceroyalty of New Spain (Mexico) until independence was declared in 1821. Immediately following independence, Nicaragua became a part of the Mexican empire under Iturbide and then a part of the short-lived Central American Federation. Even though the Federation broke up in 1838, aspirations for Central American union live on—a party supporting that end even ran in the 1990 Nicaraguan elections.

Nicaragua's unique geographical position heightened interest in the country by larger outside powers, including the United States. The country has coast lines along both the Pacific and the Caribbean/Atlantic. The navigable San Juan River connects the Caribbean with Lake Nicaragua, a large body of water that extends to within ten miles of the Pacific coast, reducing the land bridge from one sea to the other to just a few miles (compared with the thirty-six–mile length of the Panama Canal). In the continuing search by great powers for an isthmian crossing, the country could serve to provide easy access from one ocean to the other. The possibility of such a crossing in Nicaragua appears to have intrigued foreign leaders as early as the 1840s or even before, predating the focus on Panama.

Since the country's independence was achieved in 1821, Nicaragua's internal history has been one of incessant strife between the conservative and liberal parties.[2] In most areas of the country the latter consisted of urban shopkeepers and professionals while the former group was made up of the landed aristocracy and the peasants who depended upon them. In one of these Liberal-Conservative party struggles, the Liberals invited American filibusterer (freebooter) William Walker (1824–1860) to fight for them. Walker defeated both Conservatives and Liberals, declared himself president and ruled Nicaragua from 1856 to 1857, before being defeated by a combined Central American force.

Important changes occurred after the elections of 1893, when the Liberals came to power, introducing reforms in accord with the liberal philosophy of the day. These included the separation of church and state, the establishment of civil marriage and divorce, the secularization of schools, the assurance of freedom of religion and freedom of contract for women. The Liberals pushed peasants and Indians off their land, which had been held either individually in small plots or in common, in an effort to develop large coffee holdings in the northern and central highlands. Foreigners were encouraged to invest in the planting of coffee. While in the main agriculture previously had been oriented toward domestic consumption, emphasis now began to shift toward large-scale production of coffee for export, thus making Nicaragua dependent upon the price-setting structures of foreign capitals. Liberal Party members and foreign investors grew wealthy from monopolies and special concessions.

When the United States decided to build an inter-oceanic canal through Panama rather than through Nicaragua, the Liberal government under President Zelaya began negotiations with Britain and Japan in the hope that one of them would build a Nicaraguan canal, finally conceding to a British firm the right to construct and operate an inter-oceanic railroad across the country. The American Secretary of State, Philander Knox, was furious, and intervened to support an opposition group in its successful effort to overthrow Zelaya. The Conservative Adolfo Díaz, who was to serve U.S. interests for many years in Nicaragua, became president. American bankers now gained financial control of the country.

There was considerable discontent about the U.S.-imposed government of Díaz and, in 1912, Liberal generals Luís Mena and Benjamin Zeledón led a rebellion against him. When the rebels began seizing American-owned ships on Lake Nicaragua and converting them to war vessels, President Díaz requested aid from the United States. On August 4, 1912, the first U.S. Marines landed at Corinto. Except for one brief period in 1925–26, the Marines did not evacuate Nicaragua until January 1, 1933. Mena surrendered in September 1912, but Zeledón fought until he was defeated, captured, and executed. A teenager from nearby Niquinomo named Augusto Sandino was, according to folklore, among those who watched the humiliating sight of General Zeledón being dragged through the streets of Masaya by U.S. Marines.

Civil war erupted again in the late 1920s and U.S. President Calvin Coolidge sent Colonel Henry L. Stimson to mediate the conflict. In 1927, all the leaders of the parties in conflict agreed to an armistice except one: Augusto Sandino, now a Liberal general. Sandino demanded the withdrawal of the U.S. Marines as a condition for laying down his arms. When that condition was not met, he returned with his men to his headquarters in San Rafael del Norte, sending a cache of arms into the mountains to be retrieved later. He told his soldiers: "We are alone. The cause of Nicaragua has been abandoned. Our enemies from this day forward will not be the forces of the tyrant Díaz, but rather the Marines of the most powerful empire in history. It is against them that we are going to fight. . . . Those who are married or who have other family obligations should return to their homes."[3]

In July of 1927, Sandino led eight hundred men to take the city of Ocotal. A Sandinista victory would have been complete if the Marines had not sent airplanes to bomb the city, forcing Sandino's troops to flee. The city was wrecked by the bombardment. The bombing from the air of towns and villages by U.S. planes was repeated all over the north. It forced Sandino to change his tactics to "a special system of war that we have taken to calling 'little war' (guerrilla)."[4]

International solidarity with Sandino was enormous. He received messages of support from Nehru and from Madam Sun Yatsen in Asia. In Latin America, Diego Rivera, José Vasconcelos, Victor Haya de la Torre, José Carlos Mariátegui and many others were among his supporters. From Europe, French Communist Henri Barbusse sent Sandino a long letter that was a source of great pride to the guerrilla leader: "General, I send you this greeting in personal homage and in that of the proletariat and revolutionary intellectuals of France and Europe. . . . You, Sandino, general of free men, are performing a historic indelible role."[5]

Liberal Party candidate José María Moncada won the U.S.-supervised elections of 1928, just as Henry Stimson had promised when Moncada signed the peace agreement. The U.S. Marines stayed on to continue the fight against Sandino and to train a National Guard, that is, to Nicaraguanize the war. Sandino's struggle was now no longer fought under a Liberal banner; rather he began to emphasize broader objectives than mere Yankee withdrawal. This may have been the result of the influence of Salvadoran Communist Augustín Farabundo Martí, who joined Sandino in the mountains. Or possibly Sandino had merely revealed another layer of his true beliefs.

Communist organizations like the Anti-Imperialist League of the Americas and the Mexican-based Hands off Nicaragua Committee worked very hard to build support for Sandino but in return they expected him to adopt the program of the Communist International. Sandino was himself committed to a broad anti-imperialist front at the very same time that the Comintern (in the wake of the Chinese debacle of 1928) was abandoning that strategy in favor of a hard line against social democratic and socialist parties.[6]

A thorough reading of Sandino's writings, interviews, and other studies, shows that Sandino used both a class and a race analysis of Nicaraguan society. He lived in a period of intellectual effervescence in Latin America in which the idea of anti-intervention was combined with a glorification of the Indian and of Indo-Hispanic culture. Various forms of populism, anarchism, socialism, communism, and spiritualism also made headway among the people. Sandino believed that Indo-Hispanic unity was necessary to throw off the yoke of oppression from the north but that Indo-America would merely light the fuse for a revolution of all the oppressed peoples of the world. When this revolution triumphed, injustice would be destroyed and "love, with its favorite daughter, Divine Justice" would rule the earth.

Sandino and his "small, crazy army," as Chilean poet Gabriela Mistral called it with affection and respect, fought the U.S. Marines and the new National Guard that they had trained until the Marines finally left in 1933. Then, Sandino negotiated a peace with Nicaraguan president Juan B. Sacasa that allowed him to keep an army of one hundred men and gave his people wide tracts of land along the Coco River, near Honduras in the north, to farm in cooperatives. But, for the new American-named head of the National Guard, Anastasio Somoza, there could not be two armies in Nicaragua. In February of 1934, when Sandino was in Managua and after he had dined with the president, Sandino was picked up by thirteen of Somoza's men and taken to the airport where he and two of his generals were assassinated. A few days later, the National Guard massacred almost all of Sandino's supporters in the mountains of the north. Carleton Beals of *The Nation* wrote after a visit to

Sandino: "The few people we met were all loyal Sandinistas, fleeing ever deeper into the wilderness. . . . They were seeking safety, a new patch of ground to clear. But one and all, they vowed never to give up the struggle, and if necessary, [to] pass it on to their children."[8] When the early fighters of the FSLN went into the mountains, they found the old Sandinistas who had survived and they learned from them how to flee from the National Guard and how to live in the jungle.

The Somoza regime was a traditional paternalistic family dictatorship (a father succeeded by two sons) that began in 1936, when Anastasio Somoza overthrew his uncle, President Sacasa, three years after the end of the American intervention. The officers of the National Guard soon became wealthy through corruption. Because of its corruption and brutality, the National Guard was feared and hated by much of the populace. When the Sandinista National Liberation Front (FSLN) was founded in 1961 by Carlos Fonseca, Tomás Borge, Sylvio Mayorga, and Santos Lopez, the Somoza family had been in power in Nicaragua for twenty-five years and had survived several earlier revolutionary onslaughts. The founders of the FSLN had broken away from the Moscow-line Socialist Party, which held the position that the time was not ripe to take up arms against the dictatorship. The "party line" of the Communist Party of the Soviet Union (CPSU) regarding Latin America was at the time one of collaboration with existing regimes, whatever their nature, presumably to maintain undisturbed the good trade relations which the USSR was then enjoying. For the Sandinistas, the Cuban revolution had indicated that new tactics were necessary and that armed revolution could be successful. For a time the Sandinistas adopted *foquismo* (attributed by French writer Regis Debray to Che Guevara), which is the belief that a few fighters in the mountains of a country may, in the short term, inspire a successful rebellion against an oppressive government. But that period ended with the Battle of Pancasán in August of 1967, in which several important leaders, including founder Sylvio Mayorga, were killed by Somoza's National Guard. Instead, the Vietnam example seemed to be the one to follow: a long popular struggle with the formation of a nation-wide subversive network of students, workers, and peasants.

Meanwhile, still in the 1960s, the Alliance for Progress and the growth of the Central American Common Market had resulted in some economic growth and industrialization in Nicaragua. There were economic opportunities for an elite, but very few economic benefits trickled down to the great masses of people. Rather, more and more peasants continued to be pushed off the land in order to expand holdings for export crops. Two-thirds of the children of the country were malnourished.[9]

The Managua earthquake of December 1972 and its aftermath brought to a head the problems that had been developing between the Somoza family and sectors of the bourgeoisie. Somoza (by this time it was Anastasio Somoza Debayle, the second son of the original dictator) stole a substantial portion of the earthquake assistance from the U.S. and other countries and made lucrative deals for his family on state rebuilding projects. By doing so he exacerbated the anger and resentment felt by sectors of the rich when the Somoza family business empire violated previous understandings about which parts of the economy were to be dominated by the family and which were to be left for other economic groups. These entrepreneurs found that their economic expansion was blocked when the voracious Somoza family moved into "their" areas. It was a uniquely Nicaraguan bottleneck. Some of the rich began to look for a way to get rid of Somoza. Alienation grew among all classes. According to Jaime Wheelock, one of the original nine-man National Directorate of the FSLN, organization in the cities increased beginning in 1973, when the FSLN began to make connections with members of the Christian movement that was working in poor neighborhoods in several cities, but most especially in Managua. Wheelock states: "This movement was composed of university students, generally from the bourgeoisie, who expressed their social concerns and their rebellion through a religious commitment. They gave up the comforts of their homes and went to live in humble houses in poor neighborhoods, generally as part of a parish or connected with the work of a priest."[10] Thus began the close collaboration between the FSLN and progressive Christians that would continue to characterize the Sandinista revolution, often to the chagrin both of traditional Marxist-Leninists and the hierarchy of the Catholic Church.

After several years of "accumulation of forces in silence," as it is commonly called, the FSLN burst upon the scene in December of 1974 with the capture of the house of a prominent supporter of Somoza by a commando of Sandinistas. A party for the United States ambassador was ending; the ambassador and his wife had already left. A number of high government officials and diplomats were taken hostage. Anastasio Somoza had to free Sandinista political prisoners (including Daniel Ortega, who had been imprisoned for seven years), turn over a large sum of money to the commando and publish Sandinista proclamations in the government media in order to free his brother-in-law and other prominent hostages. The government then declared a state of siege and began a period of repression in the interior of the country that was to arouse the condemnation of international human rights groups during the next few years.

Beginning in 1975 differences concerning strategy were dividing the Sandinistas. The Front split into three tendencies (tendencies are groups within a Marxist-Leninist party that have differences over strategy but which still maintain identification with the organization as a whole) based on disagreement about how to attain state power. The traditional Prolonged Popular Warfare Tendency continued to maintain that the armed struggle is long and difficult and involves the establishment of support committees throughout the nation but mainly in the countryside. The Proletarian Tendency believed that organizing should center around the new agricultural and industrial proletariat. Within the Prolonged Popular Warfare Tendency, a group arose that called for mass multiclass insurrection in the cities supported by the organization of a regular army to fight the National Guard. This group was known as the Third or Insurrectional Tendency. History was to bring all three tendencies together under the leadership of the third strategy.

From October 1977 to July 19, 1979, the Nicaraguan people lived through an insurrectionary period of constant military and political conflict. In October 1977, within the space of a few days, the FSLN attacked several important posts of the National Guard, something they had never done before. In November of the same year, Pedro Joaquín Chamorro, prominent opposition figure and newspaper editor (and husband of Violeta Barrios de Chamorro, who became president of Nicaragua in 1990), gave a speech in which he called on all Nicaraguans, including the FSLN, to unite in the name of democracy for the overthrow of the dictator. On January 10, 1978, Chamorro was assassinated. News of the murder provoked bloody uprisings in several cities; the most noteworthy being that of the indigenous community of Monimbó, Masaya. In August of 1978, an FSLN commando group of approximately forty people dressed in National Guard uniforms seized the National Palace along with the Chamber of Deputies then in session. Before leaving the Palace, the commandos demanded and received a large sum of money and the release of a number of political prisoners, including FSLN founder Tomas Borge. On their way to the airport, the guerrillas were witness to a great outpouring of public support as hundreds of people lined the highway to see them off.

By this time, many rich members of the opposition were giving large amounts of money to the FSLN for the purchase of arms. They expected that the Sandinistas would serve as cannon fodder in what they saw as an inevitable all-out war against the Somoza regime. In August and September of 1978, there were Sandinista-sponsored uprisings in five major cities. Somoza forces extinguished them one by one, concentrating the full brutality of the National Guard on each city in turn.

The Sandinistas worked within a system of alliances that made possible their eventual victory in July of 1979. Nicaraguan Orlando Núñez Soto says that the FSLN had the vision and the capacity to bring together armed struggle against the repression of the dictatorship with the open struggle of groups within a civil society. He continues:

During those last years, the FSLN began a policy of broad democratic and antidictatorial alliances including the National Patriotic Front (FPN) that brought together all the anti-Somoza forces, and the People's United Movement which was made up of the left forces of the country. In this way, the national liberation struggle was made inseparable from the national democratic struggle. Nevertheless, as the alliances became broader and more democratic, as it became ever more necessary that all the people rise up against the National Guard, in that same measure, the work was done to guarantee that the political-military preparations were made and that popular hegemony over the movement was maintained.[11]

U.S. President Jimmy Carter's policies of nonintervention and support for human rights meant a breathing space for the revolution. The social democratic governments in power in Latin America —Venezuela and Costa Rica—and those in Europe looked favorably on the removal of Somoza and helped the Sandinistas. Others who played an important role were Omar Torrijos of Panama, Jose López Portillo of Mexico, Michael Manley of Jamaica, Maurice Bishop of Grenada, and of course Fidel Castro of Cuba. Carlos Andrés Pérez of Venezuela and Rodrigo Carazo of Costa Rica, however, were reluctant dance partners, collaborating with the United States and other governments as well as with the Nicaraguan bourgeoisie in an effort to get rid of Somoza without the most radical Sandinistas coming to power.

The Sandinistas would not have been able to overcome these pressures if they had not been able to put an end to their division into three tendencies. At the end of 1978, a coordinating group for the Internal Front (Managua and nearby provinces) was set up, which included representatives of the three tendencies and in March of 1979, as a result of the efforts of the members of this coordinating group, the unity of the FSLN was announced to the public. A National Directorate was formed with nine members: three from each tendency. Tomas Borge, Bayardo Arce, and Henry Ruiz represented the Prolonged Popular War Tendency; Daniel Ortega, Humberto Ortega, and Victor Tirado represented the Insurrectional

Tendency; and Jaime Wheelock, Luis Carrión, and Carlos Núñez were from the Proletarian Tendency.

Carlos Núñez, who was a member of the coordinating group in Managua that brought the three tendencies together, remembered that moment in 1979, approximately three years and four months after October of 1975, when the FSLN's internal political crisis had exploded:

> Now, in this secret meeting, within a tremendously difficult political framework, with the people in the streets carrying out spontaneous actions either to protest or to attack the Somoza regime, we were finally able to announce to the world, to our enemy, to the mediators who wanted to continue to turn our nation over to the exploiters, to the organizations of the left that had expressed a lack of confidence in our organization, that Sandinista unity was the forceful step toward deepening the irreversible death agony of the dictatorship, toward opposing all the outrages. . . . At last concrete steps were being taken; at last reality was put before any political idealism [around the divisions]. This was the precise moment in which all our forces were preparing themselves to launch the attack against the enemy fortress.[12]

Humberto Ortega, who served as Defense Minister in the Sandinista government, emphasizes that for the revolution to succeed, three things needed to happen simultaneously. There had to be 1) a mass, popular uprising on a national level along with 2) a military offensive carried out by adequately armed Sandinista troops; and both of these had to be supported by 3) a national strike of both workers and owners of commerce and industry.[13] One or two of these factors had occurred several times during the previous two years but it was not until June 4, 1979, that all three converged. From that day in early June when the general strike began, until the Junta, led by Daniel Ortega, took over the government on July 19, there were six weeks of all-out war in which the dictator became weaker and weaker and vented his fury on the Nicaraguan people by bombing and strafing the cities with all their civilian population within. Thousands died and material damage was in the millions of dollars, but with the victory of the revolutionary forces, exhaustion was accompanied by a great sense of accomplishment and great hope for the future.

## SELF-DETERMINATION: THE
## PRECONDITION FOR DEMOCRACY

The Sandinistas always emphasized that a precondition for democracy was self-determination and they proclaimed themselves followers of Bolívar and Sandino in the cause of independence from outside interference and control. On various occasions they reminded the United States of the important part which its own struggle for independence from Great Britain played in the formation of its political ideas and practices. The Sandinistas believed that they too, like the emerging nations of Asia and Africa, which were struggling for independence from the European powers, were engaged in a colonial struggle to free themselves from United States domination. Victory in this neocolonial struggle was a precondition for the establishment of democracy. This was proclaimed by Daniel Ortega in 1989, in speaking before a symposium on democracy and revolution:

> When we speak of democracy and speak of revolution, we have to speak, in the first place, of the colonial policies of Europe. European colonialism threw all its power, with all its fury . . . at the peoples of America, of Africa, of Asia. . . . And against colonialism, which was the negation of the identity of the exterminated peoples, was the resistance of those peoples, which was followed by heroic struggles for independence, resistance which was directed toward achieving independence as the starting point for the achievement of democracy. Colonialism was the negation of independence and thus the negation of democracy.[14]

An end to the humiliating U.S. intervention in their country was, in the view of the modern-day Sandinistas as it had been for Sandino, a prerequisite for progress in all other areas. Decisions in any area, whether political, social, or economic had to be made in Managua, not in Washington. In a recent interview, Alejandro Bendaña, a former high-ranking Nicaraguan Foreign Ministry official with a Ph.D. in history from Harvard who is now director of a Managua think tank, examined the theoretical origins of Nicaraguan democracy, and explained that Nicaragua did not experience the European immigration at the end of the last century that brought revolutionary social theories to the United States, Mexico, and Argentina along with immigrants. He said that the most revolutionary, the most democratic Nicaraguans were the liberals. He went on further:

> It was a liberalism that could become radical at certain times but it was not based on the radical origins of liberalism: the French Revolution, the ideas of Rousseau. What made the Liberals [of Sandino's time] radical was the phenomenon of nationalism and U.S. intervention—radical in the sense that they began to connect the nation and democracy with anti-imperialism. . . . A theoretical analysis tells us that the self-determination and sovereignty of a nation are the preconditions for an effective democracy.[15]

Nicaraguan radical thought, therefore, has a great deal in common with early American radical thought. It was similar to those ideas penned by Thomas Jefferson and Patrick Henry, including the affirmation that the law of nature entitles nations to separate and equal status (Jefferson) and the slogan "Give me liberty or give me death" (Henry). The latter is almost identical with Sandino's "Fatherland or Death" and the Free country or death" of the FSLN. Sergio Ramírez, former vice-president of Nicaragua, has spoken of "the right our countries [of Latin America] have to change, and to choose freely the forms in which to carry out those changes."[16]

For Sandino, Nicaraguan liberation from United States intervention was necessary before the Latin American republics could unite in fulfillment of the dream of the liberator Simón Bolívar. Lenin's thoughts were similar, if expressed differently. Nationalism and the formation of nation states are a necessary complement to the development of modern capitalism[17] and thus a stage on the road to the unification of the world's workers and the coming of socialism. This similarity must have been evident to the FSLN from the beginning. Nationalism is not in contradiction to internationalism but rather a precondition for it.

Once the basic precondition of national sovereignty to democracy was accepted, the Sandinistas were ready to proceed to the discussion of other aspects of democracy. This also put them into conflict with the United States government which, through many decades and in violation of its own history, insisted both on denying the precondition of sovereignty to Nicaragua and then on imposing its own specific forms of democracy.

Nicaragua's historical experience with democracy was not productive of any genuine political tradition. While the forms were familiar to everyone, the substance was viewed as yet another form of corruption and exploitation. Elections had been held, presidents held office, legislatures passed laws, judges ruled on cases in line with the constitution. But the elections were perceived as rigged, the laws and judicial rulings as self-serving. Any different theory that based itself on the negation of formal democracy was not unwelcome.

# 2

## Political Democracy?

### INTRODUCTION

Consideration of what democracy is and how to make it work goes back to the ancients in western thought. Democracy for the ancients meant rule by the people, which the rich often saw as equivalent to rule by the rabble or the mob. While Nicaraguans proudly count themselves a part of the Third World, western thought is most definitely a component of their tradition through the "madre patria," Spain. "Platón" and "Aristóteles" and some of the modern democratic theorists are a part of the training of most educated Nicaraguans. But what would democracy look like in Nicaragua? Would it be similar to that practiced in the United States, with regularly scheduled elections and legal protection from arbitrary government actions? In actuality there was great difference of opinion. Time had not stood still for Latin America. The writings of Locke, Rousseau, and Jefferson remained present in the thinking of intellectuals. But the nineteenth and twentieth centuries had brought new forms of social understanding in the writings of Marx, Bakunin, Plekhanov, Kautsky, Lenin, Gramsci, and many others. While this is not the place to trace the origins and development of socialist thought in Latin America,[1] it is important to note that none of the states of this area was left unaffected by European radical thought and movements. The success of Lenin and Stalin in transforming a backward nation into a superpower also had profound repercussions, as did the Cuban model, and the efforts of Ernesto "Che" Guevara.

With respect to formal democracy, some Sandinistas adopted the orthodox Marxist-Leninist position that the revolution had placed the workers and peasants permanently in power. If elections were to be held, they could not be elections to dispute that possession of state power by the vanguard party representing the oppressed people of the nation. Other Sandinistas felt elections and other liberal forms were unnecessary in themselves. However, if they were needed to ensure continued international support, especially from the European social democratic governments, then Nicaragua would have them.

A third group of Sandinistas was philosophically committed to elections and to the stated FSLN policy of political pluralism. The free expression of ideas was not foreign to socialism, they believed, and the people could better choose what course they wanted for their government if they were exposed to a full range of ideas. Elections were a check on the government and on how well it represented the needs and interests of the people as the people themselves saw them. They were also a check on bureaucratization and corruption in government. Sandinistas who held this view had not necessarily abandoned the vanguard concept. The FSLN was, for those Sandinistas, a true vanguard, representing the general will of the people. It could submit itself to free and fair elections, and be confirmed in power. There were conflicts and controversies around these three positions, as we shall see.

## REJECTION OF "BOURGEOIS" ELECTIONS

Nicaraguans had disappointing experiences with political democracy before the 1980s. In the nineteenth century, elections were held and presidents of the Liberal and Conservative Parties succeeded each other in office. But one party turned over control of the state to the other party only when removed from office by force of arms. In the twentieth century, U.S. intervention and supervision of elections became the rule. General José María Moncada laid down his arms in 1927 based on the promise from the U.S. representative, Henry Stimson, that he would have the presidency of the country in 1928. And sure enough, U.S. supervised elections of that year were "won" by General Moncada.

Carlos Fonseca, late founder of the FSLN, summarized this state of affairs: "1928—electoral farce in the country, controlled directly by the North American interventionists."[2] Fonseca maintained that this long-standing experience of electoral fraud predisposed Nicaraguans against elections and toward armed rebellion.

Two months before he was assassinated in January of 1978, Pedro Joaquín Chamorro, who was not a Sandinista but who was involved in some armed rebellion himself against the Somoza regime, called for unity among all opposition groups, specifically including the FSLN, and said that:

> Throughout the forty years of the dictatorship we have lived a legal fiction of democracy and a reality of dictatorship. Power has not resided in the people, not in the popular will, but in fraudulent electoral processes protected by the repressive force of arms . . . in the interests of a ruling minority. And in the same way, the popular will as a legitimate source of political power has been misrepresented . . . all the institutions and procedures of democracy have been corrupted.[3]

Such was the Nicaraguans' experience with political democracy in their own country and it made them cynical about formal democracy. The Sandinistas also analyzed democracy in countries where it was supposedly functioning properly and found reasons for doubt in those cases as well. Daniel Ortega said in 1989 that there was still a long way to go before those countries reached true democracy because they opened up their system only to "certain political forces," keeping others from participating and, in effect, exercising a political monopoly. Participation was limited to those groups who could afford access to monopoly-controlled media. He stated:

They may say: "We have freedom; here we have a press that says what it wants, television is private and says what it wants." That is a lie. How many people can pay for television time? . . . That opportunity is only given to those parties with the most resources, to those parties which are part of the dominant system. . . . They are the ones who are also the owners of the communications media. . . . A third force does not have the opportunity to express itself, to get its message to the people. That is a privilege only for the few. And that is not democratic.[4]

On August 23, 1980, during closing ceremonies for the National Literacy Crusade, the National Directorate of the FSLN, announced that elections would be held in 1985. It was the FSLN that announced the elections, not the Government Junta. Indeed, the document emphasizes that it was the National Directorate of the FSLN which had decided to install a Government Junta and it now resolved that the economic and social backwardness and destruction of the nation demanded that that Junta continue to lead the government until 1985. The document states further, "once and for all, [that] democracy does not begin with elections. It is a myth to want to reduce democracy to that."[5]

For the Sandinistas, a true democracy required more than elections. It began, according to the FSLN, "in the economic order, when social inequalities begin to weaken, when workers and peasants improve their standard of living."[6] Most of all, it required the participation of those masses of people who in the past had been denied access to the public life of the country. The arena in which democracy would be carried out would change from that of electoral campaigns to those of the activities of the popular organizations of the revolution: union halls and neighborhoods. It was the view of the Sandinistas in the years immediately following the triumph of 1979 that once the people were fully involved through their organizations in the economic, cultural, and defense projects of the nation, they would then become interested in participating in another aspect of democracy, that is, electoral democracy.[7]

The August 1980 statement mentioned above was read by Humberto Ortega at the closing rally. In addition, in his own words, he expressed the early Leninist position which rejected bourgeois elections and which seemed to foreshadow, if not an eventual one-party system, then certainly restrictions on the political pluralism that the revolution was proclaiming at the time. The document continues:

> [T]he Sandinista Front believes that constructive criticism is the only kind of profitable criticism. Disagreement and pluralism will continue to be essential components of the Sandinista democracy, but [the FSLN] points out that the criticisms that ought to be taken into account are, fundamentally, the criticisms made by the workers, because these are the most disinterested, genuinely sincere and revolutionary, kinds of criticism.
>
> The National Directorate of the Sandinista National Liberation Front reaffirms to the Nicaraguan people and to the world that the revolutionary process taking place in our country cannot go backward, and that it will continue onward to the ultimate consequences. There must not be the slightest doubt that it is a revolution that is underway today. . . . Once in power, the Sandinista Front, as the true vanguard and leader of the Nicaraguan people, decided to install a Government Junta. . . . In January 1984, the Junta of the Government of National Reconstruction must, in order to make this victory of the people of Sandino a reality, begin the electoral process by which Nicaraguans will determine the Government that will continue to build the New Nicaragua.

Ortega then added:

> As you will all have understood, the elections that we are talking about are very different from the elections sought by the oligarchs and traitors, the conservatives and liberals, the reactionaries and the imperialists, the "gang of villains," as Sandino called them. . . . Our elections will not be those imposed by the American gringos. They are the elections imposed by you, by the working people, by the Sandinista youth, by the National Directorate of this Revolution. Such will be our elections. Remember that they are elections to improve the power of the revolution, but they are not a raffle to see who has power, because the people have the power through their vanguard, the Sandinista National Liberation Front and its National Directorate.[8]

This is as clear an enunciation of the role of the vanguard party as any Leninist might have wished. Today, of course, many Sandinistas are critical of this vanguard position, a few even to the degree of forgetting and/or discarding their early, still-valid criticism of formal democracy as being easily manipulated by economically powerful forces. Most continue to give high priority to participatory and economic democracy but have now elevated political democracy to equal importance. Sergio Ramírez has said that, at the beginning of the revolution, there existed in Nicaragua what he called the "hegemonic vocation" of a vanguard power that had to lead the society, and that had a monopoly on power. He maintained that it was the economic and social realities of the nation which broke that mold and opened up to the Sandinista Front the realization that the only possibility for Nicaragua was true political pluralism. The idea that the revolution had put the workers and peasants in power forever was part of a now-closed period, one which reality had destroyed.[9]

The analysis of former FSLN National Directorate member Luís Carrión is similar. He has said:

> I think that we on the left underestimated and minimized for a long time the importance of political democracy and in some ways this was reflected during our period in government when, in spite of a platform of political pluralism, the Sandinista government closed political spaces. And we even justified this closing of political space for other forces and organizations. This contributed to the feeling on the part of some sectors of the country that they had no other way to express their opposition to the Sandinista government than by joining the counterrevolution.[10]

In other words, the FSLN's position of minimizing political democracy contributed to the growth of the counterrevolution. But, because there was always a kernel or undeveloped seed of democracy at the core of the FSLN—arising out of Marx, social democratic, and New Left thought and the empowering ideas of Liberation Theology—the party was able to put into place democratic forms at the same time that its commitment to them was still evolving. There was the geopolitical factor of the U.S. military and economic power that would have been launched against them to an even greater degree if a more authoritarian model had been followed, as well as the desire to maintain the support of European social democratic governments. Some Sandinista leaders had spent time in the Soviet Union and did not like the repressive atmosphere they found there. FSLN National Directorate member Henry Ruíz has talked about the time he spent at Patrice Lumumba University in Moscow, mentioning that things were never what they seemed, that people could never trust others or take things at face value.[11] Those who came to the FSLN from the revolutionary Christian and student movements were accustomed to open forms of participatory or electoral democracy.

## ACCEPTANCE OF ELECTIONS AS TACTICAL

In 1983, within the Council of State (the corporatist-style legislative body that functioned before the elections of 1984), a debate was going on concerning the clauses of the Political Parties Bill. Most vanguard movements which had taken power in other countries had established one-party systems and many persons inside and outside the country assumed that the Sandinistas would try to do the same. The 1980 announcement of elections and the preliminary introduction of a political parties bill in November of 1981 had indicated that such might indeed be the case. The question before the Council of State was: What should be the object or goal of political parties within the revolutionary process? There was a certain excitement and nervous sense of expectation about the question and its two possible answers. If the FSLN decided that opposition political parties could aspire to the winning of state power through elections, then this would be breaking the mold for Marxist-Leninist parties which had achieved power through force of arms. If, on the other hand, the FSLN decided that such parties could not aspire to political power, then this would give the lie to the Sandinistas' much-touted political pluralism and "prove" that they were indeed totalitarian. And, while that was an important factor to consider, an even more important factor was the question of faith in the people. How could a vanguard party continue to claim to represent the people if it did not trust them to freely confirm it in power? And, in 1983, the FSLN had absolute faith that it could be confirmed in power by the people.

Mariano Fiallos, a member of the committee of the Council of State, which considered the Political Parties Bill, and later head of the Supreme Electoral Tribunal (now Supreme Electoral Council), answered the following question, posed by an interviewer in 1983:

> Q. With relation to the Political Parties Law, how should the goals and purposes of political parties be defined within our revolutionary process?
>
> A. In my judgment, the political parties within our revolutionary process have the right to aspire to obtain political power by the legal means set out in the laws or to aspire to participate in the exercise of political power if they do not have the strength to gain power alone. Besides this, they must be parties that respect the fundamental principals of the revolution such as anti-imperialism, democracy and popular power. I believe also that they should not support the return to the political system of the Somozas or to any similar political system. Within this framework, political parties should be able to act with all the liberty that the circumstances permit.[12]

Although it took time to convince the Sandinista leadership of this position, this was finally done. Angela Rosa Acevedo, who was a representative in the Council of State in 1983 and later legal counsel to the Sandinista bench in the National Assembly, says that there was a very "big" discussion within the majority Sandinista delegation at the time. Acevedo says that it was decided that the parties should have the status in the society of public entities, but others wanted them to be able to aspire to political power. That, of course, is the nature of political parties, she maintains. Many did not understand this at the time.

We felt that we, in the Sandinista Front, were the owners of the revolution. At least we were able to realize that if we were going into elections, it was not in order to steal them; we were not the owners of the elections. And if parties were going to exist, it was for this, for elections. Commander Carlos Núñez, Dr. Mariano Fiallos, Father Alvaro Arguello, Dr. Milú Vargas and a number of other lawyers were able to clear things up for [the leadership of the] Sandinista Front about why parties existed in a democracy. And with this debate we were able to delegitimize the epithet that was always thrown at us that we were totalitarian. . . . It is true that this debate was very wide-ranging, because it is true that many people wanted a Leninist revolution and that others wanted a national, Sandinista revolution. . . . I think that it was lucky that we never had to define ourselves. The [contra] war kept us out of these great ideological debates. The important thing was to survive.[13]

Dora María Téllez, who was a vice-president of the Council of State at the time the Political Parties Bill was being considered, remembers that discussion as having been more ideological and she maintains that the debate over the significance of elections continues to the present day. According to Téllez, the FSLN has lived always within the contradiction between the theoretical platform of a vanguard party pursuing a goal of socialism and the reality which is Nicaragua. The great virtue of FSLN practice has been its ability to respond more to the national reality than to the "romantic model," as she calls it. For her, those within the FSLN who now, from the opposition, say that the Sandinista Front is not an electoral party and that it is not important to win elections, are making the same argument as those in 1983 who did not want other parties to aspire to political power. The result of this attitude now, she says, would be to see the FSLN soon reduced to a minority "sect." For Téllez, the discussion remains the same as in 1983: "Are elections or are they not the mechanism for deciding who should exercise political power in each period of time? I believe that they are and besides, it was the revolution that established this system in Nicaragua. Nobody had established it here before. We could say that the revolution gave birth to it. . . . So the same discussion goes on. It takes a different turn, but, in essence, it's the same problem."[14]

In an attempt to justify to the left the continued Sandinista commitment to political pluralism (including elections) and to a mixed economy, Humberto Ortega said in a 1984 interview that "We cannot in a voluntaristic way give drastic and profound blows to forms of basic production, to forms of social accommodation, to private productive sectors which give strength to the country, in the name of mechanical, orthodox criteria. We must definitively base our perspectives on the actual world, the world from which we cannot escape."[15]

Many persons on the left questioned the Sandinista's apparent compromise with their former position, which had been critical of "bourgeois" elections. In other words, not only was there pressure from the right within Nicaragua and from the United States for the specific type of elections that were wanted, and from friendly social democratic governments and parties in Europe for other types of democratic forms, but there was also pressure from the Marxist-Leninist left both within and without Nicaragua not to go along with elections in which the revolution could be voted out of power. The Sandinista leadership denied that its decision on elections had been in response to pressures from anyone outside the nation.[16]

But, in a speech that became famous because it was recorded and made its way into U.S. government hands, Bayardo Arce defended the above-mentioned Sandinista decision before a meeting of the Socialist Party of Nicaragua, which at the time (1984) followed the "Moscow-line." In that speech, Arce made a convincing argument for the tactical necessity of holding elections. He saw elections as a low-cost way of defending the revolution against U.S. aggression. One could argue, he continued, that these elections were a nuisance. But the revolution's policies of international nonalignment, mixed economy, and political pluralism had made it possible for it to gain much international support. These policies carried with them certain commitments, one of which was the holding of elections for the purpose of electing a constituent assembly which would write a new constitution for the nation. Yes, the elections could be seen as a nuisance. What a revolution really needs, he said, is the power to act.

It is the power to act that is "precisely what constitutes the essence of the dictatorship of the proletariat—the ability of the [working] class to impose its will by using the means at hand [without] bourgeois formalities." But, given the international situation of U.S. attacks, elections could be turned to the advantage of the revolution. Arce said that the United States demanded three things of the Sandinistas. These were that they abandon intervention in other countries, that they abandon their ties with the Soviet Union and other socialist countries, and finally that they become democratic. Abandoning internationalism (that is, support for other revolutionary struggles) and abandoning self-determination were out of the question, but bourgeois democracy contained elements that could serve the interests of the revolution:

> [T]he superstructure aspect, democracy as they call it, bourgeois democracy, has an element which we can manage and even derive advantages from for the construction of socialism in Nicaragua. . . . The main thing about elections, as far as we are concerned, is the drafting of the new constitution. That is the important thing. The new constitution will allow us to shape the juridical and political principles for the construction of socialism in Nicaragua. We are using an instrument claimed by the bourgeoisie, which disarms the international bourgeoisie, in order to move ahead in matters that for us are strategic.[17]

Looking at the panorama of numerous mini parties without any grassroots base in the country, Arce assumed a Sandinista victory in the 1984 elections. He felt that, even without strong opposition, the elections would become something of a plebiscite on Sandinista governance. The Sandinistas would not change what they were doing in order to prepare for the elections. The people would vote to confirm agrarian reform with its confiscations, nationalization of the banks and foreign trade, adult literacy and free education, Soviet and Cuban advisors, and so forth. Arce said with tongue in cheek:

> Imperialism says that Sandinismo means totalitarianism, Sandinismo means Marxism-Leninism, Sandinismo means the spread of Soviet-Cuban influence, Sandinismo is an imposition on the Nicaraguan people. . . . The people will ratify, in a bourgeois-type exercise, this

Sandinismo, which is totalitarianism, which is Marxism, which is the end of freedom, which means the spread of Soviet-Cuban influence, which is everything that gobbles up little children.[18]

Not everyone within the FSLN agreed at this point that the party should hold elections. Some *compañeros* believed, according to Arce, that there was still a long way to go in terms of rebuilding the country before elections could be held. All the time and energy that would be used on elections would be better spent on defense and rebuilding the damage caused by the attacks of the counterrevolutionaries. However, the opposition of those Sandinistas did not mean that they were opposed to all elections, Arce said. "Our political reality," he maintained, "does not permit us to think in terms of a one-party system."[19]

Victor Hugo Tinoco, Vice-Minister of Foreign Affairs under the Sandinista government and now a member of the National Directorate of the FSLN, maintains that it was not hard for the Sandinista leadership and middle level cadres to accept the idea of elections because so many of them had been involved in student elections at the universities. He states:

> Although we in the Sandinista movement were strongly influenced by Marxist philosophy and more specifically by the Leninist idea of a single party . . . , although we did not like very much having to adapt to the idea of a democratic process, of elections in a multiparty system, it was not a big problem for the leadership or at the grass roots. Because, on the one hand we had alliances with intellectual currents which did not have such strong Marxist influence and, on the other hand, our Marxists came from the university sector, that is, the petit-bourgeois intellectual sector, and had had a lot of experience with periodic elections. So, for us it was not so strange or difficult to maintain revolutionary positions and move the revolutionary project along by means of elections. The Sandinista movement for ten years maintained control of the university student bodies through elections, in competition with political currents of the right, Social Christian currents, etc. So it was almost like translating that university experience onto the national scene. We were going to compete again against Social Christians, against the right, by means of a process of periodic elections,

that is, through the formal aspects of democracy. It was not so difficult.[20]

So, elections in which the opposition political parties would, in theory at least, be able to win government power, were accepted as useful. They were useful as a tactic for maintaining important internal and international support and, in an important sense, as part of revolutionary strategy in the struggle to institutionalize the revolution through the establishment of a new constitution of the republic. They were moved up several months in an attempt to undercut anti-Sandinista propaganda on the part of the United States. And on November 4, 1984, two days before the U.S. elections of that year, the Nicaraguan people gave the FSLN 67 percent of the popular vote. Opposition parties both to the left and the right of the FSLN were on the ballot. However, an important opposition coalition which was closely allied to the U.S. decided not to participate, and probably never intended to participate, in spite of ample Sandinista concessions to its demands. Recent analysis of abstention levels of 1984 in comparison with those of the 1990 elections have led some Sandinistas to believe that, if the opposition coalition *had* chosen to participate, the Sandinista margin would have been substantially less.[21] But the important thing was the elections themselves. They were free of fraud and declared by international observer groups to have been as fair as possible in a country at war.

## ELECTIONS ON PRINCIPLE

Alejandro Bendaña has stated:

> A good argument can be made that the democratic thought of the FSLN is to be found in the document that is known as the Constitution of 1986 [1987]. . . . There it is with its radical parts: participatory democracy, the idea of an army which is national and not exclusionary, and a very important part that says that we are going to work toward the elimination of exploiters, toward the elimination of the relationship exploiter-exploited. This is a way of saying socialism but

its presentation is conspicuously democratic, constitutional; nothing about a single party as was proclaimed in the constitution of the Soviet Union. . . . There is where you can find the set of beliefs of the FSLN.[22]

Nicaraguans seem to be basically agreed that it was in the process of writing the Constitution in 1985 and 1986 (which was proclaimed on January 9, 1987), that formal democracy truly came into its own and became valued in its own right within the Sandinista movement. The journal *Pensamiento Propio* interviewed Rafael Solís before the elections of 1984, when he was Secretary of the Council of State, and then again before the 1990 elections, when he held the same position in the National Assembly. Before the 1984 elections, in answer to the question "Why is the FSLN calling for elections?" Solís stated: "The celebration of elections in Nicaragua is a response to our need to keep our promises. . . . This does not mean that this is a question of principle for us. Our principles turn on the participation of the people at many other levels and through different mass organizations and through other instances of popular democracy."[23]

And in late 1989, in answer to a question about political pluralism, he said:

[T]he electoral campaign is proof that pluralism is functioning. It is true that in the first years of the revolution there were problems because we were still not clear if pluralism was a tactical or strategic policy. But now, nobody is in doubt that it is strategic: the revolution will be strengthened as a pluralist project [by the elections]. The FSLN has promoted two types of democracy: the representative that is carried out through a legislature, and participatory which has developed— and needs to be deepened—through a series of organizations which represent directly the different sectors of the population.[24]

In the interval between those two interviews, the National Assembly elected in those 1984 elections had gone through a complex consultative process in order to write a constitution which represented the broadest possible spectrum of public opinion. Three subcommittees of the Special Constitutional Committee visited countries in Latin America, and Western and Eastern Europe to study the constitutions of those nations. (The delegation to the U.S. was denied visas.) Others compiled the opinions of Nicaraguan political parties, trade unions, business and professional groups, religious denominations, and women's and youth groups around the issues that the members of those groups felt were important to address in the new document. It was not until after this had been done that the committee began writing the constitution. When the committee had prepared a document that had the support of the majority of its members, it was sent to the plenary which, in its turn, sent the document to a special Constitutional Advisory Commission. Public consultations were then held in which the proposed constitution was discussed at seventy-five public forums throughout Nicaragua. After the national consultations, the Advisory Commission met during August and September of 1986 and, taking into account the results of the public forums, the opinions of the Supreme Court and the Supreme Electoral Council, it suggested numerous changes in the proposed constitution.

The document was debated for ten weeks in the National Assembly by the representatives of all of the seven political parties which had participated in the 1984 elections. For the opposition parties, that participation had been the subject of substantial internal controversy. The FSLN held bilateral dialogue sessions with the parties before the debate began. In the end, the parties decided to participate, evidently agreeing with an Independent Liberal Party leader who said, "The worst error a democratic party can make is to absent itself from participation in a democratic opening."[25]

The President of the National Assembly, Carlos Núñez, summarized this constitutional debate:

> [T]he representatives . . . distinguished themselves by the seriousness of their speeches and by the motions they presented . . . supported by historical, sociological, political and legal analysis. As a general rule, we observed flexibility and respect between those of different ideological currents. . . . We have left record of all the votes, the unanimities, majorities, and votes against in the minutes and reports . . . 48 articles were approved unanimously, 117 articles by 80 percent of the vote; 19 articles with 70 percent of the vote.[26]

With some differences, the constitutional model chosen was

Latin American. Dora María Téllez said in 1992:

> We grabbed hold of the Latin American model: strong executive, a rel-
> atively weak legislature, with its legislative function quite limited
> (some more than others), direct territorial election from party lists,
> typically Latin American, typical. Why? Because if you analyze the
> question of where we got our political institutions you will see that we
> inherited them from the Spanish Crown. When independence oc-
> curred, there was no rupture in the institutions. . . . What existed was
> an authoritarian model that functioned through the Crown and after-
> wards through the Creole government. . . . Here we have not had a *par-
> liamentary culture,* what we have had is an *authoritarian culture* that is
> 500 years old where the one who is on top is the king, he who has con-
> trol over the lives and goods of everyone.[27]

With the adoption of the new Constitution, one begins to see
more references to the necessity for democratic forms in order to
advance the goals of the revolution in other areas. Orlando Núñez
Soto, the principal socialist theorist within the FSLN, who admits to
"always having been a radical in theory and practice"[28] on the subject of democracy, wrote in 1987: "[D]emocracy is not just part of
the class struggle and only for that reason to be unfurled by revolutionary sectors of the left, but along with that, democracy can only
favor the construction of popular power, social transformations
and the advance of the revolution."[29]

Núñez identified himself with those who made constructive criticism of actually-existing socialism and rejected those on the left
whose criticism ended in bitter anticommunism and in apathy with
regard to anything that smelled of revolution or Marxism. People
such as Reich, Marcuse, those of the Frankfurt and Budapest
Schools, as well as Gorbachev himself, Núñez wrote in 1988, have
confronted the verticalist and totalitarian tendencies of socialism
and reclaimed individuality and democracy in the face of an authoritarian past.[30]

Of course, the level of commitment of the FSLN to formal
democracy as part of the Sandinista project was not truly put to the
test until the elections of February 25, 1990. Those elections were

lost by the FSLN to a coalition of fourteen political parties, known by the acronym UNO for Unión Nacional Opositora, headed by Violeta Barrios de Chamorro, the widow of the slain newspaper editor, Pedro Joaquín Chamorro. The margin was 55 percent to 41 percent. On the morning of February 26, Daniel Ortega said in a speech to the Nicaraguan people: "[T]he government of Nicaragua will respect the popular mandate that flows from these elections. I consider that this is, at this moment, the principal contribution that we Sandinistas, we Nicaraguan revolutionaries, can make to the people of Nicaragua; that is to say, guarantee a clean, pure electoral process that lifts up our consciences and lights up, like the sun that shines today, the road to the consolidation of democracy."[31]

Although Daniel Ortega quickly and decisively made the decision to respect the electoral results, it obviously was a terrible, wrenching decision for him and for the FSLN leadership. The Sandinistas assumed that they had achieved ideological hegemony over the population and would be confirmed in power in spite of economic problems so serious that they would surely bring down any other democratically-elected government. They were devastated to discover that they had not achieved an ideological hegemony powerful enough to overcome such major barriers.

Dora María Téllez, always an astute analyst of her nation, wrote in 1991:

> Without any doubt, the FSLN developed a model for Nicaraguan society that was profoundly democratic, at the same time that we developed methods, forms and instruments as a party in the exercise of power that were in contradiction with the scheme that we promoted in the society as a whole. Parallel with the political pluralism that we, in fact, did develop, the FSLN grew after 1979 as a vanguard party with the consciousness of a vanguard party. In spite of having organized the electoral process of 1984, this step was not enough to overcome the contradictions between the political pluralism of the society and the single party idea of the FSLN. Political parties exist to aspire to political power. The elections that make this reality concrete enter into contradiction with the idea of permanency in power and with that of absolute power.[32]

When one analyzes the speeches of the time and the handwring-
ing analysis afterward, it appears that the leadership of the FSLN
and much of the rank and file of the party believed that, as the leaders of the Nicaraguan people in the struggle against the Somoza dictatorship, as those who had returned national dignity to the
country, and as the party that had finally brought free and fair elections to the nation (which they had freely and fairly won in 1984),
they were truly the vanguard of the people and that, in fact, they
reflected the general will of that people. The FSLN, they believed,
was a vanguard party that could win free elections and that did not
have to resort to dictatorial methods, because it represented, as Sandinista leaders said again and again, "the highest aspirations of our
people." Carlos Núñez said to a gathering honoring new FSLN militants in 1981: "[T]he Sandinista Front . . . is the soul of the Revolution, its undisputed strength, the energy that stimulates
transformation; it is the will of the people that assures that their demands are satisfied. The Sandinista Front, as a party, is the light that
guides the whole people on the path that leads to a promising future, to the promised land, longed for by the abandoned, by the dispossessed, by the hungry. It is vigor, honesty, wisdom, confidence; it
is the people represented by their best sons and daughters."[33]

Elections and other forms of representative democracy, which
had served the Sandinista student organizations so well in the universities, also served to advance the revolution on the national level.
Many Sandinistas failed to see the contradiction, noted above by
Dora María Téllez, between representative democracy and the vanguard concept of permanence in power. Lenin's statement of 1905,
which emphasizes that the workers' party must be "at the head of
the whole people," may be said to encapsulate this aspect of Sandinista thought: "At the head of the whole people, and particularly of
the peasantry—for complete freedom, for a consistent democratic
revolution, for a republic! At the head of all the toilers and the exploited—for socialism! Such in practice must be the policy of the
revolutionary proletariat, such is the class slogan which must per-

meate and determine the solution of every tactical problem, every practical step of the workers' party during the revolution."[34]

In other words, while they were breaking with Leninist practice, the Sandinistas felt they were putting into effect some aspects of his most revolutionary (and democratic) thought! The break with the Leninist model came reluctantly and partially, accompanied by the attempt to combine the mystique of the vanguard with formal democracy in the society as a whole. The discussion going on today is about how to modify the internal procedures of the FSLN as a party so that, with more democratic methods of work, it can in fact (and not just in fancy) reflect the will of a majority of the Nicaraguan people. At the present time the FSLN is certainly the largest and best organized political party in Nicaragua. There are those within what is known as "Sandinismo" who believe with Dora María Téllez that the vanguard concept must be abandoned. But there are still many who believe in some aspects of the vanguard party concept and rebel at the thought of becoming just another electoral party.

One can in conclusion cite the words of Orlando Núñez Soto, who believes that the socialist commitment to the objective interests of the majority must be maintained, but that that commitment must rest upon the consensus-building processes promoted by a democratic party. He says:

> We believe that we must analyze in greater depth the erosion of the vanguardist-statist model, as well as some of its limits in the present circumstances of the class struggle. At the same time we should not undervalue the potential of a revolutionary model of socialist orientation, in which a combination exists between the possibilities of a vanguard organization with the support of state power and a model based on the consensus that can be achieved by means of ideological hegemony within civil society. The electoral defeat of the FSLN does not lead us to search for a way to strengthen the vanguardist-statist model, for which democracy is an unnecessary and dangerous impurity, but rather to emphasize with even greater conviction the democratic qualities implicit in the Sandinista break with that model.[35]

SUMMARY

Sandinista thought on electoral democracy passed through three phases of development: from a minimizing of elections or outright rejection of them as "bourgeois forms" easily manipulated by capitalist interests, through acceptance of elections as tactically necessary and even useful, and finally to commitment to free and fair elections as a way of making government accountable to its citizens. The first announcement in 1980 of elections to be held in 1984 was accompanied by Humberto Ortega's statement that the elections would not be about which party holds power because, he said, "the people" held power through their vanguard, the FSLN. It seemed at the time of the announcement that the answer to the question with which this study began, that is, "What is the role of political or representative democracy in a society (aspiring to socialism) where the working class is not in the majority?" would be the Leninist answer. Power would not be placed in the hands of a democratically-elected government (a republic, as forseen by Marx, who believed, falsely as it turned out, that workers would soon be a majority in the industrialized countries) but rather in those of a vanguard party in control of state bureaucracy. However, at the time of the writing of the political parties law and the electoral law in 1983 and 1984, the decision was made that all political parties could aspire to government power. Elections were seen as tactically necessary and useful. Bayardo Arce's secret speech to the Socialist Party of Nicaragua reflected this outlook. This position was aided by the fact that the Sandinistas honestly believed that they could win democratic elections, which they did in 1984.

Most Sandinistas report, however, that the majority of party members did not develop a true commitment to electoral democracy until the writing of the 1987 constitution. Large numbers of people were consulted using public forums throughout the country and, if so much faith was to be shown in the people during the writing of the document, certainly the government structure chosen had to reflect that confidence. As Victor Hugo Tinoco pointed out, many Sandinista leaders were predisposed to accept elections since they had participated in student government in the universities, where, as members of organizations affiliated with the FSLN, they were elected to office in hotly contested elections against students representing other political forces in Nicaragua. This participation did not prepare the FSLN, however, for the loss of the 1990 elections to an opposition coalition. The Sandinistas had set up a democratic political system while retaining many of the beliefs and methods of work of a Leninist vanguard party that expects to remain in power indefinitely because by definition it represented the general will of the people. Dora María Téllez has been most incisive and self-critical in analyzing this phenomenon. She ties in the early rejection of elections by many party members with the reluctance to accept renovation in the party today. Téllez accepts representative democracy completely and rejects the Leninist alternative. Orlando Núñez Soto would retain some aspects of the vanguard model but would emphasize the democratic qualities of the Sandinista break with that model. He maintains that political pluralism (which represents the fact that Nicaraguan society is not a society of workers, but rather of peasants, workers, petit-bourgeois merchants, artisans, professionals, and others) strengthens democracy for the popular majorities. Not everyone in the party has recognized the value of democratic elections, but only by accepting representative democracy as a value in itself will the FSLN be able to move into the future with confidence. One cannot work to improve people's lives without giving those same people the opportunity to chose for themselves how they want to live. Formal electoral democracy, while it may not be sufficient in itself to assure free choice, is an undeniable prerequisite for this choice.

# 3

## Participatory Democracy in Action

### HISTORICAL BACKGROUND

*Popular Participation in the Anti-Somoza Struggle*
In order to understand what participatory democracy has meant in Nicaragua,[1] it is necessary to follow the history of the role of the popular or mass organizations in the struggle against the Somoza dictatorship and afterwards. Mass organizations have been defined as collective associations that represent the fundamental interests of a particular social or demographic sector of society.[2] In Nicaragua, the FSLN "gave birth to the mass organizations . . . as their mother and father," as Dora María Téllez has noted.[3] Several student organizations; the Farmworkers Association (ATC); AMPRONAC, which was a women's organization with the tongue-tying title of Association of Women Confronting the National Problem; the health workers and teachers unions; and the Civil Defense Committees (CDCs), organized mainly in poor neighborhoods—all of these played an important role in the overthrow of Somoza. Substantial numbers of people joined these organizations or worked with them in order to participate in that successful struggle. The feeling on the part of so many people that they had had a role in destroying the dictatorship shaped their attitude toward the popular organizations

and, in spite of later verticalist mismanagement of the groups by the FSLN party and the Sandinista state, they have survived and, in many cases, flourish today. After a survey of the history of these organizations, we shall look more closely at two of the most important of such movements.

Joaquín Cuadra points out that when, in October 1977, the FSLN attacked posts of the National Guard in several important towns simultaneously and "the entire political situation was shaken up, many social and political sectors sought to form connections with the FSLN. [This was difficult because of the clandestine nature of the Sandinista Front.] Confidence in its fighters was reborn. New structures were created to permit the participation of the masses in the struggle."[4]

The FSLN had more success organizing workers in the neighborhoods where they lived, however, than in the factories where they worked. Jaime Wheelock points out that the workers in a society with high unemployment, like Nicaragua at the time, consider their jobs to be of enormous importance for the security of their families and they are unwilling to risk losing those jobs just "to post a flier." Wheelock continues: "They thought that clandestine organizing in the factory would be detected and they did not have confidence in the ability of their fellow workers to resist the pressures of management and the National Guard."[5] Although health workers' and teachers' unions and several others became more militant, Sandinista industrial unions would not be established until after the victory in 1979.

Several Sandinista leaders (including Jaime Wheelock, Humberto Ortega, Dora María Téllez and Joaquín Cuadra) have remarked on the fact that the Sandinistas had to run to stay ahead of the masses of people who were revolting against the long reign of the Somoza family. The assassination of opposition newspaper editor Pedro Joaquín Chamorro in January of 1978 had been a detonator for a series of uprisings. Here is Humberto Ortega: "We went with the September [1978] insurrection because of the political situation that existed, in order not to let the people be massacred. Because the people, just as they had done in Monimbó [in January of 1978], were rising up alone."[6]

Ortega points out that the January uprisings were not entirely the work of the FSLN, that they were "spontaneous reactions of the masses" which the FSLN began to lead with its activists and military units. FSLN organizations grew as more and more people became convinced that 1) only by force of arms could Somoza be overthrown, and 2) only the FSLN was prepared to take up those arms. Besides the organizations listed above, there were militias organized massively among the people by all three tendencies of the FSLN. The Civil Defense Committees supported the militia by distributing leaflets with urgent information, putting aside food and water, making first-aid kits, organizing first-aid and sanitation courses, digging and preparing air-raid shelters, putting up barricades, digging trenches, and breaking holes in walls to make movement possible between houses without going out into the street.

Dora María Téllez points out the difficulty in combining popular spontaneity, with planning by the vanguard for a successful revolutionary movement:

> Spontaneous things have an advantage: you do not have to be measuring the state of enthusiasm of the masses. But when it is the vanguard that convokes a rebellion, you have to measure well, because you can be mistaken. You have to be able to measure if the state of enthusiasm of the masses corresponds, at that moment, to an insurrectional state, ready to sweep away the existing power structures. That is difficult to determine. The problem is the moment, and that is what Lenin indicated when the date of the insurrection was discussed within the leadership of the Bolshevik party.[7]

The Sandinistas gained the confidence of most of the people by being able to measure that moment and by looking after the civilians under their control. In this sense, retreat was a serious concern because, after a battle, the Sandinista combatants could leave a city with its collaborating inhabitants at the mercy of the "clean-up operation" of Somoza's National Guard. By September of 1978, that "clean-up" meant the murder of almost all males between the ages of 12 and 25. So the Sandinistas opted in some cases for retreat with civilians in tow. Téllez explains:

> Without a doubt it is difficult to retreat with hundreds, thousands of people like "Ruben" retreated from Estelí: with old people, women and children. It seems crazy to retreat with so many people, but how are you going to leave the people behind? You have to make a very difficult decision. "Ruben" decided to retreat with half of Estelí for the jungle. I do not know if that is the best solution. . . . [I]n other cases, who knows if it would be the best. Because that strategy has a disadvantage which is that those people are without arms and you have to feed them. But there is one great advantage and that is that the people do not lose faith in their vanguard because it did not leave them to die alone.[8]

The major retreat with civilians in town Téllez mentions is the famous June 28–30, 1979, "*repliegue*" from Managua to Masaya which continues to be commemorated each year with an all-night twenty-six kilometer walk. Somoza was brutally bombing the neighborhoods of Managua and the Sandinistas decided that they had to get their many militia members and supporters who needed to receive militia training out of the city. Six thousand people made the trek from Managua to already-liberated Masaya, where civilian militia could be trained in safety and the struggle could continue, as it did in all the regions of the country, until the July 17 departure of Somoza and the July 19 victory and march into Managua.

### The Popular Organizations and Sandinista Power

Because so many people had taken part in one way or another in the overthrow of Somoza, they felt they had a stake in the revolution. Many of them joined the popular organizations in order to continue their participation in the change that was taking place in their country. Even if they had not been members of the FSLN before the Sandinista victory (and there were few of those), they felt a sense of ownership in the revolution. In spite of verticalist mismanagement of the organizations, in which all activities were decided at the top and orders passed down to the members, and of which many Sandinista leaders were to be extremely self-critical in later years, the idea of popular ownership of the revolution was not lost. In fact, some said that the 1990 electoral loss was an attempt to bring the FSLN back to its original vision of popular ownership of the revolution, "to oblige the Frente to change, to recover the Frente as a revolutionary party, a party of the poor," as one Sandinista wrote.[9]

After the Sandinistas took power on July 19, 1979, they began the task of organizing a government and, at the same time, organizing the people to participate in the Sandinista version of democracy, which at the beginning was seen as participatory and economic with only limited priority given to aspects of electoral democracy. From the start, the popular organizations were given a contradictory mandate. In an April 1980 speech, FSLN National Directorate member, Carlos Núñez said: "With the guidance of the Sandinista Liberation Front the mass organizations will follow, we could say, two important paths. In the first place, our mass organizations must protect and work to strengthen the political project of the Revolution; and in the second place, they must be true instruments for the expression, channeling and reception of the most urgent demands of the masses."[10]

By this time, according to Núñez, there were 15,000 Sandinista Defense Committees (CDS) organized in neighborhoods in much of Nicaragua; 160,000 members of the new Sandinista Workers Central (CST) formed by 360 unions; 80,000 members of the Farmworkers Association; 15,000 members of the Luisa Amanda Espinoza Nicaraguan Women's Association (which had previously been the Association of Nicaraguan Women Confronting the National Problem) and a similar number in the 19th of July Sandinista Youth Organization. All this in a country containing a little over three million people.

These groups, Núñez said, should be capable of autonomously expressing the demands of the social sector that they represent, even to the point of using "unusual methods" if their demands are not heard. But, at the same time, Núñez added, those organized in revolutionary movements must sacrifice to support the revolutionary project and defend it from its enemies at any cost. Workers were called upon to develop a new attitude toward productivity in the publicly-owned businesses where some workers had shortened the working day, increased the number of holidays, and so forth, under the premise that the farm or factory belonged to the revolution. Núñez pointed out that it was precisely because the business belonged to the revolution and to the people that the workers should work harder to achieve its economic goals.[11] All workers and others who supported the revolution should participate in the activities organized by the mass organizations, such as the literacy crusade and the militias, in order to move the process forward.[12] Thus, from the beginning, the leaders of the mass organizations found that the needs and aspirations of their members were often at cross-purposes with the "higher" interests of the revolution as interpreted by the National Directorate of the FSLN.

*Leninism in Action*

After the seizure of power, each of the nine members of the National Directorate of the FSLN was assigned one or more of the mass organizations to supervise. In turn, the leaders of the organizations, appointed by the FSLN, looked to the National Directorate for guidelines as to what their principal tasks should be at any given moment. These leaders brought to the operation of their organizations the same verticalist methods of work that they had used within the FSLN during the period in which they had worked underground and were in imminent danger of discovery and death from Somoza's National Guard. FSLN founder Carlos Fonseca (who was killed in battle in 1976), had insisted, as had Lenin, that the need to protect members of the revolutionary organization from being captured or killed by government forces precluded the openness needed for full democracy in the party. A compromise was thus necessary. Fonseca wrote in 1975:

> As is evident, clandestine methods predominate in the activities of the Sandinista Front. But it is necessary that our clandestine methods do not excessively limit the political life of the organization. . . . [I]t is good to

bring out the points that reflect the political concerns of the organs and members of the party.... It should also be made clear that in attempting a constructive political life, neither should one fall into the other dangerous extreme which is ultra-democracy. Neither ultra-centralism, nor ultra-democracy. Our guide must be democratic centralism, and the conditions under which the Sandinista Front works demand that we do not neglect for a moment the necessary centralism.[13]

It is completely understandable that the FSLN would consider the vanguard model and democratic centralism (free political discussion of all issues within the party but iron discipline after decisions on those issues have been made) as the best model for the period of underground military struggle, but that model ran into problems when the time came for the Sandinistas to set up a democratic political structure. Certainly there was a contradiction between the view of participatory democracy promised to the popular organizations and the verticalist structure set up by the party, in which orders were "sent down" from the National Directorate of the FSLN to the organization leaders, who had been named by that very National Directorate.

"The 72 Hours Document," which circulated among FSLN members after the First National Assembly of Cadres in Managua in September of 1979, reiterated Fonseca's policy of democratic centralism and extended that verticalist method of work to the mass organizations. The document refers to the "proper role" of the mass organizations, which was "to see to it that the government policy set forth by the FSLN is carried out in every respect."[14] The document further states that:

We must realize that instead of aiming for an acritical approach, excessive democracy or excessive centralism, our organization should seek to function scientifically in accordance with revolutionary principles. . . . [O]ur goal is to have our people recognize their vanguard and undertake the tasks that it has set before them, the fundamental premise being that the FSLN is the legitimate leader of the revolutionary process. It is thus extraordinarily important to point this out to each politically and organizationally independent group and clearly explain the policy that the FSLN is pursuing to unite people around it, as well as the need for a single set of organizations of a clearly revolutionary stripe to make headway in the appointed tasks.[15]

The Sandinistas had taken over a country in ruins, with factories systematically bombed by Somoza forces from the air, and a lost cotton harvest for the 1979–80 season. It was true that the nation had to pull together in order to move ahead economically. But this document sounds almost as if it had been copied from one of Stalin's directives. Stalin said that the party must transform "each and every non-Party organization of the working class into an auxiliary body and transmission belt linking the Party with the class," and that "the highest expression of the leading role of the Party, here, in the Soviet Union . . . is the fact that not a single important political or organizational question is decided by our Soviet and other mass organizations without guiding directions from the Party."[16] It may seem too strong to compare Sandinista management of popular organizations to that of Stalin, but in light of subsequent criticism by Sandinista organizers themselves, it appears justified. A popular slogan of those early years was "National Directorate, give us your orders!"

One clear order from the top of the revolutionary leadership was for unity within the country's small working class. Then National Directorate member Luís Carrión addressed a May 1st gathering in 1981:

> The Sandinista Front supports the revolutionary slogan that says "For a single social class there must be one single workers' federation;" but we are convinced that this great united federation cannot and must not be the result of bureaucratic decisions or of agreements among leaders. This federation can only be the result of true unity at the base among the workers. We must begin forging it from below, as the workers begin to understand that unity is their only strength, that it permits them to defend and deepen their revolution, the Sandinista Popular Revolution. Long live the unity of the working class![17]

Thus the vanguard was to lead the working class in its formation of a consciousness that went beyond the interests of any one sector, beyond demands related to one workplace or one type of industry. The revolution, in these early years, was seen to be threatened internally by political foes opposed to the radical transformations carried out by the new Junta, as well as externally by the organizing of escaped National Guard members across the border in Honduras. Since Nicaragua had been invaded and occupied so many times and for so many years by the United States, intervention by the U.S. was seen as a possibility even before the election of Ronald Reagan at the end of 1980. The Sandinista leaders assumed that if the supporters of the revolution were not united, the enemies of the revolution could easily triumph before the new government consolidated its power.

The double mandate of the popular organizations was reiterated again and again: 1) defend the interests of the nation and the revolution as defined by the National Directorate of the FSLN; and 2) represent the particular interests of the members of the organization. The contradiction is apparent. The organizations were to represent the aspirations of their members but at the same time to make those members understand when the higher interests of the revolution as decided by the leaders might supersede their interests and needs.

### The Council of State

Especially confusing was the fact that, at the same time, that "National Directorate, give us your orders!" was an ever-more-popular slogan, an open vision of participatory democracy was being promoted by this same FSLN. The Council of State, called a *co*-legislative body because it shared some legislative functions with the Junta of National Reconstruction, was inaugurated on May 4, 1980. It included representatives not only from the existing political parties in the country, but also from all the mass organizations and unions as well as professional and business organizations, some of which were opposed to the radical reforms of the revolution. But, by adding nine Sandinista Defense Committee (CDS) representatives (three from Managua and one from each other region of the country) to the formula agreed upon with conservative political parties before the triumph of the revolution, the Sandinistas made certain that their representatives formed a solid majority.

Sergio Ramírez, at that time member of the Junta of National Reconstruction, gave the inaugural speech at the first session of the Council of State:

> This [revolutionary] struggle, these battles, this victory were all necessary so that here in this assembly these seats would be occupied by the peasants, workers, teachers, combative women, journalists, young people; these [indigenous] Miskitos, Sumos, and Ramas whose needs until now have been forgotten and postponed; the army which won this war, the armed forces of the people; the popular representatives of the neighborhoods, organized in the CDS; so that the political parties, allied with the revolutionary project in the Patriotic Front, and those who are not allied with this project; the guilds, the businesspeople participating in national reconstruction, would have seats here in this assembly.
>
> This is truly a democratic exercise, truly a pluralistic exercise, that was made possible only by the ceaseless struggle, sacrifice, and blood shed by our fallen brothers and sisters.[18]

Members of the Council of State from the Sandinista organizations did not always agree with each other because their constituencies had different interests. Even though FSLN representatives met every Wednesday to discuss and coordinate their tactics, the debates and votes on the floor of the legislature revealed those differences.

AMNLAE, the Women's Association, developed a methodology of open political forums at which bills that the organization was preparing to present in the Council of State were discussed in cities and villages around the nation. The meetings were open to any and all citizens, all spoke their minds and notes were taken of everything that was said for possible incorporation into the proposed legislation. This was done with the Family Support Bill and with the bill on parental authority. The first of these mandated financial contributions from absent fathers to their children and was strongly opposed by many Sandinista men who maintained that it would divide the nation into camps of men and women at a time (1982–83) when the people needed to be united for defense. The bill passed but was never signed into law by the Coordinator of the Junta, Daniel Ortega. In contrast, the second, the Parental Authority Bill, which had symbolic meaning but little in the way of practical implications in ordinary people's daily lives, was passed and signed easily. It changed previous law which said that fathers had sole authority over children and instead divided that authority between mother and father. For example, before its passage, in order for children to travel outside of Nicaragua their father had to give signed permission; after its passage, both mother and father had to give permission. Both bills were important to women, and symbolized the idea that the struggle for women's rights and equality in Nicaragua would now move ahead along with the attainment of economic equality for workers and peasants. Women's rights, Sandinista women believed, would not be postponed, as had happened in so many other revolutions that aspired to socialism.

### The Contra War Accentuates Verticalism

After the Sandinista victory in 1979, about four thousand members of Somoza's National Guard were imprisoned, but several thousand escaped to Honduras and to the United States. As time went on, the Sandinistas released about half of the guardsmen they had imprisoned because they could not be proven to have been involved in the worst crimes of the dictatorship. These men left for Honduras as well. Meanwhile, in the United States, the Republican Party platform of 1980 stated: "We deplore the Marxist Sandinista takeover of Nicaragua. . . . [W]e will support the efforts of the Nicaraguan people to establish a free and independent government."[19] Within a month of President Reagan's inauguration in January of 1981, former members of Somoza's National Guard were training in Florida to fight against the Sandinistas. National Guard camps in Honduras received U.S. financial support and training as well. In 1982, attacks across the border into Nicaragua began. Several bridges in the north of the country were destroyed by bands of "contra-revolucionarios"—soon to be known in both English and Spanish as "contras" in a linguistic victory for the Sandinistas. From this time on, until the signing of the Central American Peace Accord (for which President Oscar Arias of Costa Rica received the Nobel Peace Prize) in 1987, the United States funded and trained the contra army, carried out covert military operations against the Sandinista government, cut off all U.S. foreign aid to Nicaragua, stopped the multilateral lending agencies from lending money to Nicaragua, and from 1985 on, carried out a trade embargo against Nicaragua. The Reagan administration was not fazed by international criticism or even by a decision against the United States at the International Court of Justice in the Hague. The administration even risked impeachment in the notorious Iran-Contra affair in order to continue its campaign against the Sandinista revolution when Congress prohibited "covert assistance for military operations in Nicaragua" by passing the Boland Amendment.[20]

The Sandinistas responded by building up a large military establishment with aid from the socialist bloc countries and from several other countries, including France. They instituted a draft for young men and armed hundreds of thousands of militia members, mainly women, grandfathers, and children. And, if the influence of Leninism and democratic centralism led to verticalism in the relationship between the FSLN leadership and the mass organizations, the contra war made the situation worse. Dora María Téllez explains:

> Every war, just, injust, more just, or less just, all presuppose a single command, vertical action, and absolute authority. All wars. There has never been a war that did not presuppose this. . . . What philosophy strengthens that idea? The philosophy of command. The philosophy of the defense mission. That is a product of representative democracy. It is objective. Like it or not. It is produced as a natural and also necessary phenomenon in organizing for defense. The authoritarian mentality is strengthened. And that is when the problem begins. At what moment do you return from a defense mentality to a more or less normal mentality? That is where there is a difference of opinion.

That is where we made mistakes. Perhaps it was not necessary to continue some measures for so much time; perhaps in some cases less time was necessary.[21]

All the popular organizations were called to participate in the defense of the revolution from outside aggression. Unity of the revolutionary forces was prized above all else. As the war situation became more and more serious, with 50 percent of the national budget going to defense, priorities changed in many areas. Women's issues, for example, were placed in second or even third place by the revolutionary leadership. Now, AMNLAE began to work more and more with the mothers of the soldiers in the Sandinista Army and with the organization formed by the mothers of those who had been killed in the war. "The women's movement was in large part a mother's movement" during the war, noted journalist Angela Saballos.[22] Its original aims were subverted by the Sandinista Party and state in the interests of defending the revolution against its attackers. The mobilizing of women for work in health campaigns and neighborhood nightwatch (called revolutionary vigilance) was important activity as well, but the pressure on the government around essentially women's issues became ever weaker as the postponement which Nicaraguan women had vowed would not happen, did happen.

FSLN founder and member of the National Directorate, Tómas Borge, answered criticism about verticalist management of the popular organizations in 1985:

> [T]he errors that have resulted in a waning in certain aspects of popular participation would have to be attributed to the leadership of the revolution. But, one also needs to understand that these errors are almost inevitable in a situation like the present one, with our revolution under attack by an especially aggressive U.S. government, not only as a natural aspect of imperialism, but because of the particularly visceral hatred of Nicaragua on the part of President Reagan.[23]

However, in the mid-eighties there were few Sandinistas who were criticizing FSLN management of the popular organizations and the resulting decline in participation. Also, although some foreign observers pointed it out, there were few Sandinistas who noted the effect of the 1987 Constitution on participation. As a result of the promulgation of that document, the legislative body changed from one in which representation came from the popular organizations, unions, business groups, and parties to one in which the representation was by party from geographical districts. Some foreigners noted that this gave the popular organizations a lesser role, but most Nicaraguans maintain that the geographical representatives were also members of the popular organizations and, thus, the effect of the change was marginal.

### The Electoral Defeat of 1990

The Sandinista electoral loss in 1990 was liberating but disorienting for the popular organizations. The loss of the powerful mechanism of the state to support the needs and interests of the organizations was a blow. But now the organizations did not have to function as "para-state" groups, carrying out many functions that in other times and places would have been performed by government functionaries. Now they did not have to take orders from Sandinista Party officials, or at least there was nothing to make them do so. Unions no longer were obliged to consider the "larger interests" of state and nation and could strike when worker interests in their factory or industry demanded it. Other organizations could be formed or their functions expanded without party approval, as happened with the proliferation of women's groups. Suddenly, people were more interested in attending meetings of the mass organizations than of the party itself, since the organizations might actually be able to obtain something that people needed at their workplace or in the neighborhood where they lived. The party, in contrast, could no longer deliver the same benefits it had provided when it controlled the state. And, possibly most interesting of all, criticism of past methods of work on the part of the FSLN appeared everywhere. Sandinista leaders themselves were critical and self-critical to the degree that one marveled that the mass organizations still existed at all, so badly had they evidently been mismanaged.

In a 1992 interview, Dora María Téllez said, "We wanted everyone to sing the same song in the same way." She described a conversation with a major contra leader (now dead) whose nom de guerre was "Franklin." Franklin told the FSLN leaders, "We rose up against the Sandinistas, not against the revolution, nor against agrarian reform. We rose up against 'sandinismo' because we felt that we had no space. All our space had been closed."[24] Téllez says that it was that kind of criticism from the people that needed to be listened to. She feels that no future Sandinista government would even try to maintain the same kind of subordination of the popular organizations that it had in the 1980s. The party and the state had complete hegemony, according to Téllez, over everything, one hundred percent. But, at the same time as its control over the instruments of power, over the organizations, increased, the FSLN was losing ideological hegemony over the people on the street. Those people hadceased to identify with the FSLN. Membership and attendance at meetings of the party and the mass organizations haddropped.

With relation to how much the top-down management of the organizations could be justified by the conditions of war, most Sandinistas agree that some of the measures were necessary. Their verticalism was philosophically based but it was reinforced by the needs of defense. Although he makes a scathing critique of the strict Leninist handling of the popular organizations, Community Movement (successor to the Sandinista Defense Committees) national coordinator Enrique Picado does maintain in contradictory fashion that it was necessary to pass through the period of verticalism during the contra war: "If not, we would have been fried yuca. So, I believe that without that subordination, that verticalism which is bad and which I do not like, it would not be possible for us to be sitting here today talking of democracy! That is to say, that bad part had also its good part and that is how we come to be here today."[25]

Luis Carrión criticizes the use of the organizations as "transmission lines for orders to go from the top down to mobilize the people for the tasks of the revolution" but he maintains that, in spite of this misuse of the organizations, there truly was a space for the people to mobilize around their own interests. Some analysts, he says, have described a caricature of the mass organizations, described them as if they had been merely robots. But, according to Carrión, they were not. He goes on:

> There was a space. What happened was that it was constricted. They were under pressure, but people tried to use those organizations and the proof is in the fact that they were authentic. In spite of everything, they were authentic. They are still here and they are the most feisty and the best organized with the greatest ability to mobilize people. And that is not because they are supported or financed by the Sandinista Front, not at all. One has to recognize that the revolution taught the people to defend their rights and they have rapidly learned to do just that in the new situation. If one goes to Eastern Europe, one would probably not see even a sign of the labor organizations that were there. They broke apart. The top levels of these organizations disappeared. But here they are all intact.[26]

Sandinistas seem to agree, therefore, that 1) at least some of the vertical management of the popular organizations during the war was necessary; 2) the organizations were distorted and weakened by this type of management; and 3) in spite of verticalism, the organizations did offer to the people some real space for participation.

The popular organizations that grew out of the Sandinista revolution were the only organizations in the Latin American region that were close to state power. They were often viewed by other Latin Americans as adjuncts to state bureaucracy, carrying out tasks that in other times and places would be performed by official bureaucrats or employees. This has changed markedly since the Sandinista electoral loss in 1990. The question may be asked: If the Sandinistas were to win the elections in late 1996, what would be the role of the popular organizations? Would they revert to being paragovernmental entities? Involvement in activities like the giant Literacy Crusade of 1980, where there was "a harmony of wills between the government and the population," would be appropriate according to Dora María Téllez, but not health campaigns and other such activities, which belong in the domain of government.[27]

A more likely role for the popular organizations is participation in cabinets of consultation at the national and especially at the local levels. Monica Baltodano, who is the head of a non-governmental organization which works with municipalities in Nicaragua (and one of the women members of the FSLN National Directorate elected at the 1994 party congress), would like to see this participation institutionalized in the Constitution. The Sandinista government, she said, set up education councils where the community was to take part in decision-making on education issues but they never became fully functional. Now, she says, not only education councils but economic councils, agriculture councils, and health councils should be established, especially at the municipal level where, she feels, participatory democracy can function fully. One must question how effective participation of the people can actually be at the local level, however, when the problems are national or international. But, Baltodano emphasizes that the local level participation would be only a stepping stone leading to participation at the national level as well. "The government should not be able to make decisions about the economy without consulting with the affected sectors," she states, "especially in such areas as credit policy, where small and medium-sized farmers should have their say."[28]

The idea of popular participation remains very much alive in Nicaragua, along with a faith in the possibilities for its institutionalization in the future. However, with a few exceptions, there is a paucity of ideas about how to formally combine participatory and electoral democracy. Under the administration of Violeta Chamorro, the popular organizations have exercised their right to petition their government for redress of grievances, carrying out protest marches to the presidential offices and to the National Assembly. But there is no formal mechanism which mandates their inclusion in decision-making and President Chamorro tends to consult with such organizations as the Superior Council of Private Enterprise (COSEP), a business group, and the organizations representing large farmers rather than with unions and peasant organizations. If the FSLN returns to power in January of 1997, it is to be hoped that the popular organizations would have a more substantive role in policy-making.

## FROM SANDINISTA DEFENSE COMMITTEES
## TO COMMUNITY MOVEMENT

The Sandinista Defense Committees were formed before the Sandinista revolution to help the people prepare for the final offensive. After the revolutionary triumph of 1979, the committees were organized in blocks and neighborhoods throughout the country as the grassroots participatory organizations which would represent people where they lived. Enrique Picado rose through the ranks of the Sandinista defense committees beginning with the Sandinista victory. He held regional and national positions in the organization that became the Community Movement and in 1991 was elected to a four-year term as national coordinator. He was re-elected in 1995. He makes a searing criticism of the early methods of work of his organization, saying that, up until 1988, it had very vertical organizing methods. "It was a totalitarian mentality and style, totalitarian!" he says. The CDS was the only neighborhood or community organization that existed, he declares, adding:

> Because we were totalitarian in philosophy and practice, we did not permit anyone else to organize. What is more, within the CDS, we were so totalitarian that people who wanted to join the CDS could only do so with the permission of the local leadership. Within the organization the notion that anyone should come up with an original idea was frowned upon.... Even less would it occur to anyone to start a new organization.... So what [people] did was, since they knew that the steamroller would roll over them if they expressed an original idea and they would be seen in a bad light, they said nothing and they withdrew from the CDS. Within the CDS there were fewer and fewer of us.[29]

An awareness was building that the verticalism under which the Sandinista Defense Committees were being run (no Sandinista at that time would have dared to call it "totalitarianism") was reducing them to insignificance. Something had to be done if they were to be salvaged. In April of 1988, Omar Cabezas, whose autobiographical book about the guerrilla struggle in the mountains of northern

Nicaragua had won the Casa de las Americas Prize for 1981, was nominated by the FSLN National Directorate to be national coordinator of the Sandinista Defense Committees with the mandate to bring them back to life.

Cabezas, who waited to take office until an assembly of representative member committees had confirmed him, said that what he found upon taking office was not a vast mass movement but rather small groups of activists who were doing the work that the organized population should have been doing. The people in the neighborhoods were waiting to be told what their next tasks would be. "The community has lost the capacity to develop its own projects," he said in an 1988 interview.[30] Cabezas wanted to revive this capacity so that, "based on the efforts of the community, on their own creativity as active subjects, participants in their own reality, the people will see and study their own problems. Then, out of the community itself will come a great variety of forms of participation, without the rigid organizational schemes that have been the bane of the CDS movement for the last few years."[31] Instead of having to get permission even to "express an original idea," as Picado says, the new groups would organize themselves as they saw fit, according to Cabezas, "for the good of the community, [and] they do not have to ask for permission from anyone at all."[32]

Cabezas set three priorities for the new community movement: 1) that the organization in each neighborhood be inclusive of all who lived there, "independent of their political or religious beliefs"; 2) that the organization be democratic from the bottom up, with leadership changes whenever the people thought necessary; and 3) that the local groups address the issues that concern their neighborhoods, and not be used to carry out tasks mandated from above by government bureaucrats. Cabezas took over the CDS movement at a time of severe economic crisis. The inflation rate in 1988 was over 30,000 percent, poverty was increasing, people were weary and desperate. For Cabezas, this was the best time to do grassroots organizing: "Anyone who believes that a situation of economic crisis like the one we are going through leads people to be individualistic, to search for their own methods of survival, is mistaken. This is a view that leads to impotence, defenselessness, defeat and helplessness. I believe that the opposite is true. The more economic difficulties there are, the more united the population needs to be—not as individuals but as a collective—to work for solutions."[33]

Thus, in an attempt to ward off their virtual disintegration in the late 1980s, the Sandinista defense committees were "let go," as it were, from the FSLN tether. "We're going to forget about Papa State and Papa Government," said Cabezas. If the government could help the committees, fine. "But we maintain that it will be the community which solves problems with the help of the government, and not the government with the help of the community."[34]

One might argue that the Sandinistas were making a virtue of necessity, that now that the government and party no longer had the resources to assist the neighborhoods, the latter were declared capable of helping themselves. But Picado argues that there was a philosophical change in that year as well. The CDS should no longer continue to carry out tasks for the government, the reformers thought at the time, because, as Picado iterates, "the government was grown up enough now to do those things for itself," and they should no longer carry out tasks for the army "because that was what had turned the organizations into hollow shells." Picado goes on to say that most people were happy that the CDS was going to change but that there were doubters within the FSLN who accused the CDS of "turning social democratic" because they would no longer carry water for the party, the government, and the army. "Many comrades became thoughtful, and began to doubt the CDS," Picado says, "but we knew that historically we had right on our side."[35]

No one, according to him, expected the electoral defeat of 1990. But, he adds, thanks to the radical changes made in 1988 from CDS to Community Movement, "we were able to confront the major structural and political changes and changes in peoples' consciousness that came with the elections." Other organizations became weaker or broke up, but the Community Movement, based on practical philosophical premises of true popular empowerment adopted in 1988, "was able to stretch after the electoral defeat."[36]

The 1990 electoral defeat of the Sandinistas did not mean that controversies were at an end concerning the proper role of the Community Movement, especially with relation to the FSLN Party. Father Miguél D'Escoto, foreign minister under the Sandinista government who had had considerable neighborhood organizing experience as a Maryknoll priest in Chile in the 1960s, was now named national coordinator of the Community Movement. (Omar Cabezas was elected to the National Assembly.) D'Escoto and his associates had an altogether different vision of community organizing from that of Cabezas. "'Organize yourself as you see fit' [which had been the slogan of Cabezas's reforms] is not a good motto," said D'Escoto.[37] His report on the year 1991 stated that, besides being in debt, the Community Movement suffered from the consequences of a prolonged absence of organizational leadership, which had produced a diversification of methods and styles of work including different conceptions in each of the departments (provinces) of the country. This, of course, had been Cabezas's goal: to let communities organize in the way they thought was best in order to solve their own problems. The goal for 1992 on the part of the D'Escoto team was to organize the movement in such a way that it could confront, "in a vigorous, harmonious and coherent fashion," the negative effects of the economic structural adjustment programs that the Chamorro government was then applying.[38] In other words, some of the organizational autonomy that had been so difficult to achieve in the 1980s was to be discarded in the 1990s. Ernesto Torres, coordinator for the Department of Granada, says that D'Escoto "wanted to use the same old verticalist style of organizing, and he wanted a Movement that relied more on the FSLN for its positions."[39] Toward the end of 1991, D'Escoto was replaced by René Núñez, the secretary of the FSLN National Directorate, and a few months later by the first democratically elected national coordinator, Enrique Picado.

In assessing his ouster and subsequent personnel changes, Father D'Escoto asserts that an opportunity was lost. For him the enormous national economic problems facing the Nicaraguan people could not be countered by a movement that was fragmented. "I favor a big power structure parallel to that of organized labor," he has said. "Territorial unionism is popular empowerment. The Movement could have become a solid united organization. Instead it is still the fragmented one that it has always been."[40] D'Escoto was thinking on a large scale, believing that for the massive threat of the Chamorro government's neo-liberal economic policies, a massive revolutionary response was required.

D'Escoto rejects the argument that the FSLN would again dominate the Community Movement as it had during the days of the Sandinista Defense Committees. He says that he would rather that the party "turn itself into a coalition of groups, and that its goals should become identical to those of the organizations."[41] In other words, the FSLN would take as its positions those of the mass organizations instead of the other way around. But although D'Escoto is nothing if not sincere, his position is unrealistic. He is confusing the roles of party and popular movement. Each one must have its separate and distinct role in the struggle for a more just society. (For a more complete discussion of this matter, see chapter 7 on democracy in the FSLN.)

D'Escoto also wants to believe that there exists one great, agreed-upon solution toward which all should work. Picado's response is that, since the left does not now possess a macro-solution for the economic problems of Nicaragua, of Latin America, or of the Third World, "therefore, in the Community Movement, we are thinking small. We think that the strengthening of communitarian values in the heart of the sector that we represent is of strategic importance for any positive change. Along these same lines, it seems to us that we must work like little ants in the community, in the neighborhoods, engendering confidence in the people that together we can solve our problems."[42]

This difference between those who are thinking big and those who are thinking small is one of the major ideological divisions in the revolutionary sectors of Nicaragua today. Within the first group, which believes that the choice is still between different grand philosophies, between socialism and capitalism, there are two factions. The first asserts that it is necessary to continue the good fight against capitalism and for socialism, while the second faction maintains that there is now only one world system—capitalism—and that we must find a way to work within it. But there are others, like Picado, who think small and reject the grand philosophical solutions, opting for an extreme democracy that emphasizes the participation of the people in the organizations of civil society in all their diversity of forms.

Picado says that he used to be one who believed that it was only the workers and peasants who would go all the way to the end, as Sandino's slogan had said in the 1920s. But now he says:

> Look at Nicaragua. Nicaragua is not made up of just workers and peasants. Nicaragua is made up of artisans, artists, intellectuals, professionals, workers, peasants, housewives, of the unemployed. And the peasantry is made up of people who are in the countryside but who have no land, who just live there. That is to say that Nicaragua is a mosaic. And out of this mosaic, progressive political parties that call themselves revolutionary must put together a project for this society as it is. The moment that I give a privileged position to workers and peasants, I am being sectarian. I don't want to be accused of revisionism, but in my view, that old analysis just doesn't fit, not in Nicaragua or in the rest of Latin America.[43]

Nicaraguans with views similar to those of Picado are to be found in both currents within the Sandinista movement today—that surrounding former president Daniel Ortega as well as in that surrounding former vice-president Sergio Ramírez, even if they are more commonly associated with the latter. Those who hold such views also insist that the attempt to find a solution for Nicaragua's problems by bringing people together at the grassroots level can only work if there is a coming together of these grassroots organizations on a national level to influence national policy. What the relationship to the FSLN should be is a subject of some controversy, but most would agree with Picado that it should be "a horizontal relationship, not a vertical one."[44]

## THE WOMEN'S MOVEMENT: FROM
## SUBSERVIENCE TO INDEPENDENCE

It is not often noted that Nicaraguan feminism began long before the Sandinista revolution. Mention of women's rights goes back to the 1830s. Josefa Toledo de Aguerri, often referred to as "the mother of Nicaraguan education," publicly called herself a feminist in 1920. In 1938 she wrote that "One of the characteristics of feminism is that it considers woman able to find in themselves their means and their end. They can live independently from men if they wish and can earn a living."[45] Support of women's rights came from the Liberal Party in Nicaragua and women finally achieved the right to vote in 1955 under the Liberal Party president and founder of the Somoza dynasty, Anastasio Somoza Garcia. Because the vote was achieved under the Somoza dictatorship, Sandinista women for many years ignored the struggle for women's rights that took place in that period.

Like many other Sandinista women, FSLN National Directorate member Mónica Baltodano maintains that with the revolution, for the first time in Nicaraguan history, great numbers of women discovered themselves as human beings. She says that they found that they had rights and possibilities, as independent beings with their own opinions, their own need for achievement, their needs for their own space, and for their own individual lives. But, she said in a 1991 interview:

> I believe that we were too timid in many things and this was as much because of the perpetual threat under which the revolution lived as because of a series of internal mechanisms in our political life. We were unable to develop and strengthen democracy in our own house. Many struggles were not even begun because of fear of the war and of U.S. imperialist attacks and, if we can say that some of those decisions were correct, others were not. I believe that the threats of imperialism took away from Nicaraguan women the right to advance more in our development. At this moment, I feel that we are very much behind and disjointed and that our women's organization, one of our most important instruments of struggle, is very weak. This lost ground in the struggle for women's rights is lamentable.[46]

The criticism Baltodano makes is particularly significant because she is considered to be among the more traditional of the FSLN women leaders. "Our women's organization" to which she refers, AMNLAE (the Women's Association), was one of the grassroots groups that showed the greatest promise at the time of the 1979 Sandinista victory, but became one of the most subservient to the dictates of the FSLN leadership.

Ileana Rodríguez says that during the first years of the revolution, the mission of AMNLAE was to bring women's energies to the various tasks of rebuilding the country after the destructive war of 1977–79. This effort presumed, she says, an identity of interests between women and the nation as a whole. Later, an ideological debate developed among the more highly educated women who saw two roads to women's equal integration into society. The first assumed that gender equality is dependent upon the prior realization of revolutionary goals for the whole society and at best would advance simultaneously with the realization of those goals. The second wanted to attack the vestiges of sexism and gender stereotyping within the revolutionary movement itself, here and now, maintaining that this is a necessary first step if gender equality is ever to be achieved in society as a whole.[47]

However, as the contra war heated up, Rodriguez says that defense of the homeland and the revolution became the first priority. If the revolution were to be lost, all would be lost. The FSLN leadership pointed out that revolutionary transformations and benefits for the whole society had to be deferred because of the war, and consequently so did the struggle for women's equality. She explains further that "The integration of women, all agreed, was first of all an economic question. And since there was little economic development, women's integration was postponed. It became a kind of utopia; it was put into the future."[48]

With a postponement of the struggle for women's full equality, there was uncertainty about whether an organization that represented women as a gender was necessary. Would it not be better if women were organized in their workplaces, in their neighborhoods? AMNLAE was downgraded from an association to a movement. "In a sense," says Magda Enríquez, an FSLN party diplomat who is now the party's representative for the United States and Canada, "AMNLAE became close to being the women's branch of the FSLN but without real quotas of power." One of the main functions of AMNLAE was to reconcile mothers to the loss of their sons in battle against the contras, and to involve them in the activities of their organization, which was called The Mothers of Heroes and Martyrs.

In the mid-eighties, the other popular organizations began forming "women's sections," among them the Farmworkers Association (ATC), the Union of Farmers and Ranchers (UNAG), and the Sandinista Workers' Central (CST). While officially under AMNLAE, these sections became ever more independent. As Rodríguez points out, it is ironic that it was the war, which was responsible for the postponement of their struggles as a gender, that also brought women to the forefront of economic activity because so many of the men were off fighting. The organization of women in the workplace became important. Later, women's collectives addressing women's health, domestic violence, and other issues began to appear in Managua and Matagalpa.

By the late 1980s, according to a document prepared by prominent Nicaraguan feminists María Teresa Blandón, Lillian Levi, and Sofía Montenegro, there were conflicts within AMNLAE based on "the lack of autonomy, the absence of our own discourse, [and] undemocratic styles of work," that provoked major discord between the official structures of AMNLAE and other women who had begun to draw nearer to feminism. Steps were taken in 1987 toward democratic elections within AMNLAE for the first time in the organization's history. FSLN leadership called for a postponement of the elections, however, when the nation's presidential elections were moved up after the signing of the Central American Peace Accord in that year. "Once again," the document says, "the FSLN imposed its priorities."[50]

Six months after the February 1990 Sandinista electoral defeat, women from AMNLAE and other organizations met to try to re-shape the women's movement, establishing new work priorities, new forms of organizing, and new leadership. They held a series of workshops and planned to finish off with a national women's "en-counter." The "encounter" was never held, however, because the leaders of AMNLAE decided to retain their traditional methods of work and leadership. The feminists' document states:

> Because of this, the other organizations involved in the process broke ideologically, politically and organizationally with AMNLAE and or-ganized the "Festival of the 52%." This break marked a new moment for the women's movement: We broke with the guardianship of AMN-LAE and, as a result, with that of the FSLN. For the first time, we called ourselves together for an open interchange that was pluralistic, di-verse, and without the desire of any one group to dominate. We had the public presence of the lesbian women's collective and initiated the process of breaking away from the fears and taboos around sexual preferences.[51]

The First National Encounter, called "United in Diversity," was finally held in January of 1992. In attendance were more than eight hundred women. Some wanted only an opportunity for interchange and reflection, while others sought to establish some permanent or-ganizational structure, making clear that they firmly rejected orga-nizational schemes that were verticalistic, authoritarian, or exclusive.[52] Since no organizational mechanism came out of that conference, those women who were dissatisfied formed the Na-tional Feminist Committee in May of 1992. In October 1993, the Committee called another national encounter and, in March of 1994, a third.

Meanwhile, perhaps making a virtue of necessity since the FSLN could no longer support it financially, AMNLAE, at its August 1993 assembly, declared itself an autonomous movement that was not subordinate to any political party. The assembly recognized that, for a long time, the circumstances of history had distracted the women's organization from working on tasks related specifically to problems of gender. AMNLAE had instead taken on tasks of national interest, which had often given the movement a political and at times even a political-military character. The document that came out of that AMNLAE assembly lists the present priorities of the movement: "The struggle for democratization of present power relations both in the public and private spheres, the struggle against unemployment, against violence against women, the struggle for our education and training, the struggle in defense of the environment, of the right to our own sexuality, to freely chosen maternity, for responsible paternity, for economic autonomy, for integral health care, and for laws which make possible women's exercise of their rights, are all priorities for AMNLAE."[53]

Several of these priorities were new to AMNLAE, the most prominent being the struggle for the democratization of power relations between men and women in both the public and private spheres, women's right to their own sexuality, and to freely chosen maternity. The organization had worked for some years in the prevention of violence against women but without addressing the issue of unequal power relations between men and women.

At the May 1994 Extraordinary Party Congress of the FSLN, women achieved several victories. They had begun preparing for this congress immediately after the one in 1991, at which they had been unable to place a woman on the FSLN National Directorate. This time the women were organized both at the leadership level and at the grassroots level. They achieved, by popular vote of the delegates, a mandated "quota of power" of 30 percent women at all leadership levels. This meant five women on the National Directorate out of fifteen. The five elected women were Dora María Téllez, Mónica Baltodano, Benigna Mendiola, Dr. Mirna Cunningham, and Dorotea Wilson.

While at first glance, it might appear that Sandinista women are coming together, there are still major philosophical differences between them, especially around the question of which of the priorities of the women's organizations should be emphasized in their work. At the risk of oversimplification, one could say that the women of AMNLAE, in the main, still feel that women are doubly oppressed and that class economic oppression is as important as (and for some, more important than) the struggle for more equal power relationships between men and women. The independent feminists believe that the unequal power relationships between the sexes must be addressed first, but that ethnic issues also divide Nicaraguans and must be addressed along with class economic oppression. Both groups address gender and class issues but each tends to accuse the other (sometimes unfairly) of not giving sufficient attention to the set of issues to which it gives prime importance. There is even controversy over the term "feminist," which the independent feminists routinely use to describe themselves, but which party-identified women tend to avoid because of its connotation of separatism. Magda Enríquez says that the concept of feminism continues to be unacceptable to many FSLN party members, that women's participation in leadership positions in the party (before the quotas adopted in 1994) had fallen drastically with relation to the percentage of women in the party, and, "to be a party militant and of the feminine sex still does not guarantee a feminist vote."[54]

The more party-identified women are less willing to address the difficult, often recalcitrant personal issues than are the feminists. Mónica Baltodano, of the former group, believes that one of the greatest problems of revolutionaries has been a contradiction between their global positions and their everyday ones. This, she says, has not been resolved by any revolutionary movement in the world. Many revolutionaries are divided into two parts: the lives they live in public are revolutionary, but their personal lives are not. She goes on to say that "one of the most important aspects of this is the question of discrimination against women. . . . In my opinion, we have not worked on this enough. This is because it touches the most intimate part of our lives, the most difficult to change. It is much easier to give out land or carry out a political revolution, than to carry out a revolution in the intimate lives of humans in the most profound parts of their beings."[55]

For Baltodano exaggerated feminism, which ends up denying the different conditions of women, is extreme. To try to do everything that men do, in exactly the way they do it, does not mean women are advancing at all and certainly means that they are hurting their families and especially their children. She says:

> If you carry out a struggle only on the level of thought, in the end you have carried it out badly; you have not been effective; you remain in small circles of intellectual discussion. In all struggles there are objectives, enemies and allies. I believe that in a woman's struggle, her principal allies must be her own world, her husband, her children, her family, her brothers and sisters, her friends, and with them she should establish alliances which permit her to overcome historic cultural and material obstacles. Otherwise, her struggle is individual, one against all, and it wears one out.[56]

Sandinista women knew about and were shocked by things going on in the personal lives of revolutionary men and women. The Sandinista woman commander of the National Police was suffering from a husband who beat her; a member of the National Directorate drove attractive Sandinista women out of active participation in the party because of his insistent demands for sexual favors.

Militant feminists have not been afraid to denounce the continuing sexist attitudes of many Sandinista men and the legal system that perpetuates sexism, which the Sandinista government changed very little. The feminist document prepared for the 1993 conference by Blandón, Montenegro, and Levi challenges the classification of women as bodies specialized in the reproduction of other bodies and in the care of young bodies, sick and dying bodies, and for the satisfaction of the erotic appetites of other non-feminine bodies. It calls for a slogan of "Free bodies . . . or death!" taken, of course, from the Sandinista slogan of "Free homeland or death!" This would appear to be a liberal demand for basic individual rights. However, liberal demands are for political rights, including the right to vote and to equality before the law. What these women are demanding is something more radical that moves beyond the liberal demands for political equality and socialist demands for economic equality. The women want rights over their own bodies, rights that are not denied them by law or economics but by social custom. The document says:

It is absolutely necessary for women to reclaim their own bodies for their legitimate owners. The struggle for property in general begins with our claiming our rights of property over ourselves, the right to freedom and sovereignty over our own bodies. These rights over our own bodies are an integral and inalienable part of universal human rights. . . . Therefore any conditioning of these rights of women over their own bodies is unacceptable whether it be for religious, ideological, moral, political, economic or State reasons.[57]

A further point needs to be made about the above-quoted statement. The political left in the South (the Third World) has wanted to dismiss birth control and abortion as a plot by the North and the political right to limit the growth of the poor population and thus stave off revolutionary change. Population control campaigns are also seen as racist. But the taking of this position places the left on the same side with conservative Catholics and others who advocate the restriction of women's equality. Nicaraguan feminists refused to go along and demanded the control over their own bodies as a basic individual right, a control which includes access to birth control and abortion. During the period of Sandinista government birth control became more available, but the question of abortion was not addressed. The Chamorro government, dominated as it has been by the Catholic Church, has not addressed the question either.

The more traditionally inclined women in the party find the discussion of the independent feminists too theoretical and too intellectualized to be of use to the great masses of poor women in Nicaragua struggling to keep their children from dying of malnutrition. They also find that after fighting the struggle against hunger, landlessness, and all the other overwhelming immediate problems of underdevelopment, they have very little energy left for tackling those other, much more recalcitrant, personal aspects of life.

For Benigna Mendiola, a peasant leader who is head of the women's section of the Farmers and Ranchers Association and a member of the Sandinista National Directorate, the struggle is for equal opportunities for women, for access to land and to credit. Even under the revolution, she says, agrarian reform titles were given mostly to men. Only 500 women received land under the revolution, Mendiola says—"Too little!" Under the present government of Violeta Chamorro, she adds, 366 women have received land as a result of the efforts of her office. Mendiola explains that the UNAG Women's Section has a rotating fund with which it makes loans to women. "It's not a gift," she explains, "We're trying to end paternalism." She adds that the women in several cities have already paid back their first loans and have profit left over from the chickens they have raised or the vegetables they have grown. The Women's Section has also started a rotating fund with over 600 women who were supporters of the resistance (the contras) so that they can begin their own agricultural projects.[58]

Mendiola questions whether many of the issues important to some feminist groups are important to these peasant women. "It's not the same to be in the reality of the countryside as it is to contemplate philosophical questions. . . . It's all right to promote sex education. But, tell me, why am I going to talk to a woman about sexuality if she is starving? First I need to talk to her about health, housing. . . . [Peasant women] are interested in getting land and bank loans so they can produce food. If I tell them to make their husbands cook and wash dishes, they'll chase me away with their brooms."[59]

However, the issue of democratic decision-making, a central issue for feminists, is important to Mendiola as well. In a 1993 visit to the United States, Mendiola criticized a women's agricultural project being supported by groups in the U.S., saying that the Nicaraguan organization in charge of the project gave limited decision-making authority to the women in the cooperative. Agricultural specialists told them what they had to do, and they did it. She promised to see to it that the women were organized in the Women's Section of UNAG, where the emphasis is on women taking charge of their own lives.

The women of AMNLAE have agreed with the independent feminists on the seriousness of the problem of what is called in Nicaragua the "double day's work," and even the triple day's work for those women who not only work outside the home and do the housework, but also, during the Sandinista years, participated in the activities of the revolutionary organizations such as the CDS and the militia. There was even an attempt, in a bill sponsored by AMN-LAE, to put into law a provision that men and children (the latter so far as they were able) had to help with the work of the home. Some women challenged Marxist orthodoxy, which maintains that housework is not true labor. Ileana Rodríguez said that that philosophical system marginalized women with the concept of the salaried family, in which the principal breadwinner was the man and the woman was in the home, "where the door is closed on the labor theory of value" and women's work is thus devalued.[61]

The above critique led the feminist intellectuals to move farther in their analysis. If the working class was seen as the revolutionary class and the workers were mainly perceived as being men, then the revolutionary project was downplaying the participation of a great part of the Nicaraguan population, which was not male and not working class. The document by María Teresa Blandón, Lillian Levi, and Sofía Montenegro referred to above, which was prepared for the 1993 feminist meeting, laments that "a Eurocentric and androcentric perspective is what has led to the systematic disregard of the true composition of the Nicaraguan people who in their majority are peasants, women, and of indigenous and multilingual origins."[62]

The document goes on to say that feminists believe that negotiation among a plurality or a diversity of interests—rather than between working class and capitalist males—is what constitutes democratic policy-making: "Democracy is the negotiation of conflicting interests, not the imposition of one interest that denies or destroys the others. . . . Our vision of leadership is based on the recognition of the differences among women, of their autonomous condition, of the capacities of each and of their parity (a political relationship that supposes that all have the same value and are associates holding fundamental ideas in common)."[63]

The document presents an analysis of the Sandinista period of government from a feminist perspective, criticizing for example the concentration of government power at the national level with very little initiative allowed at the local level. But, surprisingly, the authors give no critique of the Sandinista economic model, with its lack of interest in peasant production, its decision-making concentrated in the state bureaucracy, its emphasis on modern high-technology agricultural methods and large scale agri-industry. This is especially disturbing because the introductory part of the document is so strongly critical of the FSLN for its failure to realize that the nation is made up of a majority of peasants. It makes one suspicious that, even though peasants are included in the feminists' analysis, the peasants' problems are not felt and understood by them in the same way that urban women's problems are felt and understood. Mendiola's criticism seems to gain added validity. Not only do the intellectual, urban feminists not understand the daily lives and problems of peasant women, they have not formed a critique of Sandinista agrarian policy that would help support their analysis of other "Eurocentric and androcentric" aspects of the revolutionary government's years in power, especially as they relate to participatory democracy and the role of the popular organizations.

The 1993 feminist document notes that a majority of women supported the revolution even though they felt that they were not considered participants with full rights but rather added factors. This situation created a personal and collective conflict of loyalties for them, because they were investing both energy and hope in the revolution while at the same time failing to achieve a corresponding satisfaction of their specific demands. The document goes on:

> This conflict of loyalties has been a divisive factor in the women's movement between those who adhered to leftist thought and those who, while continuing to be revolutionaries, enriched their thinking and their practice with feminist thought. The latter are cut in half because they continue to be loyal to a revolutionary project that is being questioned and is in crisis, in spite of their recognition that that project does not include addressing the problems of unequal and hierarchical relations between the genders. It is, however, a project to which these women have given so much effort and which they cannot easily abandon.[64]

The document charges that women end up reducing feminism to a series of themes or generalized policy problem areas, such as the campaign to end violence against women. This "ignores both in theory and practice, the struggle against the unequal and hierarchical relations between the genders." Such an agenda is therefore not threatening to men in the "mixed" organizations, such as the Farmworkers Association, where these women work. In the end, the women's issues are co-opted by "the instances of masculine power."[65]

The independent feminists maintain that the autonomy of the women's movement is of the utmost importance. They insist that the role of women's organizations is to work on the issues that concern women *as women,* and not to be social service agencies. When women's organizations spend their time and energy on helping women with their demands connected to economic and social problems (such as access to bank credit, fully-funded schools for children, day care, etc.), which it is the obligation of the state to fulfill, they will not be able to address issues of gender oppression (such as sexual harassment in the workplace, domestic abuse, irresponsible paternity, tolerance of rape, etc., especially by men who in other aspects of their lives are revolutionary). In order to achieve results on social and economic issues, the women's organizations may have to collaborate with the established powers to such a degree that issues of gender oppression are not raised at all.

Traditional left women counter that if women do not work to achieve these socioeconomic goals for themselves, all the bank credit will go to male farmers, day care centers will not be funded, and so forth. The obvious answer is that both tactics are necessary for the advancement of women. And although many in Nicaragua express the desire for the women's movement to unite, this might not be a good thing. If all the women unite under the banner of the independent feminists, they could all be dismissed as extremists, as many men (and women) of the traditional left already do. If the independent feminists joined the traditional left women, the economic and social issues they raise would constitute the extreme position and could also be rejected, as they were during the contra war. As things stand now, the FSLN party addresses with some seriousness the issues raised by the women's sections of the unions and UNAG and by other women of the traditional left exactly because they seem moderate in comparison with the "extreme" positions of the independent feminists. Alliances and coalition building among women's groups while preserving their diversity appears to be the best road. Dora María Téllez, who is more active as a member of the National Assembly than in any women's organization, agrees: "They are all part of the women's movement," she says, "and they are all revolutionaries. It is not dispersion of efforts but rather division of labor."[66]

The autonomy and respect for diversity that progressive Nicaraguan women declare as their guiding principles, they also see as principles for a healthy, functioning participatory democracy. Autonomy is understood as the capacity of a person to develop her own strength in a way that permits her to overcome any oppressive power that is exercised over her. An autonomous woman is free of restrictions over her actions, but she is not free in absolute terms, since freedom always presupposes acting responsibly in relation to others, and recognizing the existence of collective obligations.[67]

Sofia Montenegro, a leading feminist theorist, says that she has a very radical vision of democracy. For her, democracy is a permanent process of negotiation in which one group cannot impose its will on others but rather has to negotiate differences. She adds that "this is what brings one to develop a democratic attitude, an attitude of tolerance, of respect. . . . I do not see how we can arrive at this process except insofar as we recognize the other person as a subject with full rights, as an equal."[68]

A document prepared for the March 1992 women's meeting also expands the classical liberal origins of the claims of Nicaraguan feminists. It states:

> Our gender rights are the political rights of citizens. A democracy that does not recognize us as protagonists of our lives, of our acts and of the life of the country is not democratic. The democracy to which we aspire implies the freedom to decide about our own bodies, about our own organizations and our own destiny. We demand a political role

that is based on our specificity, because we do not want our needs to be eternally diluted in the general interest nor do we want to be eternally at the service of others. On this foundation, we can build new relations between men and women, based on dialogue between equals. We call on all men to assume as their own this liberating and humanizing proposal.[69]

Montenegro adds that from this perspective it is possible to find the real meaning of the French revolutionary ideals of liberty, equality, and fraternity. This means a revolution in thought and culture, because as long as the power of patriarchy lasts, there will be no room for these ideals. The elevation of half of humanity to a position above the other half poisons all human relationships, she emphasizes. If we are able to recognize the interconnection between us, we can open the doors to human emancipation.[70]

## SUMMARY

Ideas on participatory democracy within the Sandinista movement have changed radically since 1979. Ordinary citizens played an important role in the overthrow of the Somoza dictatorship and massively joined the popular organizations set up by the FSLN. But it was a Leninist method of work that governed the numerous popular organizations after July 19, 1979, and the Leninist tendencies were exaggerated by the contra war of the 1980s. The partial changes of the late 1980s, most particularly in the neighborhood-based CDS, prepared some groups better to face the Sandinista electoral loss in 1990. Many Sandinistas seem unembarrassed today, after losing those elections, to admit to having used "totalitarian" methods while in power. However, even those who are most critical of their own past practice insist that some of the verticalism was necessary given the contra war. They also insist that tens of thousands of people were organized and that all space for free thought was not closed. To prove this, they point to the revival of these organizations after the electoral loss. However, it is unclear to this writer that more open organizations might not have served the revolution better even in wartime by including more people rather than driving them away. It is obvious that many Sandinistas were simply blindly following Leninist dogma in expecting the mass organizations to unquestioningly obey orders sent down from above. As was the case in several policy areas under the Sandinistas, recognition of error came too late. By the time changes appeared in the Sandinista Defense Committees in 1988, for example, too many people had become disillusioned and carried their resentments into the voting booths in 1990.

The principal controversy within the Community Movement since 1990 has been over whether to form a cohesive national organization to do battle with the government over national problems of neighborhood dwellers or one in which each neighborhood organizes itself in the way it sees fit with only a certain amount of guidance from the national office. At the moment, under the leadership of Enrique Picado, the latter tendency is dominant. Obviously, there must be a compromise between the two positions. A movement needs to be strong and coherent enough to exercise influence on government policy at the national level but not run in a dictatorial fashion with all orders coming from the head office.

The Sandinista women's organization, AMNLAE, became subservient to the FSLN Party during the years of the contra war and this subservience led to the present division between traditional left women and the more radical feminists. Traditional left women feel that women's organizations must help women solve their economic problems, while feminists maintain that women's groups must dedicate themselves to changing the power relationships between men and women and not become "social service agencies." Both of these types of women's organizations are necessary for women's interests to be advanced. While some would like to see unity in the "women's movement," both the economic and the gender tasks will have more chance of being successfully addressed if the two tendencies within the women's movement continue their work separately.

# 4

## New Radical Thought on
## Participatory Democracy

### INTRODUCTION

Within Nicaragua, the concept of participatory democracy has changed substantially from what it was in 1979 when the Sandinista revolution took power. At the time of "the triumph of the revolution" the Sandinistas emphasized that their vision of democracy was not the same as "bourgeois democracy," which meant only manipulated elections every few years but lack of involvement of the people between elections. Theirs would be participatory democracy in which "the people" would become the "architects of their own liberation," as the Sandinista anthem states. It was the Leninist version of participatory democracy that was superficially imposed, however, with top-down management from the uppermost reaches of Sandinista leadership. In fact, as was stated above, each member of the FSLN National Directorate was assigned the supervision of one or more popular organizations and most members learned to look to the National Directorate for orders and directions to follow. But the imposition of the Leninist model was not absolute, partly because so many participants in the revolution at all levels were not Leninists at all but rather sympathizers of a New Left vision who chafed under authoritarianism and partly also because the Sandinista revolution came at a time in Latin American history when popular organizations were forming in all countries among poor people under the influence of Liberation Theology and other democratic and empowering ideas. Nicaragua was not immune to these tendencies and, in the end, Leninism did not stick. Father Xabier Gorostiaga, S.J., a naturalized Nicaraguan, who is now the head of the Jesuit University of Central America in Managua, says that:

> [T]he decade of the eighties was the decade of civil society. The irruption of the organized popular sectors in civil life, in a revolutionary manner in Nicaragua and El Salvador and to a certain extent in Guatemala as well, but particularly in a new civic presence of the impoverished and marginalized masses is a phenomenon that has definitively changed the region's social fabric. . . . Their organizational strategies are manifold; nevertheless, one notices in all of them a rejection of verticality and hierarchical vanguardism. Organizational Leninism collapsed in Latin America prior to the crisis of the East. The tendency to search for alliance, consensus, participation, and dialogue is a cultural as well as a political and economic phenomenon.[1]

Gorostiaga finds that the most important characteristic of these movements is their autonomy with regard to the organizations that created them, which, in the case of Nicaragua, means the Sandinista Party and the Nicaraguan state. Other characteristics include efforts to achieve internal democracy, accountability, and ethical coherence. The organizations show a notable lack of interest in winning state power directly through armed action (as in the past) or even through elections. Rather, according to Gorostiaga, the concern is with "the creation of an alternative social power capable of defining negotiating positions with capital, State, culture, and international relations." Organizations representing diverse constituencies form alliances within countries to work for common goals and networks of non-governmental organizations (NGOs) within individual nations form alliances with other national networks in the region to play a role in international economic and social policy. Gorostiaga points out that there is "networking throughout Latin America of organizations formed by peasants, indigenous communities, women, environmentalists, urban dwellers, and the emerging student (particularly university) movement."[2]

This international solidarity and movement building can be seen as an antidote to provincialism, local corruption, and other problems often faced by the organizations of participatory democracy. In Nicaragua the women's movement has struggled against sexism, racism, and discrimination based on sexual orientation. The use of combinations of democratic voting with consensus-based decision-making mechanisms, which is common in Latin America, can minimize the threat of majority tyranny in popular groups. Neither Gorostiaga nor other Nicaraguan commentators on the development of participatory democracy in Latin America appear to be much concerned with some of the other problems bothering writers in the North. Most of the countries are emerging from years of military dictatorships and are excited about their burgeoning organizations and the possible roles they can play in what everyone is now calling "civil society." Few social movements have had time to become bureaucratized into limited interest groups. Nicaraguan organizations which may have suffered from bureaucratization became "liberated" with the Sandinista electoral loss of 1990.

Nelly Miranda, professor of sociology at the Central American University in Managua, attempts to put ideas about civil society into a theoretical perspective. She speaks of the 1980s as the decade in which democracy took the form of a space reserved for a set of autonomous social actors, who were characterized by their opposition to the excessive growth of the state. Projects that saw the state as the principal agent for the resolution of social problems entered into crisis. In Nicaragua, the Sandinista experience, according to Miranda, resulted in the development of civil society (which here means those organizations outside the political structures but at the same time, she says, the revolution co-opted its possibilities of expansion by limiting the autonomy of its diverse expressions.[3]

Miranda explains how, in Europe, the development of a capitalist market economy put an end to the authoritarian and hierarchical order of feudalism; how the collective class actors (lords, peasants, clergy) of the feudal period were replaced by the individual as the basis of public life. She says that, for Kant, reason, conceived as a transcendental universal present in all human beings, guarantees the development of democracy, as it articulates the individual rights of equality and liberty. Miranda does not pursue here, as might be expected, those whom we might call the liberal theorists of civil society, most especially Rousseau and Jefferson, whose ideas contributed to and rose out of the French and American revolutions. Those ideas, of the Enlightenment and of the French Revolution, as we have seen above and will see below, are important as well to Nicaraguan revolutionary thought. Jefferson, in particular, should have been mentioned as a major theorist of what is today called participatory democracy.

Miranda continues: In the Hegelian model, civil society as a normative order can only be realized through the state, which is the space where the ethical is made concrete and within which public and private interests come together. With the writings of Hegel, Marx, and Engels, she says, the idea of civil society as a center or core of solidarity based on inherently human moral principles disappears. Miranda says that the antinomy between public and private, according to Hegel, is resolved in the absolute state. (It should be noted, however, that Hegel conceived the state's power as absolute, but not arbitrary, exercised as it was under the forms of law.) For Marx, says Miranda, the solution to this contradiction is found in the reunification of civil society and the state with the coming of the socialist revolution.[4]

Miranda states that Antonio Gramsci, whom she calls the "theoretician par excellence of civil society," incorporated into the theory of the state, developed in part by Lenin, the concept of hegemony as the moral and intellectual direction of civil society. Gramsci says that civil society together with the coercive apparatus of political society, constituted the integral state, that is, hegemony plus coercion.

But Miranda, in her analysis of the relationship between civil society and the state, wants to give particular emphasis to the critical theorists, especially Jürgen Habermas. She says that the central concern of Habermas consists in developing a critical theory of modernity which is based on the design of new forms of social emancipation. For Habermas, as for Kant, Miranda says, the public sphere is the space in which human beings develop their autonomy. In order to make an end to the pathology engendered by modernity, critical theory must achieve the "de-colonization of the life-world"—the universe of communicative action—through the realization of noninstitutional collective actions, such as those carried out by social movements of all types. The idea is to strengthen civil power through the rescue of the individual and the processes of social integration, to make the state an instance of power at the service of its citizens. She goes on: "The democratic alternative for Nicaragua for the last decade of the 20th century, then, is to make a useful instrument of the State, minimizing its bureaucratic aspects and its elitist policies, invoking the notion of civility in the face of the tendency to concentrate political power in few hands, articulating the reactive and proactive interests of the most disadvantaged sectors of society."[5]

Miranda's work puts into perspective for her Nicaraguan students the theoretical background to the discussion of civil society heard at many levels of life in Nicaragua today. Her preference for critical theory over postmodernism is typical of many other Nicaraguan writers and thinkers, who cannot accept what they consider to be a demobilizing ideology. There is a question, however, about whether the majority of the poor in Nicaragua have not, in fact, been demobilized by economic desperation into a concern about individual and family survival only, because they are unable to find time and energy to mobilize with others for change.

Philosopher Alejandro Serrano, president of the National Autonomous University of Nicaragua, gives a more complete analysis of postmodern thought while at the same time providing a critique. He says that ideological incredulity and moral skepticism in the face of all universal, rational philosophical and political constructions and lineal interpretations of history are replaced in postmodern thought by an emphasis on the present, on difference, tolerance, and dialogue and what he says some have called the sociology of fragmentation. He calls rather for a "unity in diversity" and calls on Nicaraguans and all Latin Americans to attempt to rescue their plurality of cultural and political expressions. He goes on to say:

> Only on the basis of this concept can the idea of universality have meaning. The universal is not equivalent to the homogeneous or to an archetypal standard into which we must assimilate ourselves, dissolving our particularities, rather, on the contrary, the universal is the integration of multiple expressions. Identity and universality are two terms that cannot be disassociated: one only has identity to the degree that one's particular cultural expressions are integrated into the universality of cultures. Universality can only be achieved when it is formed by the convergence of multiple contributions: that is unity in diversity.[6]

Serrano wants to see Nicaraguan expressions of civil society (the popular organizations and movements) come together around a platform of democracy, pluralism, and freedom in order to struggle for social justice as part of what he calls "the search for the Possible Nicaragua," in other words, the Nicaragua that it is possible to achieve.[7]

## SOFÍA MONTENEGRO: A DEMOCRACY CONSCIOUS OF GENDER AND ETHNICITY

Sofía Montenegro is a feminist theorist who, as we have seen in chapter 3, is one of the moving forces in the independent feminist movement. She moves beyond the problems of women in her analysis and applies her vision to the whole of society. Montenegro is a journalist and writer. She was editor of the supplement *Gente* of the Sandinista-oriented daily newspaper, *Barricada,* until she resigned in protest when the FSLN leadership removed the paper's general editor Carlos Fernando Chamorro in late 1994. She is now executive director of an agency that does political polling.

She begins her analysis of Nicaraguan society with a critique of how traditional Marxist analysis failed in Nicaragua. She then describes how she differs from postmodernist thinkers and, finally, offers her own ideas on what kind of revolutionary project would be successful in her country. Her ideas are important and relevant because they lay out a vision of participatory democracy that is more inclusive in terms of gender and ethnicity than the original Sandinista project.

Montenegro sees a crisis in the whole of rational western thought including the two great philosophies—"daughters of the enlightenment"—liberalism and socialism. According to her, these philosophies were mechanically applied to areas outside Europe and were confronted with a powerful reality which overwhelmed them. She gives credit to western feminists who, she says, elaborated the theory explaining how patriarchal discourse had left out the language and category of gender. She adds to this that they also omitted the category of ethnicity which, in the case of Latin America, means primarily the Indian, but which also includes the African American. One of the principal differences between the indigenous civilization of the Americas and that of Europe is the concept of nature and the human relationship with nature.

As a part of Western thought, Marxist analysis also devalued nature and saw it as an enemy to defeat, Montenegro says. Humans were the highest beings of the universe for Europeans and the farther a society had removed itself from nature, the more advanced it was considered to be. According to Indian thought, in contrast, human beings are integral parts of the cosmos and the realization of their fullest potential consists in their adjusting themselves in a harmonious fashion to the order of nature. Humans exist only as a moment in nature, not as the masters of nature.[8] Montenegro goes on: "Those of us who studied Marxism worked with two categories. Surplus value expresses the value that the labor of men (literally) gives to natural materials. This undervalues nature and makes its role invisible. In the same way the work of women is made a part of nature and its contribution to the economy ignored. The awareness of this omission necessarily brings us to reevaluate that thought and to include what has been omitted in the past."[9]

Marx, of course, does refer to production in the family and in the clan (see, for example, *The Grundrisse*) but once he moves into his analysis of capitalism, family labor, insofar as it is not involved in exchange, is no longer considered. This analysis, which undervalues much of women's work, has been adopted by most followers of Marx.

Montenegro says also that the differences between the basically white urban centers (now mestizo but historically white), which were symbols of European colonization, and the rural areas which in Nicaragua have been historically indigenous, were ignored. She says:

> The left here did not incorporate anthropological concepts because it was married completely to the strict classical scheme: bourgeoisie versus proletariat without analyzing the cultural differences and the "civilizing" conflicts that took place. And so the contradiction city/countryside or city-dweller/peasant has a variation here. The indigenous is permanently in revolt, in rejection of white, western modernity and progress. Within each peasant in Nicaragua exists the Indian, culturally speaking.... What has happened here is not a mixing of the races but a clash of two civilizations, the Occidental and the indigenous, in which one imposed itself on the other but was never able to completely conquer it.[10]

Montenegro says that she was prompted to investigate exactly who the Nicaraguan people are when the Sandinistas were confronted by a loss of support from rural peasants and especially from indigenous groups in the Atlantic (Caribbean) coast region of the country. The former joined the "contra" army in substantial numbers in protest over agrarian policies while the latter formed their own armies to fight the government for autonomy for their ethnically distinct area. In researching Nicaraguan history, she says she discovered that the state was established before the nation existed, and that the state, in actuality, founded the nation. In 1910, Liberal Party president Zelaya, in effect, "abolished" the Indians of Nicaragua. He imposed Spanish as the official language and accepted as "Occidental" all who dressed in European fashion. Indians abandoned their dress and customs in order to participate in the economic life of the country. Marxists did not analyze this reality and their project under the Sandinistas ran amuck. The Sandinistas, she says, saw women, peasants, and Indians as added factors to the basic capitalist/worker contradiction. They were not subjects in their own right as were the workers. Montenegro maintains that there are many Sandinista leaders who to this day do not recognize these errors.

One thinker who did give importance to race and ethnicity as well as to class was Augusto Sandino, the hero of the struggle against U.S. intervention of the 1920s and 1930s. But modern day Sandinistas have emphasized Sandino's class analysis and ignored his race analysis and his solidarity with the indigenous people of his country. Montenegro wants to rescue his heritage, even at the risk of being called an *indigenista* or one who glorifies and romanticizes the Native American heritage.[11]

There is no doubt that the complexity of the societies of Central America much more closely resembles the categories identified by Montenegro than they do the austere polarities of European Marxism. As I have stated elsewhere, the success of Augusto Sandino in appealing to his countrymen and countrywomen was based largely on his inclusion of these indigenous traditions. Marx himself, late in life, began to study other, non-European systems and to examine the question of alternative routes to human emancipation. Also, wherever the Sandinistas entered into dialogue with the local, most particularly rural, population, their policies were successful and they won in the 1990 balloting. But wherever policies were imposed vertically by those who "knew" what was right, the revolution was not successful and the FSLN lost in the 1990 elections.[12] Montenegro fails to acknowledge the successes of the Sandinistas in those places, such as the towns of Wiwili and San Ramon and the cities of Esteli and Leon, where the party did not impose outside categories on the local traditions and won in the 1990 elections.

In contrast, however, with some others who emphasize traditional identities and differences, Montenegro makes clear that she disagrees with most versions of European postmodernism which she calls a "demobilizing ideology." She states that some people

announce that we have arrived at "Post-Modernity" and they say that it is a new era in which we must forget the libertarian ideals proposed by the French Revolution, and in which the main tenets of modern rationalism no longer apply: the category of subject and the category of totality. It is the "death of the subject" in any of its manifestations (man, class, party, humanity) that makes sterile any proposal to change the world. They recommend that we retreat into individual self-realization, into our private lives, and that we reject all types of revolutionary utopias that can only lead to frustration. They tell us that the all-encompassing narrations which defended global explanations of the evolution of society and nature have fallen and they declare the death of ideology. The only valid ideology, then, is theirs.[13]

Montenegro maintains that there can be a global explanation of the crisis of civilization that is both interdisciplinary and interconnected. For her the cure for the ills of Enlightenment philosophy is more enlightenment. Liberty and equality must be made compatible. Instead of the imposition of European culture upon American indigenous culture, Montenegro wants a synthesis of what she calls the paternal (European) and the maternal (Indian) cultures, a true *mestizaje,* a mixing of cultures based on equality and liberty. We have to see indigenous culture, she says, not as a backward vision, which is how traditional peasant farming methods were seen by many in the Sandinista Agrarian Reform Ministry, but as having the intrinsic value of another culture that could generate a third, valuable, hybrid culture.

This is far from a separatist vision. It is a necessary one, Montenegro feels, for the *mestizo* nations of the Americas if they are to come to terms with their mixed identities. She continues:

> The paradigm for true democratization of a society is not a question of the proletariat and the bourgeoisie, but rather a deeper problem of the human species. There exist tremendous inequalities in human society. Men cannot be free while women are not free. This has often been repeated but the true economic implications are rarely noted. Women were the first excluded group. After that other men were excluded from equality because they had dark skin or were otherwise different. . . . I believe in the possibility of creating a viable utopia by including all those who have been excluded in the past.[14]

Montenegro thus joins thinkers like Martin Luther King, who built on the basic tenets of classical liberalism, maintaining that contained within that system of thought was the possibility, even the philosophical necessity, of expanding individual rights and liberties to include all members of society and not just male property-owners of European descent. Montenegro says that racial, religious, and class prejudices exist within the Nicaraguan women's movement. But, she adds, "We have to pull up those prejudices by the roots and ensure the political recognition that each person has rights that are intrinsic and inalienable."[15] Marx himself did not stray from these premises, but rather added economic rights to those political rights so important to his predecessors Locke, Rousseau, and Jefferson. Montenegro says that she has a radical vision which sees democracy "not just in political and organizational terms but rather in economic, social, and real terms and which sees it as a process of negotiation and pact-making among equals."[16]

Montenegro maintains that a new vision can come out of the diversity that exists in the Nicaraguan women's movement and out of the diverse Sandinista movement in Nicaragua. The Sandinista Party itself will really change, she says, when it feels enough pressure from the popular organizations. It will then modify its statist vision of the economy toward one that will include all sectors of society as active economic subjects and will incorporate the value of nature in a way similar to the vision of the eco-feminists. It is the popular organizations, and most important for Montenegro, the women's movement, that represent the force for true democratic change in Nicaragua. Just as the women's movement brings together women from many different walks of life, the popular organizations must work together as equals, without renouncing their primary identity, to find a new national project for Nicaragua.[17]

It is the nature of this new national project for Nicaragua, including the role of the popular organizations and their relationship to the party, that is the object of such controversy within the Sandinista movement today. Montenegro is among those who are reminding Nicaraguans of the tasks yet to be completed in the area of including all their countrymen and women into the revolutionary project on an equal basis, one of the few who recognizes that there are still inequalities left from the imposition of Spanish colonial rule over the indigenous peoples of western Nicaragua 470 years ago. (More recent grievances stemming from early 1980s government policies with relation to the Miskito Indians of the North Atlantic region were more fully addressed by the Sandinistas with the granting of autonomy to that part of the country. Regional councils in two regions have substantial decision-making power in such areas as natural resource development.) But it is the combination of the intellectual work of Montenegro with the work of people like Beniana Mendiola in the rural areas that will make the difference for Nicaraguan peasants, women, and indigenous and mestizo peoples. While Montenegro theorizes, Mendiola works for reconciliation between demobilized men from the contra and Sandinista armies and obtains land titles for peasant women.

## ORLANDO NÚÑEZ SOTO:
## THE POPULAR ORGANIZATIONS AS
## THE NEW DEMOCRATIC VANGUARD

Orlando Núñez Soto worked with the Center for the Study of Agrarian Reform under the Sandinista government and is now director of CIPRES, a center that trains participants in the new worker-owned agricultural and industrial enterprises of Nicaragua. He has a Ph.D. in political economy from the University of Paris and has published several books.

Núñez Soto emphasizes the importance of the popular organizations, the organizations of civil society, to democratic development even more strongly than does Montenegro. He agrees with her that the Marxist left has concentrated on the worker/capitalist contradiction to a degree unwarranted by the reality of the class structure in Latin America and especially in Nicaragua. And, like Montenegro, Núñez wishes to build on the Enlightenment values of liberty, equality, and fraternity rather than destroy them. He speaks of three revolutions or revolutionary routes. The third revolution he calls the insurrection of consciousness. The nature of the first two revolutions for Núñez changes from his early thought to his later ideas, but the force behind the third revolution in both cases is, he believes, a third force in the population that is broader in its makeup than merely workers and peasants. In pushing for a revolution of consciousness, Núñez makes use of the ideas of Antonio Gramsci, "Che" Guevara, and of critical theorists of the Frankfurt School. He rejects Kautsky but not Marx, especially not the Marx of the "Economic and Philosophical Notebooks of 1844" and the "Ethnological Notebooks."

In the 1980s, Núñez Soto wrote of three processes or strategies leading to socialist revolution. He said that Marxism stipulated that the development of material productive forces would prepare the conditions for revolution and socialism. The active subject of change would be the proletariat. Later, Leninism put its hopes on political revolution which, from the position of state power, would make the changes in the social relations of production that are necessary for the transition to socialism. In this case, a worker-peasant alliance under the leadership of a vanguard party would be responsible for the movement toward change. And finally, in a third moment, a cultural revolution would attempt to make changes in civil society and in the daily lives and thought of citizens with the motor for change being a large and varied representation of "the people."[18]

The second and third processes or roads to socialism are based on the belief that it is not necessary to wait for economic and technological development to reach the level at which revolution is inevitable. "People in the underdeveloped countries got tired of paying the costs of waiting for economic advancement while barbarism proceeded," Núñez said. And those who lived under socialist regimes could not continue to accept a strategy of revolution which first resolved the economic problems of development, then later moved to resolve the political problems and finally, at the end, would "build a new culture, a new civilization, with new values, a new organization of daily life, a new way of relating to one another."

The political (Leninist) revolutions that have occurred in this century are necessary but not sufficient to change alienated relationships, Núñez maintains.[19]

But, in some cases, he adds, the critique by the left of "actually existing socialism" has ended up in a reactionary anti-Soviet and anti-communist position which has included a bitter apathy toward everything that smells of revolution or Marxism. Núñez rather supports

> a critique of the model . . . that reclaims individuality and democracy in the face of authoritarian and statist tendencies. This position has been fed by the new Marxist humanism influenced by psychology (Reich, Marcuse, the Frankfurt and Budapest Schools). These thinkers have confronted the verticalist and totalitarian tendencies of socialism as well as the criticisms that are made of communism from the right because of its lack of democracy. Finally, we can include in the democratic critique of socialism the entire process of renovation, rectification and opening-up which is happening in the Soviet Union under the leadership of Gorbachev.[20]

Núñez adds that the Sandinista experience shows that transformations in the state and in the economy can be accompanied by substantial changes in cultural values, in new kinds of relationships in people's daily lives, instead of the latter having to wait for completion of the former.[21] To this day he tends to emphasize the positive aspects of the transformations of the Nicaraguan revolution, such as the distribution of land to tens of thousands of peasants, which definitely occurred, and to minimize the errors, such as the failed large-scale agricultural model and the excessive growth of the state bureaucracy. There were changes in values and relationships in Nicaragua, but they were far from universal among FSLN leaders, militants, and organizations. As we have seen above, many people left the popular organizations precisely because the new values of equality and participation were crushed by excesses of Leninist verticalism that did not allow members to have any democratic input into their functioning.

It was the Argentine/Cuban Ernesto "Che" Guevara who believed that socialism could be seen not simply as the inevitable result of class contradictions in highly developed societies, but that the revolution would be made by inspired men and women. "Man is the conscious actor of history," Guevara wrote, citing Marx's 1844 Manuscripts to support his position. He said that Marx believed that the end to human alienation which would take place under communism would come about by conscious human action.[22] Núñez makes clear his debt to "Che" when he says:

> How much time did we revolutionaries lose, as "Che" very correctly asks, in waiting for the . . . famous maturation of the objective conditions of capital . . . ? And how much time have we also wasted waiting for state planning to produce the conditions for the new man, the new consciousness, new social relationships of cooperation and solidarity? If revolution and socialism are, in the final instance, an act of conscious liberation, of human creativity freely building a new way of living, then it is only right that we not wait for society to do everything for us. Rather socialism . . . will be a product of our initiative, obviously within existing conditions and circumstances, but keeping in mind the need to supersede in a revolutionary fashion existing reality. To be scientific is to begin with reality, but to be a scientific revolutionary is to deny that reality, revive its tendencies and invite it by force and by historic persuasion to the path of socialism.[23]

For Núñez Soto, the revolution in Nicaragua was one of those in which political power held by a revolutionary vanguard had to compensate for the economic and ideological limitations of the society in order to advance toward socialism. He maintains, however, that the revolution was built on the path to socialism laid out by Karl Marx. He quotes that section of the *Communist Manifesto* in which Marx and Engels say that the first step of the revolution is to elevate the proletariat to the position of dominant class, to win the battle for democracy. He believes that this meant, under conditions present in Nicaragua, the establishment of a democratic regime governing in support of the interests of workers and the rest of the popular sectors. In contrast with previous revolutions, the Nicaraguan revolution included more representation, in the taking of power and afterward, from the undifferentiated urban masses including students, women, barrio residents, religious groups and others. Once in power, the FSLN took a series of measures which Núñez maintains did not differ qualitatively from those enumerated by Marx and Engels in the *Manifesto*.[24] (In the *Communist Manifesto*, Marx and Engels list some measures that would be carried out by a revolutionary government in an advanced country soon after taking power. These include the nationalization of banking, the centralization of the means of communication in the hands of the state, free education for all children in public schools, the combination of agriculture with manufacturing industries, and the confiscation of the property of emigrants and rebels. These measures were carried out by the Sandinista government. Others, such as the abolition of property in land and of all right of inheritance were not.)[25]

Núñez sees the "Third Revolution" as being the project of what he calls a third force. Writing with Roger Burbach in 1986, he said that it was assumed that the motor of the revolutionary process in developed countries would be the working class and in developing countries, a worker-peasant alliance. Marx and Lenin were aware that other social sectors—including segments of the petite bourgeoisie—could play a role but neither of them developed a program for their incorporation. Núñez and Burbach explain:

> History compels us to broaden revolutionary theory and practice. Diverse political experiences, ranging from the Cuban revolution and the political ferment in the United States in the 1960's, to the May 1968 rebellion in France, and the 1979 Nicaraguan revolution, have made it increasingly clear that the impetus for revolutionary change no longer comes only from Marx's working class or Lenin's worker-peasant alliance. Today a *third* social force comprised of a variety of groups— the middle classes, the intellectuals, the urban poor, the petty bourgeoisie, and the ethnic and social movements—often plays a highly original role in social change.[26]

Núñez and Burbach describe in some detail the component groups of the third force. They include the economically marginalized sectors of society, those who live in the barrios and the *favelas* and are often unemployed or underemployed. The social movements form another important part of the third force and within this category Núñez and Burbach include those who struggle for "civil rights, gender equality, opposition to nuclear power and environmental degradation, peace, the right to housing . . . and so on." Included are the new communities of religious activists influenced by Liberation Theology, especially, in Latin America, the Catholic *comunidades de base*. "In many countries," they point out, "Christians and Marxists are forging a common front against exploitation, oppression, imperialism, even capitalism."[27] Núñez saw these groups as leaders on the third road to socialism. However, while their members are struggling to make human relationships more just and this is at the core of what Núñez called the "third revolution," it is not at all certain that all of them see their goal as socialism or that they could agree on what socialism as a goal would mean.

Writing in 1992, Núñez continues to speak of a third revolution but characterizes it as coming after the bourgeois and socialist revolutions, rather than following the two routes (material and political) to socialism to which he had referred before. Those years between 1988 and 1992 had seen the fall of the Berlin Wall, the breakup of the Soviet Union and, most significant of all for him, the Sandinista loss in the elections of 1990. He takes the longer view— "actually existing socialism" has become, with a couple of exceptions, a thing of the past. Núñez says that "the bourgeois revolution had not been fully consummated, nor the possibilities of state planning fully explored when a third revolutionary wave was unleashed, this time for autonomy and self-management."[28] Now he sees the liberal and socialist revolutions as being steps on one positivist route, that of reason and work, of science, technology, and progress. The other road, that "of love, of play, of ethics, of aesthetics, of art, of the conscience, of the spirit, of the best values of humanity," has not yet been fully explored.

Núñez maintains that liberty has now been freed from its principal obstacle, which was the realm of necessity. Objectively, humanity can feed the world. What is missing, he says, is the will, the free-dom, the organization. Humanism must follow its route now, ac-cording to Núñez. The contribution of humanists, of utopians, he believes, is more important than ever in the midst of the confusion and uncertainty of the present-day alienated social consciousness.[29] It appears that Núñez here is confusing humanity's ability to pro-duce enough food for everyone to eat, which may technically exist, with the ability to set up economic structures in all countries that would allow people to sustain themselves and their families through productive labor, a capacity which does not presently exist. This is an important distinction because while will and inspiration are im-portant (and here enters the influence of the utopians), very con-crete changes in economic structures need to take place and in most cases we do not yet know what those should be. We cannot change defective economic structures merely by changing alienated social consciences; in fact, the reverse may well be true. We can, however, put the "best values of humanity" to work to help guide the search for concrete economic alternatives, and this is where Núñez's "third force" organizations in civil society have a role to play.

Liberalism gave us the individual citizen who, Núñez says, speak-ing colloquially, "is now five hundred years old," and built represen-tative democracy. But, along with individual citizens, there exist as well "collective subjects, which are also a creation of western civi-lization." These collective subjects want to manage the factories, the unions, and the federations and have a say in government more sig-nificant than merely casting a ballot every four years. This involve-ment, which appears to mean having their organizations consulted by government officials when decisions are being made but remain-ing free to criticize government policies later, is what Núñez means by participatory democracy. It is this surge in participation at the level of civil society among women, ethnic minorities, environmen-talists, neighborhood residents, and so forth, in Latin America and elsewhere that he sees as a manifestation of the Third Revolution.[30]

Sometimes it is unclear, when Núñez speaks of the Third Revo-lution, whether he is referring to changes in people's personal lives, in how they relate to their mates and their children, for example, or to societal changes, such as people's increased role in making management decisions in their workplaces or their participation on city-level commissions to decide questions of local government. He reiterates several times, however, that he means all of these: "We think that a new way of living must simultaneously include personal projects, joint projects at the level of couples, community projects and social projects."[31] He quotes what he calls "the phrase that energized the 1960s, 'the personal is political and the political is personal,'" which he says symbolizes the recognition that basic power relationships have to be challenged and changed, not just at the level of the state, but in civil society and in daily life as well.[32]

In support of this position, Núñez quotes from Marx's "Theses on Feuerbach": "The chief defect of all hitherto existing materialism—that of Feuerbach included—is that the thing, reality, sensuousness, is conceived only in the form of the object or of contemplation, but not as human sensuous activity, practice, not subjectively."[33] If the struggle against the previous regime must include the struggle to change that social system, Núñez goes on to say, then the latter must include the fight against the alienated, inherited cultures, and civilization. And, he adds, this struggle finds its battlefield in our daily lives.[34]

Socialism has always included at its heart, Núñez says, the conflict between a project that was more statist and one that was more communal and libertarian, between the party in power and individuals organized in grassroots structures, between centralization and decentralization.[35] It is the latter in each case that can bring to fruition the revolution of consciousness. Certainly in the Soviet Union and other countries of the former Eastern Bloc, the former triumphed and Núñez would be the first to argue that a revolution of consciousness did not take place in those countries. But, he would also argue that the Soviet experience does not preclude it happening elsewhere.

But is Núñez not being too optimistic? When he says that values such as the traditional family, religious and political doctrines, paradigms of personal conduct, and so forth, are being challenged by new democratic, egalitarian, and fraternal values, is he taking into account the strength of the right, in Nicaragua and in the rest of the world? What about the growth of religious fundamentalism, both Protestant and Catholic in Nicaragua, and of fundamentalist groups within other religions in different parts of the world? Núñez answers, in effect, that it is exactly because of the strength of the new movements for change that the right-wing and the fundamentalist religious groups are waging such a desperate counteroffensive: "The reaction of the dominant classes against these protests has been that of a beast that feels itself mortally wounded." But, he adds, the struggle will be long and difficult and we could be well into the next millennium before the new values take root.[36]

Popular organizations must overcome formidable barriers, even apart from the counteroffensive of the right, according to Núñez, such as the isolation of one group from another, interference in their internal affairs by political parties, and undemocratic internal structures in which officers are put in place by these same parties rather than by direct election of the members.[37] These and other undemocratic practices, in fact, did take place in most cases in the popular organizations in Nicaragua under the Sandinista government, as was noted above. Núñez Soto was not to be found at the time among the most severe critics of these practices, as were Sofía Montenegro and other feminists. In the late 1980s he made general criticism of authoritarian tendencies in countries with vanguard parties in power, but showed a definite reluctance to apply these criticisms directly to Nicaragua.

It is indeed ironic that, as we have seen above, the popular organizations founded by the Sandinistas, which were foundering under the revolutionary government, have blossomed since the revolutionary government was turned out of power in 1990. Núñez says now, in a more outspoken fashion since the electoral loss, that the role of the Marxist-Leninist vanguard parties may diminish due to the rejection of their verticalism, "but the struggle against exploitation and power is as strong as ever" and the fight for social justice must go on despite adverse conditions. He maintains that there could very well occur in Nicaragua a revolution that does not include mediation by government, but that develops instead within civil society. The popular organizations, liberated from party control, can carry out a revolution in neighborhoods and on farms and in factories, independent of the party in power. As Gorostiaga also described above and as will be seen below, networks of popular organizations and other networks of non-governmental organizations have trained worker-owners of farms and factories and have provided financing for their projects. This is a new version of participatory democracy that is taking place on the ground in Nicaragua and in other parts of Latin America as well. Theorists like Núñez Soto have been looking upon these developments as an encouraging new sign. The new forces, says Núñez, raise the traditional banners of all revolutions, such as liberty, equality, and fraternity, either in their bourgeois/democratic expressions or in their socialist expressions, and also demand a share in the management of capital, of power, and of life in general.[38]

Núñez rejects postmodernism in a fashion similar to that of Sofía Montenegro. He says that the philosophy of progress is not resolving the problems of alienation from which people suffer and that they therefore are looking for a refuge in their own individual, personal lives. But refuge from the world cannot be found by "hiding in your room alone because the television will follow you in there! We have to be in the street again!" He goes on to describe what this means politically: "We think that we have to combine individuality and the objectives of each social sector with the joint coordination of all the sectors, taking ownership of universal values and developing alternative organizations that will help us to realize those values. But we believe that isolated struggles by those sectors, even if they are very legitimate struggles, will not be able to resolve their problems. It is difficult for any group to save itself alone."[39]

Núñez says that if there is a force in the world that could be considered to be a democratic vanguard, we should not hesitate to point to these new social movements which struggle every day to transform the lives of their members, "without waiting for objective conditions or for a dominant political or ideological figure to tell them what to do and how to do it."[40] This is a dramatic change from the position of "Che" Guevara, Antonio Gramsci, and others who have influenced Núñez, because for them it is the vanguard party and its members that forge the new man and woman and provide the inspirational force with which to carry out the radical changes of the revolution.

As a "democratic vanguard," as Núñez calls them, it is very possible that these popular movements do represent "the highest aspirations of their people," as the Sandinistas were wont to say about the FSLN. But they do not represent those aspirations through any mysterious process of political osmosis, as did the vanguard party. If they do reflect the general will of their members, it is in a true Rousseauean sense through the direct participation of all in the operation of the organizations. One must remember, of course, that Rousseau disapproved of mediating organizations in society. The general will thus formed would be that of each organization rather than that of the people as a whole. But in modern diverse societies, possibly the most one can hope for is the formation of a general will within the different groups and for some institutionalized way to bring these views into the governing process. Rousseau did add that, "if there are sectional associations, it is wise to multiply their number and to prevent inequality among them. . . . These are the only precautions which can ensure that the general will is always enlightened and the people protected from error."[41]

Núñez thus charts a major change in socialist thought: participatory organizations as the "democratic vanguard" of the revolution (now a peaceful revolution) bringing egalitarian values to the workplace, the neighborhood, and even to the family. The very meaning of the word "vanguard" changes, back to its dictionary meaning of "the forefront of a movement" and away from the Jacobin and Leninist versions of coercive leadership bodies. The new way of thinking is based on the upsurge in the organizations of civil society in Latin America. Núñez Soto is not the only theorist or political activist dealing with this upsurge. The parties of the Latin American left meet regularly in what they call the Forum of São Paulo to discuss these changes. Some of the newer parties, like the Brazilian Workers Party, appear to have an easier time dealing with the new political realities than do the formerly military vanguard parties like the FSLN.

The principal question now becomes, what is the role of the party if the social movements are the democratic vanguard? And this is the question that the FSLN has been considering since the party's electoral loss in 1990, and even more with the flowering of the popular organizations that followed that loss. Should the FSLN become an electoral party which would represent a broad range of citizenry in the way a European Social Democratic party does, making political compromises in order to win elections and in order to govern afterwards? Or should it instead remain pure, a type of post-vanguard (because everyone says the vanguard party "is dead or should be") vanguard, a network or coalition of popular organizations representing the poor and dispossessed, forswearing all collaboration with the haute bourgeoisie, and possibly abandoning hope of government power as well? This question will be examined in Chapter 7.

## SUMMARY

Xabier Gorostiaga, Nelly Miranda, and Alejandro Serrano began this chapter of new ideas on participatory democracy among Sandinista thinkers. An introductory examination of their ideas was followed by a more in-depth look at work on participatory democracy by Sofia Montenegro and Orlando Núñez. Both of the latter emphasize that recognition of the ethnic, gender, and economic diversity of Nicaragua's population is necessary for participatory democracy to function properly. Both could be accused of having an idealized view of the popular organizations. Montenegro believes that the women's movement has the potential to show the

FSLN how to become again the force for democratic change in Nicaragua and Núñez sees the popular organizations as the new "democratic vanguard." However, the variety and diversity of these organizations makes them virtually the opposite of what is traditionally understood as a vanguard. One is prompted to ask if these writers are not so enamored of the popular organizations precisely because the party, the FSLN, is in such disarray. The organizations appear to know whom they represent and what their members need. The party does not. As pointed out by Gorostiaga, the popular organizations and NGOs believe that they can do effective work for their constituencies whether a party sympathetic to their needs is in government or not. The national and international networks that they have formed are now playing varying roles in influencing policy at both the national and international levels. As Enrique Picado said, the organizations are now grown up. The Leninist vision has been left far behind. Many Nicaraguans feel that it is these organizations which, with all their diversity, are working toward realizing the democratic and revolutionary vision that they are not ready yet to abandon.

# 5

## Economic Democracy:
## The Revolutionary Years

Dora María Téllez says that "it is impossible to imagine a political democracy without a lessening of the gap between those who have the most and those who have the least."[1] Economic democracy has been one of the most important principles of the FSLN since its founding. In the early period, many Sandinistas believed that economic democracy was much more important than political or formal democracy. Most Sandinistas, however, have come to agree with Alejandro Bendaña's description of Sandinista thought and practice as "liberal democracy squared, that is to say, civil and political rights and freedoms but also social and economic rights."[2]

Economic democracy was defined in the introduction to this volume as a system under which there is an equalization in the ownership of wealth and in which the people of a nation have control over the use of the resources of the nation and over the type of economic system under which they will live. Certainly there is no question about Sandinista commitment to the idea of a greater equalization of wealth in their country. However, considerable difference of opinion arose among Sandinistas around the role of the people in *deciding* economic policy. The controversy was between those who "knew" from studying correct theory and political economy what policies were best for the country and those who believed that the people themselves, through their own organizations, should have the major role in the formation of economic policy.

In this chapter we shall examine in detail the views of the main participants in this controversy during the Sandinista years in power and then, in the next chapter, consider the possibilities for a new Sandinista economic model to fit the present period. In order to provide a sound basis for theoretical discussion, we must first review the recent economic history of Nicaragua. As in previous chapters, the statements of the participants themselves are the primary sources.[3]

## HISTORICAL BACKGROUND

According to Jaime Wheelock, minister of Agriculture and Agrarian Reform under the Sandinista government, there are two important aspects of Nicaraguan economic history that have to be taken into account in the formation of an economic plan. The first is that the country's economic formation after 1850 was strongly influenced by the United States, by U.S. bankers, corporations, and the U.S. government. The second is the fact that Nicaragua did not follow the classical model of capitalist development, but, as is true in so many other Third World countries, capitalism was imported and began mainly in the area of export agriculture. An agricultural proletariat developed, Wheelock maintains, before an industrial proletariat arose. Plantation agriculture brought about the dissolution of the indigenous community, which was moved from its traditional lands and converted into a seasonal agricultural workforce. Other Nicaraguans argue that the members of this seasonal farm-worker population did not cease to be peasant in their class orientation and that their desire was always to again have a piece of land of their own on which to plant corn and beans. Agrarian capitalism promoted not industrialization, but rather the importation of manufactured goods.[4]

In the 1960s, the formation of the Central American Common

Market and the investment promoted by the Alliance for Progress resulted in some growth and industrialization in Nicaragua. There were
economic opportunities for an elite but few benefits trickled down to
the great masses of people. Wheelock asserts that, in countries where
an economic model is in force that concentrates wealth in the hands
of a few, the coming of boom years does not result in any improve-
ment in the lives of the poorest sectors of society. And so it was that
the climax of the revolutionary struggle against the dictatorship occurred during years of excellent prices for Nicaragua's export crops
on the world market and excellent harvests in those crops.

In 1969, the FSLN presented to the Nicaraguan public what is
known as its Historic Program. In this program the FSLN promised
that upon taking power it would put into effect the nationalization
of the foreign mining and timber companies, of the landholdings
and business enterprises of the Somoza family, of the banks, and of
foreign commerce. The document promised to give land free of
charge to the peasants who worked it, to promote the organization
of cooperatives in the countryside, to give credit for the first time to
peasant farmers for seed and machinery, to cancel debts to usurers,
to protect the small and medium-sized farmers and those who had
collaborated with the armed revolutionary struggle, and to provide
free medical care to the entire population with clinics throughout
the country. All of these promises were fulfilled by the FSLN upon
taking power—an extraordinary phenomenon in the history of revolutionary struggles. Other, even more ambitious, promises were
not fulfilled, however, such as providing adequate housing for all
and eliminating unemployment. Only partially fulfilled was the
promise of control and participation by the workers in the administration of industry and other nationalized units.[5] The adherence
of Sandinista leaders to the 1969 FSLN Program when they took
over the government in 1979, however, gives the lie to the claims of
some that the Sandinistas, in order to gain popular support, hid
their true goals.

When the Sandinistas came to power they found that two thousand large landowners, *latifundistas,* owned half of the land under cultivation. Small landowners, *minifundistas,* who were 70 percent of the total number of farmers, held only four percent of the land in properties of seventeen acres or less. Medium-sized farmers, a strong sector in Nicaragua, held the remaining 46 percent. The terrain of the small farmers and sharecroppers tended to be of marginal fertility, located in areas isolated from markets. There were also growing numbers of landless seasonal agricultural workers who harvested the coffee, cotton, and sugar.[6]

By means of two decrees issued in the first days after taking power, the Sandinista government nationalized the properties of the Somoza family and its closest associates. With the properties from these first decrees, which put over 2.7 million acres (approximately 7.5 percent of the land area of the country), as well as factories and other businesses, into government hands, the state sector was set up. It included sugarcane plantations with their refining plants, coffee plantations with their corresponding operations to prepare the beans for export, and other enterprises of high-technology export agriculture. At the time, most revolutionary leaders agreed that it was appropriate to turn over only a very small part of this property to the peasants.[7] No one suggested that the Somoza family factories and businesses be turned over to the workers. Edmundo Jarquín, minister of foreign cooperation in the Sandinista government, now says with some irony that the state sector was set up based on political rather than economic criteria: "We expropriated the Somocistas. This meant that we got an airline, a cotton plantation and gin, a grocery store, a house of prostitution. . . . Very quickly in the name of economic democratization we should have gotten rid of many of these small and medium-sized businesses and farms that introduced irrationality into state administration."[8]

In the two years following the victory of the revolution, worker productivity went down precipitously, credit was disbursed to small farmers without much care taken as to its use, food prices were subsidized and, where national production was not sufficient, food was

imported. As a result of the latter policy, malnutrition among in-
fants and young children virtually disappeared by the close of 1983.
It was not to reappear until the economic crises of the mid- and
late-eighties. Infant mortality dropped precipitously. Staffed health
centers were set up in all the most remote rural areas as well as in the
cities. International assistance was consumed in such necessities
rather than being invested in productive activities. The short-lived
results of these policies were phenomenal, but they were short-lived
only. Orlando Núñez says in explanation that "the desire for justice
of the popular sectors who had just won the war of liberation was as
great as their hunger and hopes for improving their lives with the
Revolution."[9] On the other hand, Edmundo Jarquín says that
Nicaragua's straightened circumstances after the overthrow of Somoza should have prompted policies that were less distributive in
nature and at the same time more attention should have been given
from the beginning to maintaining macro-economic equilibrium.
He points out that he and Henry Ruíz, member of the FSLN National Directorate and minister of planning, were the only ones who
insisted that the nation could not continue for long to operate with
fiscal deficits and balance of payment deficits.[10]

In 1980, the Sandinistas put together their economic plan for the
next few years, under the assumption that the prices on the world
market for Nicaragua's principal exports would stay the same or decline slightly. Instead, beginning in 1981, coffee dropped from $1.80
per pound to $1.12, cotton from $.95 per pound to $.62, and in the
steepest drop of all, the bottom fell out of the sugar market with
sugar falling from $0.60 to $.04 per pound. Some crops, such as cotton and sugar, cost considerably more to produce than they would
bring on the world market. In fact, in the case of sugar in the early
1980s, the transportation to the port, which was nearby, cost more
than the value of the sugar. The drop in export prices, combined
with rising prices for the oil the country needed to import and
growing protectionism in the developed countries wrought havoc
with the Nicaraguan economy and the Sandinista economic plan.
Even though the 1982–83 coffee harvest was the largest in history

and that of cotton the second largest, the economic benefits to the nation did not reflect this.[11] The recession of the early 1980s hit all of Latin America very hard. Wheelock estimates that the region as a whole lost over $27 billion in 1983 due to deterioration in the terms of trade alone.[12] Núñez Soto says that between 1980 and 1985 Nicaragua alone lost $150 million from this same cause.[13]

The 1985 U.S. trade embargo also had damaging effects on the Nicaraguan economy. For some products traditionally sold to the U.S., such as bananas, markets were quickly found in Europe. But finding markets for other products was more difficult. Suppliers had to be found for industrial products and consumer goods traditionally bought from the U.S. There were other results of the trade embargo, as former Minister of Foreign Trade Alejandro Martínez Cuenca points out:

> The U.S. embargo effectively forced a more acute dependence on the countries of the East, more than was originally intended. For my part, I always thought that our way around the blockade should be found in Latin America, but unfortunately, the crisis of the 1980's made it impossible for even the richest countries of Latin America to be able to commit resources to Nicaragua in the amounts and at the times they were required. Therefore, we had to increase our economic dependence on the Soviet Union especially, and on the countries of Eastern Europe, such as the German Democratic Republic and Bulgaria, and also on Cuba. Great inconveniences were created with the extension of trade towards the east, but without a doubt, it was better than remaining completely isolated.[14]

Because the first confiscations of the property of the Somoza family and its closest associates had produced so little land appropriate for use in peasant production, the revolutionary government issued an Agrarian Reform Decree in 1981 that was intended to put idle, abandoned, or poorly managed agricultural land into the hands of landless peasants. The decree affected only farms of more than 850 acres in the more densely populated Pacific and central highlands areas and 1,700 acres in the rest of the country.[15] Peasants were encouraged to come together in cooperatives to farm the land.

The most popular form of cooperation was the Credit and Service Cooperative, in which individual peasant landowners came together to receive credit and technical assistance; much less popular but favored by the revolutionary government was the Sandinista Agricultural Cooperative, where the land was owned and farmed in common. By 1982 approximately three thousand cooperatives had been formed with over sixty thousand members. Credit to peasant farmers increased almost 400 percent in the first years of the revolution with different interest levels for different types of farmers. Large owners had to pay 17 percent interest, small and medium-sized farmers 13 percent, credit and service cooperatives 10 percent, and production cooperatives 8 percent.[16] The banks of the agricultural towns and cities of Nicaragua were an interesting sight to see. There were bank branches where there had never been bank branches before and peasant farmers doing business inside them where they had never been before. Most remarkable of all, the peasant farmers were signing their full names to the documents, having been relieved by the 1980 National Literacy Crusade of the crushing humiliation of having to mark an X on the line where others could sign their names.

On the negative side of the equation, neither the banks nor the Ministry of Agriculture had the capacity to oversee these loans properly, or provide technical assistance or equipment, and when the small farmers could not repay their loans because of low prices, drought, pests, or plain mismanagement, the government, committed to not foreclosing on small farmers, declared that the loans would be forgiven. It is regrettable that the lack of trained specialists prevented the government from supervising the use of the credit it extended. If the goal is economic democracy, however, there is, in fact, no acceptable answer to this problem.

The main focus of the first years of Sandinista government was the consolidation of the state sector. By the middle 1980s, state-owned industry accounted for 40 percent of total industrial production. Foreign commerce was nationalized and thus was wholly in government hands. Approximately 30 percent of internal commerce was in the hands of the state, along with about 23 percent of agricultural production.[17] The state farms suffered from a serious shortage of capable managers. Many farms had been stripped of their assets by their previous owners and required repairs to machinery and infrastructure. While their production was not much lower than that of private producers, their expenditures were much higher. Wheelock admits that from the very beginning all these state farms "made social investments that far outstripped their economic possibilities. Nevertheless, it was necessary to answer the needs of the farm workers who had been living so long in conditions of misery."[18] In this case, as in other areas, the roots of the transformation and of the later crisis were not economic at all; they derived instead in great part from the political need to satisfy the demands of the masses.

Large agro-industrial projects in sugar refining, milk production, vegetable processing, a massive corn irrigation scheme, and other similar projects were begun with matching monies from the Eastern and Western European countries and Cuba. Later, the start-up costs of these enterprises were revealed to have been entirely out of line with what the government could afford. Few of these projects would make it to completion. Noel Sánchez, who worked in the Ministry of Planning under the Sandinista government, points out the contradiction between these policies and Nicaragua's economic reality: "The technocracy of the Ministry of Agriculture and Agrarian Reform favored the mega-projects with sophisticated technology that were capital-intensive. This was in a country that by definition suffered from capital scarcity and that by further definition had abundant labor power."[19]

Large private farmers were given incentives to continue planting and harvesting because the foreign exchange from their crops was so essential for the economic development of the nation. Incentives were especially generous in the case of farmers growing crops that needed to be planted annually, such as cotton, sugarcane, and rice. There were fewer incentives for coffee growers, whose crop grows on a bush that produces beans for fifteen years. But with or without incentives the large private growers virtually stopped investing their own money. Many would invest the bank's money, however, so loans to large-scale farmers continued to flow even though their support for the revolution was in doubt at the beginning and was to wane as the years went by.

At the same time, the peasant sector was suffering. The subsidized prices paid for peasant-produced food crops grew at a slower rate than the prices of the goods peasants needed to buy[20]—such as machetes, rubber boots, cloth, radio batteries—and also at a slower rate than the subsidies that lowered the price of food for the city dweller. In general, the city dweller was given higher priority in economic decision-making than the country dweller. Also, large-scale production—whether private, cooperative, or state-owned—was given priority over small-scale production.

By the middle of 1984, according to Jaime Wheelock, state farms held 20 percent of farm land, cooperatives 17 percent, farmers with over 340 acres held 23 percent (down from 50 percent in 1979), medium-sized farms (the largest sector in terms of acreage) held 30 percent of the land and the small individual peasant farmer now held 10 percent.[21] Combining the figures for cooperatives and small individual farmers, the total for peasant production is 27 percent, a substantial rise from 1979.

By 1982, the economic costs of the Contra War began to be felt. Speaking in 1984, Agriculture minister Wheelock calculated the losses in production alone at $50 million per year. The CIA-trained contra troops concentrated their attacks on cooperatives, state farms, grain silos, trucks, road repair equipment, saw mills and other economically significant targets. Several important attacks were carried out by the CIA directly. Among them is the explosion of the petroleum storage tanks in the port of Corinto in October of 1983, which occasioned enormous economic losses, and the mining of the principal harbors in 1984. By the end of that year, more than 80 state farms had been attacked and totally or partially burned. Also, the labor of the 40 thousand men who had been drafted into the Sandinista Army was lost to the economy. Health and education expenditures continued while, at the same time, fully half of the government's budget had to be spent for defense. Where did all this money come from? Wheelock answers, "It came out of the budget, or more exactly, in conditions like ours, it came from printing more money with very little to back it up."[22]

A major change in agricultural policy that favored distribution of more land to individual peasant farmers began in 1984 and 1985. Wheelock states that, by the end of 1983, only 21,505 acres of land had been distributed to individuals, but that in the middle of that year the National Directorate of the FSLN ordered a change of course in the application of the 1981 Agrarian Reform Law. The leadership had become alarmed, he says, by the slow pace of distribution of land to poor peasant farmers and by the difficulty in organizing and developing the peasant cooperative sector. In 1984 land distribution to individuals virtually exploded, with thirty-five thousand families receiving land in the first ten months. Most of the land came from state farms; some came from national lands; some was land purchased from individual owners.[23]

While Wheelock says that the decision was made by the National Directorate based on the leaders' concern about the slow pace of land distribution, a more accurate description of what happened appears to be that peasants all over the country, but especially in the densely populated department of Masaya and in parts of the northern war zones, were consistently demanding land, pounding on the door of the local offices of the Ministry of Agriculture and Agrarian Reform each year when the planting season approached. The Union of Farmers and Ranchers, formed in 1981 by separation from the Farmworkers Association, took up the banner of the small peasant landowners and landless peasants and pressured for more land for peasant farmers and better pricing and marketing policies as well as greater availability of consumer goods in the countryside. Núñez and Burbach say: "Rather than try to contain these demands by pushing for . . . production cooperatives, the Frente decided to distribute land titles to the peasantry. . . . [T]his was a recognition of the basic rights of the rural inhabitants to organize their communities and their lives in the way they wanted."[24]

In 1985–86, therefore, the government made major changes in

economic policy. Besides distributing more land to the peasants to farm individually, food subsidies were ended and prices for basic grains were floated. Consumer goods and agricultural inputs needed by the peasants were prioritized over the needs of the urban population. A fiscal and monetary adjustment program reduced social expenditures, imposed a hiring freeze, restricted credit and set higher interest rates. The currency was partially devalued and tax collection improved. Large-scale, technically advanced, capital-intensive investments were funded at lower levels. In general, the cooperatives and small and medium-sized farmers responded better to the new production incentives than did large farmers, recording greater production increases than the latter or, at least, less decline in production. Several observers[25] feel that the state farms that were turned over to cooperatives were managed better under cooperative operation than they had been by the state. By 1989, 62 percent of peasant families, that is, 120,000 families, had received agrarian reform titles, half of them in individual holdings.[26] Other observers maintain that these changes came too late and that many peasants did not participate because of lack of faith in the government based on its previous actions.[27] Thousands joined the counter-revolution.

In the last quarter of 1987, Nicaragua entered a period of hyperinflation that was to peak at an unimaginable 30,000 percent the year following. To try to bring the inflation under control, the government implemented several sets of drastic measures, similar to but more severe than those of earlier years. Many called these "IMF policies without IMF money" since the international financial institutions had not made loans to Nicaragua for half a decade. The Sandinistas tried to put a human face on their stabilization and adjustment measures by conserving a minimum level of social services to thus soften the blows of the layoffs and restrictions on credit. In spite of this, there was a great deal of controversy within revolutionary circles about the correctness of the measures and about how much involvement in decision-making had been given to the labor unions, farmers, and other sectors being affected by the measures. At any rate, inflation, the great enemy of the poor, was indeed lowered by these steps, although only to 1,500 percent.

## THE MODERNISTIC VISION OF JAIME WHEELOCK

> Those who in the past were exploited and oppressed now hold power in the person of a vanguard that represents and puts forward their interests.
>
> —*Jaime Wheelock, minister of Agriculture and Agrarian Reform, 1984*

> [W]here the peasant exists on a mass scale as a private land proprietor ... where he has not disappeared and been replaced by agricultural laborers ..., the proletariat ... must, as the government, take steps as a result of which the situation of the peasant will directly improve and which will therefore bring him over to the side of the revolution, steps which embryonically facilitate the transition from private ownership of the land to collective ownership, so that the peasant will himself come to this by economic means; but there should be no stunning of the peasant.
>
> —*Karl Marx, 1874, from his critique of* Bakunin's Statehood and Anarchy

The major architect of Sandinista agricultural policy was Jaime Wheelock, one of the nine members of the FSLN National Directorate and minister of Agriculture and Agrarian Reform. Before the reunification of the FSLN in 1979, Wheelock was the major figure of the Proletarian Tendency. It was his insistence that the FSLN give priority to the agricultural proletariat in Nicaragua that brought about the first major division in the FSLN. Wheelock studied in Nicaragua and in Chile and the master's thesis from his studies in Chile became the highly-regarded book *Imperialismo y dictadura* (Imperialism and Dictatorship). This work analyzes the formation and structure of the Nicaraguan bourgeoisie, especially including the Somoza family and its closest associates.[28] What concerns us here is that Wheelock had a coherent vision of the present and future of the Nicaraguan economy and, while his vision was being put into practice after 1979, he expressed himself eloquently in interviews and essays. These later became books which have been accessible to the student of Nicaraguan economic policy for a decade. Orlando Núñez Soto presents a supporting position to Wheelock in his doctoral thesis, which was translated from the original French into Spanish and published in Mexico.

The alternatives to Wheelock's and Núñez's orthodox ideas did not have such eloquent advocates. But the alternative voices were very important and are expressed strongly here by Daniel Núñez and Benigna Mendiola, both of the Union of Farmers and Ranchers (UNAG).

Wheelock sees the Nicaraguan economy as one based on dependent capitalism accompanied by great social and cultural backwardness. From this economy, the United States and other advanced capitalist nations had extracted raw materials. According to Wheelock, an undeveloped bourgeoisie of oligarchic origins accumulated a certain amount of capital based more on the merciless exploitation of workers than on high productivity or efficiency.[29] Wheelock goes on to say, in agreement with "scientific socialism," or orthodox Marxism, that a country cannot pass from one economic stage to another before the first has matured and reached its natural limits, such that the forces of production are being constrained by outdated relations of production. From no perspective whatsoever, he says, can capitalism be perceived to have reached this point in Nicaragua. Therefore, the Sandinistas had to look at history and at the political and geopolitical situation of Nicaragua in 1979 for guidance in the making of a policy that was objective, adequate, and in accordance with the interests of the revolution. Nicaragua's situation was not appropriate for a classical socialist agrarian reform; instead the leaders had to look toward a mixed economic model, one in which private farms of all sizes would be permitted and even encouraged.[30]

The unfavorable terms of trade for Third World countries in general and for Nicaragua in particular were a major cause of concern to the Sandinistas. Wheelock notes that the Sandinista revolution occurred at the same time as the beginning of the severe economic crisis of the early 1980s. He points to the fact that, as noted above, the prices of Nicaragua's exports dropped while the prices for the country's imports rose.[31] Along with the severe crisis in the traditional agro-export model, the model based on import-substitution industrialization was also in crisis because of the costs of the imported materials and equipment needed for manufacture of these consumer goods. Nicaragua, he insists, "is the sum of two models in crisis." It is difficult to plan "when there is only misery to divide up."[32]

But for Wheelock, an opportunity to work for a patriotic future was offered. This could mean "the construction in Latin America of a way to overcome the old unresolvable problem of the domination of U.S. imperialism, which has hovered over us since the days of the Monroe Doctrine."[33] Nicaraguans could now decide what to produce and how to produce it, to whom they would sell and from whom they would buy, Wheelock maintains. This turned out to be an unrealistic assumption in light of Nicaragua's tiny size and limited economic power.

For Wheelock, land is Nicaragua's principal resource and therefore democratizing society means democratizing the ownership of land. It also means making human beings the subject of their work by giving them the material base that will allow them the means to develop freely in the economic, political, and cultural spheres. He continues: democratizing land ownership means giving thousands of hungry peasant farmers a nation they can feel a part of, something they did not have prior to the revolution. Wheelock is careful to add, however, that the special privilege granted to the peasants does not mean that other classes, including middle-sized and even large farmers, are to be excluded from the revolutionary project, which is based on a mixed economy and political pluralism.[34] What Wheelock and other Sandinista leaders seem to be reluctant to face, however, is the zero sum relationship between the interests of rural peasant farmers and those of urban workers. Urban workers want cheap food, rural farmers need good prices for the food they produce. Urban and rural consumers have demands for different goods purchased with limited foreign exchange. The famous slogan of Sandino, "Only the workers and peasants will go on to the end," and Lenin's coalition worker and peasant government have, in economic terms, limited viability in Nicaragua.

In spite of the obstacles Wheelock describes, his vision and his model are based on "faith in the future." The Nicaraguan economy, he says, is like a family that sells ice cream from its refrigerator but finds out at the end of the month that the electricity bill comes to more than the profit from the ice cream. The family has to close down the ice cream business. But "we cannot close down Nicaragua. Rather we have to find a way to open a new economic horizon."

This new horizon is a plan for development based on the "industrial transformation of [Nicaragua's] own natural resources with the agricultural sector as a base."[35] In order to escape from the two failed models of traditional agro-export and import substitution industrialization, Wheelock wants to process (at least minimally) the nation's agricultural, forestry, mining, and fishery products before export. Instead of exporting logs, Nicaragua will export lumber or furniture; instead of exporting cotton in bales, it will export cotton yard goods; instead of tomatoes, catsup.

Along with agro-industrialization, Wheelock believes that the country can and must achieve food self-sufficiency. This will not be done by providing technical assistance and credit to widely scattered small peasant farmers on infertile, mountainous terrain far from roads and silos, where they had been pushed by the large export-crop growers. He favors instead taking advantage of the fertile, level Pacific coast region where, with irrigation, two or three crops of corn, beans, and other basic grains can be grown every year or, alternatively, corn and cotton can be grown in successive harvests in the same year on the same land.

In addition to producing more food, this plan will relieve the pressure on the jungle soils of the agricultural frontier and halt the erosion of soils in the mountains. Mountain soils are better suited to coffee and pasture and the soils of the jungle are more suited to perennial crops. The peasants need to be brought down from those mountains and out of those jungles into cooperatives where they can take advantage of economies of scale while the government provides them with technical assistance as well as access to markets. With his customary idealism, Wheelock emphasizes also that an important corollary to this strategy of development is the application of methods of high technology to agriculture. He admits that his plan is controversial:

> Some maintain that we will become more dependent, others that we are using equipment that we will not be able to handle . . . 'Nicaragua cannot handle so much modernity,' they say. There is a certain amount of truth to all these criticisms. Intensive agriculture can bring more dependence because of the chemicals that we need to import; three harvests a year can wear out the soil; we may not have enough technical expertise to support this growth. . . . Nevertheless, no one has offered us anything better. . . . Each alternative has its own contradictions.[36]

Wheelock maintains that the combination of agrarian reform, changes in the use of the land, the application of modern technology, and industrial processing will place the country on the road to self-sufficiency in food and lead to the transformation of its own natural resources. "We want to leap stages," Wheelock says, affirming, "We are not a country of appropriate technology which has as its philosophy the institutionalization of under-development." In other words, he rejects the idea common among development workers on the left that Nicaraguans should limit themselves to simple agricultural tools and small-scale projects appropriate to the country's previous level of development. Wheelock feels that Nicaragua should instead move quickly to higher levels. But then, as if realizing that he has perhaps spoken too strongly, he admits that the route Nicaragua has chosen is provocative, even problematic; but for him it offers the best route to greater independence and less hunger and poverty.[37] However, as noted above, these plans when put into effect led not to a higher level of development but rather to disaster.

An essential aspect of Wheelock's plan is the large size of the agricultural and industrial enterprises he envisions and which became the centerpiece of Sandinista agricultural policy. Large state farms, large agro-industrial enterprises, large private growers, and large cooperatives—all are favored by the minister of Agriculture and Agrarian Reform. Small peasant farmers are not considered efficient producers, first of all because, as Wheelock frequently points out, they have been pushed off the best land to the infertile agricultural frontier. Secondly, within capitalist and socialist economic and political thought, the peasant is seen as conservative, bound by tradition, uninterested in producing crops in excess of what his or her family requires for subsistence.[38] Sandinista agrarian policy, therefore, favored the modern sector and with it the capitalist export-crop farmers, the haute bourgeoisie in Nicaraguan terms. Wheelock justifies this position. In his words, "We are now developing a national bourgeoisie; not one that has the capacity . . . to articulate a political project, but one that is guaranteed an economic presence."[39] The large growers are needed for their expertise and production capacity and will be given credit and other incentives to continue to produce but will not have a share of government power. Wheelock does not seem to realize that most members of the bourgeoisie would not cooperate under these conditions and that the supposed beneficiaries of the revolution, rural workers and small peasant farmers, desirous of their own plots of land, would become disenchanted and drift into the arms of the counterrevolution.

The large state farms which formed the "hub" of Sandinista economic policy were set up because the revolution "could not turn over a sugar mill to the peasants." Wheelock says that in retaining the large agro-export enterprises as state farms with their salaried workforces the FSLN was not specifically trying to turn the peasantry into a proletariat but that material and political conditions demanded this solution.[40] But, it was neither an answer to the demands of the peasants nor was it a fulfillment of the promises the Sandinistas had made to them. Once made, however, the decision resulted in a limitation of the amount of land that could be distributed to landless farmers because many thousands of harvesters were needed each year on the big farms to harvest and process the sugar, coffee, and cotton crops. Usually there was some overlap in these harvests during the November to March period, which meant that even more laborers were needed. If too much land was given to the peasants, then there would not be enough people to harvest the crops that brought in the foreign exchange the nation needed to survive. Thus theory and reality came into conflict.

The Sandinista government also undertook many large modern agro-industrial projects, such as the famous Chiltepe dairy farm, which were never completed. On the surface, Wheelock's explanation and defense of this type of project appear logical and coherent. Nicaraguans on the average do not have access to enough dairy products, especially milk, for good health. There are two ways of increasing the milk supply. The first is to work to provide technical assistance to the farmers who own the existing national herd of two million head of cattle. But since the cows in this herd produce only 120 million liters of milk per year, the second and better choice for Wheelock is to make a major investment in modern dairy projects using imported, high milk-producing cows. Over a short period of time these cows will substantially increase total milk production, improving the national level of nutrition.[41] There were several problems with this second choice, however. Access to technology was not democratized. Rather, it was limited to the few rural workers and administrators involved in the modern projects. The principal problem, however, was high costs and it was because of high costs that almost all of the high-technology projects, including the Chiltepe dairy facility, failed.

Jaime Wheelock's vision of agricultural development for Nicaragua was based on a faith in modernity and the power of modern science and technology to solve the problems of underdevelopment, on the necessity for exhausting the full potential of capitalism before moving ahead to a socialist future, and on a belief in state power as a vehicle for propelling the nation forward economically. At the time the Sandinistas began their revolution, the Soviet Union and Cuba were showing few signs of the economic problems that subsequently became obvious. Wheelock's vision was moderate when placed beside the state-dominated economic models chosen in those two countries, and it seemed possible to carry it out successfully. Too soon, however, this model was to be challenged by economic and military realities as well as by political and philosophical protests. And, in fact, it was the policies of Wheelock and others similarly inclined that, along with the war, brought Nicaragua to the economic disaster of the late 1980s.

Orlando Núñez Soto, as director of the Center for the Study of Agrarian Reform (CIERA) during the period of the Sandinista government, worked closely with Jaime Wheelock and other government officials in the area of Sandinista economic policy. His doctoral thesis in political economy from the University of Paris (Sorbonne) is a study of Sandinista economic strategy with an emphasis on agricultural policy. In general, Núñez supports Wheelock's ideas in this area, taking a Marxist and/or Marxist-Leninist position on most questions. Núñez maintains that revolutions that have taken place in nonindustrialized rural countries have had more success in neutralizing private property and the bourgeoisie than they have had in diminishing the need for capital and eliminating the different forms of division of labor. Also, they have had more success in exercising power over the political representatives of the capitalists than in controlling the market. The questions of how to accumulate the capital necessary for development; what price will be paid by workers, by peasants, and by other sectors; how collectivization should be carried out; and what the role of small private farmers should be have not changed, nor have the answers become clearer. Furthermore, these questions have always arisen under the pressure of imperialist attack, either open or covert.

Núñez reminds his readers that the main contradiction of Third World socialism is the lack of correspondence between socialized relations of production and a level of development of productive forces that has not even reached an industrialized capitalist level: "Consciousness has gotten ahead of itself and tried to overcome economic structure."[42] The market, he says, is much stronger than government planning and tends to strengthen capitalist tendencies and block socialist ones. This, as he rightly points out, has often led to an over-politicized authoritarianism in socialist societies in order to compensate for the limitations of the state and party in controlling the economy.[43]

An important question for Núñez is how to collectivize production without violating the sensibilities of those sectors most important to the revolution, either as its principal social base, such as the peasantry, small artisans, and merchants, or as its internal allies in the form of a patriotic bourgeoisie.[44] The *latifundio* and *minifundio* are both brakes on agricultural production and thus should be eliminated. The collectivization of the former offends the capitalists and the cooperativization of the latter offends the peasants, "without whose support these and other transformations cannot be carried out." In order to limit the inequalities of wealth in society, Núñez feels that it is essential to cooperativize or collectivize production. He said in 1987, "Recently, a literature has appeared which, in criticizing the low productivity of agricultural cooperatives, proposes reviving the individual productivity of the peasantry. Positions such as this, although they claim to be against capitalism and sometimes in favor of socialism, do not provide a way to avoid commercialization and a new strengthening of social differentiation [in the countryside]."[45]

He thus sees the two goals of economic democracy set out at the beginning of this chapter (equalization of wealth and popular control of the use of resources and of the type of economic system the nation would adopt) as coming into conflict. If there is to be a lessening of the differences between rich and poor in a country, then production must be collectivized to some degree. But if the peasantry does not agree to work in cooperatives, then the goal of cooperative agriculture can be achieved only by violating the second goal of giving the participants in a society a voice in the type of economic system under which they will live. Núñez does not want to do this. The only solution, as he said in a 1994 interview, is that if the people want to move ahead at ten kilometers per hour and the intellectuals and revolutionaries want to go at seventy kilometers per hour, "you have to go at twenty kilometers per hour, because it is preferable to go with the people at twenty kilometers per hour than alone at one hundred."[46] Núñez would agree with Marx's statement cited above that there should be no stunning of the peasant and that the peasant should be encouraged to come over to the side of cooperativization himself or herself.

Núñez offers three suggestions for overcoming the problem of how to obtain the resources necessary for investment and development. These are: 1) international assistance as a source of foreign exchange and investment capital; 2) industrialization of agricultural products and natural resources; and 3) internal efforts for food self-sufficiency.[47] Jaime Wheelock also concurs with these choices. And, in fact, Núñez is now one of the few Sandinistas who does not criticize Wheelock's ideas and policies during the Sandinista period in government. In answer to a question about whether the counterrevolution would have been weaker if the revolution had had a different policy toward the peasantry, Núñez answers: "If one studies revolutions during the last five hundred years, one sees that there have always been counterrevolutions. Revolutions (with justice) do violence to the existing order. That order always rejects the change. But if we had not had a revolution, if we had not tried to distribute wealth, to democratize land ownership, to neutralize the effects of the market which deepen the differences between rich and poor, if we had not tried to do those things, there would not have been any counterrevolution, it is true!"[48]

## THE ALTERNATIVE VISION
## OF THE PEASANT FARMER

Daniel Núñez and Benigna Mendiola are peasant leaders who have challenged the orthodox positions of Wheelock and Orlando Núñez. Mendiola, the head of the Women's Section of the Union of Farmers and Ranchers, who was elected to the FSLN National Directorate in May of 1994, began her work in the 1960s as a peasant organizer with the Socialist Party (Moscow line) of Nicaragua in the mountainous area of Matagalpa. She disagreed even then with the orthodox Marxist view of the peasantry. She says that the Socialists were trying to organize cooperatives among peasants who, in fact, wanted to farm their own plots of land. "It was like trying to put a bird in a cage," she says, "when what it likes is to jump from one branch to another and to fly." Later, she and her husband, another peasant leader who was killed before the revolutionary victory, joined the FSLN. But Mendiola does not believe that the Sandinista revolution treated the peasants any better.

For several reasons, neither the production cooperatives nor the credit and service cooperatives worked as well as they should have, she maintains. First, the peasants were not properly prepared or educated for cooperative farming; and second, the peasantry was the cannon fodder of the contra war. The counterrevolutionaries made the cooperatives their particular targets of attack, while compulsory military service took the young men from the co-ops off to fight and die in the Sandinista Army. In a stinging indictment, Mendiola says, "The cooperatives were born suffering from rickets. They had stepfathers instead of fathers. The cooperatives did not have health centers, or rural day care centers, or their own schools. But the state farms did have day care, schools, health centers, and good food. In the case of the cooperatives, they tried to impose a model that the peasants did not want."[49]

For Mendiola, democracy means that the people have a chance to actively plan and manage their lives and the form in which they work. Fewer people, she says, would have joined the contras if they had felt that they enjoyed such freedoms under the Sandinista government. Furthermore, many peasants believed the propaganda of the religious right, which told them that the communists ate people and that they shared their wives with other men. But the FSLN also made many errors, she says: "I am a member of the Sandinista Front but I am not closing my eyes to some of the barbarities that were carried out."[50]

Daniel Núñez, who organized peasants and robbed banks for the FSLN before the 1979 victory and has been head of the Union of Farmers and Ranchers for ten years, has been firm in his vision of his organization as one that represents small and medium-sized farmers, both individual and cooperative, and any large growers who wish to join. He uses a class rhetoric that emphasizes the interests and demands of poor peasants but which at the same time does not exclude middle peasants. While he sees cooperatives as a positive good, he envisions his role as representing his constituency, and if a majority prefers to farm individually, then so be it. He says of the beginning years of his organization immediately after it broke away from the Farmworkers Association: "[W]e made a mistake. We began to prostitute the meaning of the word 'bourgeoisie' and we started calling any small peasant who had ten cows or who harvested two hundred hundredweights of coffee a 'bourgeois,' without giving any thought to the sacrifices he had made to achieve this. . . . This meant that many peasants felt unconnected to the revolution. . . . The counterrevolution took advantage of this. . . . We had to take a line that was wider and more democratic."[51]

Daniel Núñez criticizes the policy of the Sandinista Agriculture Ministry in the early 1980s for slowing down agrarian reform in order to strengthen the state farm sector. This was rectified, he admits, in the mid-eighties, principally because of pressure from the peasants themselves, much of it through the organization he leads. But Núñez chastises the government for continuing to support large landowners "because of the ideological position of some functionaries," when the revolution has still not fulfilled its promises to poor landless peasants. For us, he says, this is a question of principle. The large landowners should be subjected to land reform, beginning with those who support the cause of "imperialism." After that, the large "patriotic producers" should also come under the reform and, Núñez states, "We will see exactly how patriotic they are!" Along with the granting of land to the peasants there must be a commitment to provide financing, technical assistance, and marketing, "all the pieces of agrarian reform."[52]

If the thought of Daniel Núñez is contrasted with that of Jaime Wheelock, it is clear that the conflict is between those who, like Wheelock, do not have faith in the ability of the peasant farmers to produce a surplus for the development of the nation, and those like Núñez and others at UNAG who do. It is between those who believe that the revolution has to pass through the stages of capitalist development, including support for large private production, before a socialist future can be contemplated, and those who believe that the revolution was made for the workers and peasants and that their needs for social justice and for economic participation must come first. It is between those who see the "mixed economy" as a tactical slogan corresponding to a particular period in revolutionary history and those who believe that a combination of production cooperatives, credit and service cooperatives, small and medium-sized individual farms and possibly a few state farms could be a valid model in itself for the present and future alike. And it is most of all between those who believe that there is a correct theory available that should be applied and those who believe that the informed decisions of the participants and beneficiaries must guide policy. Indeed, it is at its core a conflict between democracy and verticalism, between dialectic and imposition from above.

FSLN National Directorate member Henry Ruíz says that one of the aspects of Lenin's thought that is still valid today is that peasants should not be forced into cooperatives.[53] The Sandinistas did not try to do this, but they made it clear to the peasants that the cooperative model was favored over private production and that if peasants wanted the benefits of the revolution, they must join cooperatives. This was true even though, according to Mendiola, the cooperatives themselves were the step-brothers and sisters of the state farms—the favorite children of the revolution.

The agro-industrial complexes, which were also favored children, are not mentioned by Daniel Núñez or Mendiola. This is because, as Luis Carrión says, "they had no important social effect in terms of improving the technological level at which the great majority of peasants, farmers, and ranchers of Nicaragua worked." All the technology was concentrated in the projects themselves. It is important to democratize technology, Carrión emphasizes, and the very highest levels of technology often cannot be democratized. Therefore, sometimes it is better to use a lower level of technology but to make it more broadly available."[54]

Since 1990, the Sandinistas have analyzed in considerable depth the economic policy they followed while in power and are working to produce a new model which will take into account what they have learned.

## SUMMARY

All of the Sandinistas who have addressed economic democracy agree on the importance which must be given to democratization of the ownership of wealth and this, in an agricultural country, means land. During the Sandinista period in government there were serious differences of opinion about how this democratization was to be achieved, about whether the state and other modern sectors would have the primary role or whether the wishes of the peasant majority would dominate. The first of these views, embodied in the modernistic vision of Jaime Wheelock, was both unrealistic and undemocratic. The large agro-industrial complexes that he proposed and defended were too costly for the resources available to Nicaragua despite substantial foreign assistance. His vision was undemocratic because resources and technology were concentrated in the large state enterprises rather than disbursed among the majority of the people. While peasants were supposedly going to have access to modern technology when they joined together in cooperatives, the latter, as peasant leader Benigna Mendiola maintains, were always the "step-brothers and step-sisters" of the state farms. The Sandinista leadership's reaction to peasant pressure and its decision to distribute land to individual owners came too late, when many peasants had already become disillusioned and had joined the contras.

In terms of socialist theory, the vision of peasant leaders such as Mendiola and Daniel Núñez, in which peasants would own their own land in the form they preferred, whether in individual farms, cooperative ownership, or credit and service co-ops, would seem to be a step backwards toward agrarian capitalism. But a socialist like Rosa Luxemburg, for example, who opposed distribution of land in individual ownership to the peasants was also a firm believer in democracy (including the forms of liberal democracy) and it would be a violation of democratic principles to force peasants into certain prescribed forms of landholding. Possibly the more relevant democratic theorist in this case would be Thomas Jefferson, who supported democratic forms of government at all levels along with an assurance of a minimum of fifty acres of land for each family. He opposed unlimited large holdings, agreeing with Aristotle that representative democracy could not function in a society with great differences in wealth.

In practice, in Nicaragua, the large state-owned enterprises were less successful economically than were the variety of small and medium-sized farms when they were provided with proper incentives to produce. Both socialists and western capitalists have had a prolonged love affair with enormous size, especially in agriculture, believing it to be both modern and efficient. When large size is not efficient in providing for the needs of all citizens, neither socialists nor capitalists seem capable of offering an adequate explanation. Perhaps socialist and neo-liberal theorists both need to look at the East Asian model, where small farms have been preserved, contributing to more egalitarian societies (which has led to more even development) while feeding entire populations as the nation industrializes.

# 6

## Economic Democracy:
## The Search for Alternatives
## to Neo-liberalism

### HISTORICAL BACKGROUND

Although the Sandinista government's austerity measures of 1988 and 1989 were able to lower inflation levels substantially (from the astronomical high of 30,000 percent), that was not enough to win majority support for the FSLN in the February 1990 elections, given all the country's other economic and political problems. With the electoral loss, the Sandinistas were confronted with the problem of how to preserve the democratization of resources that they had achieved in their years in power. Because they had not foreseen the possibility of being voted out of office, the titles that they had given to peasant farmers were mere pieces of paper called "Agrarian Reform Titles." The changes of ownership had not been registered in the land records office of each locality, and, in fact, the names on the records in that office were most likely to be those of old Somocista landowners who, with the turnover in government, were packing their bags in Miami to return home and reclaim their lost properties. In order to prevent a rollback of agricultural land reform as well as of the distribution of urban plots to city dwellers, the Sandinista-dominated National Assembly took advantage of the short two-month period between the election and the inauguration of

Violeta Chamorro as president to pass several laws under which legal ownership was given to those who had lived on their lots or farmed their agricultural properties before February 25, 1990, which was the date of the elections.

Transition accords were signed with the new government team that spelled out which revolutionary measures would be preserved. These included the confiscations accompanying land reform, except for those judged to have been unjustly carried out. In the latter cases, compensation would be offered to the previous owners so that peasant farmers would not have to be dispossessed. In some cases Sandinista officials took over state-owned properties, farms or urban dwellings, that might have been returned to their previous owners. Most Nicaraguans agreed that Sandinistas had a right to own the house they lived in after many years of service to the nation at low salary, but where the land-grab was excessive, such as when several farms or businesses or large houses were acquired by a single political official, the public became outraged, giving the name "piñata" to the phenomenon. (In Mexico and Central America, the piñata is a children's party game in which a decorated clay pot filled with candy is strung up above the children who take turns while blindfolded to try to break it open and all rush to retrieve the candies.) Many people, including Sandinistas, demanded investigation and restitution. This, however, never came about.

For the Sandinista unions, especially the Sandinista Workers' Central (CST), and the Farmworkers' Association (ATC), the electoral loss by the FSLN meant liberation from having to support the policies of the Sandinista government even when these were blatantly harmful to the interests of workers. These groups carried out strikes to raise wages before Mrs. Chamorro's government came into office. Then, in the first few months of her tenure, massive strikes based on work-related and economic issues along with demands for demobilization of the contra army, virtually closed down Managua. New worker unity and coordination were formalized by the formation of the National Federation of Workers (FNT), which brought together both urban and rural unions.

The property question was complicated by the determination of the Nicaraguan far right to return all confiscated property to its previous owners, in spite of the fact that much of the property had been heavily mortgaged before the revolution and the money taken out of the country. When the Sandinista government seized this property it paid off the mortgages to the banking system. To help the right in its attempts to achieve its goal, members have enlisted the help of U.S. Senator Jesse Helms (R-NC). Helms has been able to hold up United States foreign aid to the Chamorro government several times by demanding that property confiscated from U.S. citizens be returned. Many Nicaraguans in the course of their stay in the U.S. had become naturalized citizens and appear on Helms's list of U.S. citizens. Their claims, however, are not recognized by international law. Other members of the U.S. Congress have achieved various degrees of success in working around Helms's obstructionism but his efforts have been extremely damaging to Nicaragua's recovery.

In early 1992, President Chamorro vetoed as unconstitutional a measure passed by the Nicaraguan National Assembly which would have annulled the effects of the laws protecting land reform passed during the interregnum. An alliance of the FSLN bench and centrist party members upheld her veto. Many properties have, however, been returned, with the police removing the peasant occupants by force. In a few cases, the police have refused to carry out eviction orders, but these have been rare. There was one positive development in the area of democratization of property ownership, however, during the first period of Mrs. Chamorro's government. Nearly half a million acres of state land, some of it land that had been abandoned during the contra war, was either given to or taken over by peasant farmers, many of them former contra soldiers. This resulted in a 25 percent increase in the total land affected by land reform. The question of whether these farmers are receiving needed technical assistance is, however, being answered in the negative.[1]

In November of 1995, a new property law finally passed the National Assembly which recognizes the property rights of those who have benefited from agrarian reform.[2] However, it also provides for compensation for anyone whose land was confiscated by the Sandinista government, excluding only members of the Somoza family. This means that gross violators of human rights under the Somoza dictatorship and people who had mortgaged their properties just before the revolution and taken the money out of the country will be eligible for compensation. The new law is thus a compromise which entirely pleases no one.

The first year of the new Chamorro government was marked by inflation almost as high as the worst year of the Sandinista crisis. By imposing strict stabilization measures, however, inflation levels were subsequently brought down to almost nothing. Stabilization measures focus on decreasing the fiscal deficit by cutting back on government expenditures, laying off public employees, and then decreasing the availability of credit. Economic adjustment measures also put in place by the new government go further and include the privatization of state-owned industry, farms, and utilities, and often the denial of credit to cooperative and associative forms of ownership because they are considered to be less efficient. Adjustment measures also include the following: the lowering of tariff barriers, production for export rather than for domestic consumption, and restrictions on labor organizing in order to attract investment of foreign capital.

Privatization of state-owned factories was a requirement of the IMF, World Bank, and of USAID and, indeed, had been a part of Mrs. Chamorro's electoral platform. But workers in the factories argued for employee ownership. Negotiations resulted in an agreement for workers to receive 25 percent ownership in previously government-owned factories and businesses. In some cases this has meant 100 percent ownership of one sugar-producing enterprise (for example) while three others have been returned to their former owners.

The Sandinistas had increased Nicaragua's foreign debt from the approximately $1.6 billion left them by Somoza to $9.5 billion. The Chamorro government has borrowed another $1.5 billion, raising

Nicaragua's total debt to over \$11 billion, the highest per capita in the world. Chamorro has been able to negotiate substantial forgiveness of the debt and to reschedule much of the remainder. This still leaves the country with a debt service obligation at 120 percent of total earnings in foreign exchange from exports.[3] Thus, Nicaragua's need for funds to service its debt has made it necessary for the government to sign stabilization and adjustment agreements with the IMF and World Bank. Because the country has not recovered economically as a result of the measures but rather been plunged into deep recession, their efficacy has been questioned by all sectors, including the most conservative, of Nicaraguan society. A joint declaration of the FSLN and the UNO Coalition (which had been Mrs. Chamorro's successful electoral coalition) in 1993 stated: "Any accord with the international financial institutions that brings with it more unemployment, cuts in social services and in business and farm credit, is not viable in Nicaragua."[4]

## A DIFFERENT KIND OF PRIVATIZATION

According to union leader Ronaldo Membreño, during the first years of the FSLN in power a dominant group within the party believed in the possibility of workers' participation through their unions in the management of state enterprises. The result, however, was continual questioning of the managers by the workers and within a short period the policy changed and the traditional functions of manager were revived and combined with those of "party man" in one individual. An interesting parallel exists between what occurred in Nicaragua under the Sandinistas and what took place in Russia during the first few years after the 1917 Bolshevik revolution, when early worker control quickly reverted to management domination of factories. In the Nicaragua case, Membreño remembers that "this closed any space for questioning the management that might have existed for the workers, and in this sense a plain vertical scheme such as what you would find in any capitalist business was established." He adds that this scheme was replaced later by "a more technocratic current," in which plans were made by professionals, specialists, and technicians, and in which workers were equally excluded from decision-making.[5]

After their defeat in the elections of February 1990, the Sandinistas declared themselves in firm opposition to the privatization of the agricultural and industrial enterprises which belonged to the state. The first party assembly after the elections issued a formal declaration on the subject in June of that year. But it soon became clear that this position was untenable. National Directorate member René Núñez remembers that, despite the intensity of their struggle, privatization was moving forward. "Given that," Núñez says, "we decided to shift gears and unite under the banner that, if state property was to be privatized, an equitable part of those properties should remain in the hands of the workers who created the nation's wealth. Out of that position came the proposal that 25 percent would stay with the workers. . . . This was a political response, without carrying out economic studies."[6] As noted above, some enterprises have been privatized with the workers being given the right to own 25 percent while in other cases factories or farms that have been privatized have gone entirely to the workers while three other similar businesses have been returned to their previous owners.

Membreño sees worker ownership as the first opportunity for the workers to be directly connected to their work in the way Marx laid out in his socialist program, a reuniting of capital and labor. Marx, of course, was speaking not at the level of individual factories but of a socialist society, where all production had been concentrated in the hands of a vast association of all the workers of the nation.[7] Membreño rightfully questions whether these plans for worker ownership can be financially successful in an era of neo-liberal economics and openness to the world market. "We will have to wait and see," he says.[8]

Others envision different types of associative enterprises, whether urban or rural, as giving some hope of economic recovery to a pauperized population. Enrique Picado, the national coordinator of the Community Movement, promotes projects for the urban areas that include bringing small businesses together in ways that are similar to those used by Benigna Mendiola in her work with women in rural cooperatives. These Sandinistas look to small-scale enterprises because they do not believe that large capitalist enterprises can provide adequate jobs and incomes to the great masses of poor people in Nicaragua. Their ideas of small-scale development are finding favor with growing numbers of development specialists internationally[9] but are still not accepted by the international financial institutions, which look to large projects and to transnational corporations as the engines of development.

Just as in the area of participatory democracy, so also in the area of economic democracy, Orlando Núñez Soto is recognized in Nicaragua and outside the country as the person doing the principal theoretical work. He combines practice with theory in his job as Director of CIPRES, which is a non-governmental organization that trains many of the worker-owners in the privatized sector. In his 1992 writing on worker ownership in the book *En busca de la revolución perdida* (In Search of the Lost Revolution), Núñez returns to his model of three revolutions: the first and second are the bourgeois and socialist revolutions and the third is the self-management revolution. It is, at first, unclear if this supplants or is merely a part of his previous (1988) Third Revolution, which was a revolution of consciousness that would change power relationships in the personal and public spheres. He speaks of the self-management revolution as "a manner of constructing alternative relations of property and of power, within the sphere of civil society."[10] It therefore would appear to be a perfectly logical expansion of the revolution of consciousness into the economic sphere. It is ironic, certainly, that this opening would occur as a result of the Sandinista loss of state power.

In the 1992 book, Núñez Soto places his ideas in the framework of Marxist analysis by giving a brief history of ideas on the subject of worker participation in management. He draws upon Marx, Lenin, Gramsci, and Luxemburg. He says in summary that, up until the present time, many Marxist intellectuals and theorists, as well as Marxist parties which never took power, have criticized the existing socialist states for not including participation and mass democracy in both the workplace and the political sphere. But this has been due, he states, to the fact that virtually all revolutions up until at least the 1960s have been carried out by a minority of the population. The revolutionary countries have not been industrialized, their workers have not formed a majority of the population or even a substantial percentage, as happened in the industrialized countries. The bureaucracy became the heir to the property confiscated from the capitalists in order to manage it in the name of all the dispossessed classes, including but not limited to the small working class.[11] The profit from what in Nicaragua under the Sandinista government was called the Area of People's Ownership (that is, state ownership) was used for the benefit of all Nicaraguans, and not just in benefit of the workers at one plant. When confronted in the new post-electoral period with the alternative between the return of farms and factories to their previous owners or their privatization to workers and administrators, the Sandinistas opted for the latter. Núñez explains: "It is not that we were mistaken in the past and now we are going to rectify that mistake, but rather how do we move best within these contradictions between social interests on a national level and social interests on the local or plant level."[12]

In an article published in mid-1994, Núñez lays out several new ideas. He maintains that every social system requires an economic subject which, working for itself, builds the social system as a whole. Feudalism had its feudal lords; the colonial system, the *encomenderos*; capitalism has had the bourgeois class; and imperialism, Núñez says, has the transnational corporations. He is obviously using Marx's idea of a world historical class which represents the interests of an entire society during a particular historical period.[13] But up until now, because workers have not been a majority and likely never will be even in industrialized societies, socialism has had to divide resources "between workers' strategic interests and the immediate needs of the whole population" and could not compete with the capitalist model. The oppressed and exploited in any society wish to shed those conditions, he says, and thus may carry the banner for a revolutionary struggle but they do not fulfill the requirements of an economic subject.[14]

The FSLN, Núñez asserts, is a political force with a political class and a party organization but must choose between two economic classes "in order to make it a viable and permanent social force." The modern national bourgeoisie "is flirting with it" but the reformed sectors of the economy "need it." Even though many Sandinistas now are owners of businesses and lead a bourgeois lifestyle, Núñez believes that the FSLN must and will choose the reformed sector as its economic subject for the new period. This sector is made up of the peasants who benefited from Sandinista agrarian reform either individually or in cooperatives. It also includes the large numbers of demobilized soldiers from the Sandinista army and from the contras (or what the entire nation now calls the "Resistance") who have received land from the Chamorro government. In addition, it includes the rural and urban workers who work on the state enterprises that are now being privatized. "All these thousands of individuals," Núñez says, "have put together a multitude of cooperatives and other associative and self-managed enterprises." They own nearly half of Nicaragua's farmland and are especially strong in basic grains, coffee, cattle, bananas, tobacco, sesame, soy, sorghum, vegetables, honey, and fish. They also own several agro-industrial processing plants. The members are organized in different types of federations, producers' associations, unions, cooperative societies, and worker-owned companies or those in which workers have a significant share of stock.[15]

Associations of individual farmers have been able to obtain foreign credits and are diversifying, moving into such areas as organic production for export. Cooperatives are coming together to form Agricultural Cooperative Unions of which Núñez says there are over one hundred as of 1994. He says that the workers' companies have organized by trade and "now include some 20,000 workershare-holders." At the municipal level around the nation, hundreds of associative businesses have been formed, many of them by ex-combatants of the army. The reformed sector receives twice as much financing from national and international non-governmental organizations (NGOs) as from the banks. Núñez states that NGOs finance forty thousand small producers while the National Bank has provided financing for only twenty thousand. And, according to him: "Perhaps the most important novelty of these new property forms is that they demonstrate that small producers can achieve an economy of scale through territorial association that opens up a competitive place for them in the national market. . . . [W]ith increasingly voluminous operations, [they] are achieving a national scale in both commerce and industry."[16]

But all is not rosy for the reformed sector. It faces two principal problems. One is that its properties have taken years to be legalized. The former owners are still pressuring for the return of their old farms and factories and the present owners are determined to prevent this from happening. Many former owners refuse to accept compensation in the form of bonds with which they can purchase shares in utilities being privatized. Theirs is an ideological rather than an economic position. Núñez states that "We have been paralyzed in this transcendental dilemma for almost five years now, and the situation does not appear to be moving toward any resolution."[17] With the passage in November of 1995 of the new property law, the question hopefully has been settled.

The other challenge the reformed sector faces is the condition of the present international economy and of Nicaragua's place within it. The international financial institutions (IFIs) impose their rules on the economies of nations that need their funds, requiring that for businesses and farms to be eligible for credit they must be of a certain size and type. (Recent "Titling Loans" to some countries from the World Bank, for example, have required that all titles be for individual ownership.) In many cases, Nicaragua's reformed sector does not meet these criteria and therefore cannot obtain funds from the IFIs through the National Bank. Poor farmers who cannot get credit are often forced to sell their land to large landowners, a phenomenon that if it becomes widespread, could lead to a return to previous levels of concentration of land ownership in the hands of a few in Nicaragua.

For Núñez, if the reforms in property ownership in Nicaragua are not legalized and preserved, "representative democracy will have no meaning." The FSLN knows "that if we do not build local and sectoral power, guaranteeing the participation of all trade and union organizations in developing economic policies, representative democracy will continue being a democracy only for holders of large capital."[18]

The decisions that came out of the May 1994 FSLN Party Congress were positive steps in this direction, he feels, establishing the priority the FSLN will give to the reformed sectors and the methods of struggle it will use to preserve them, including everything from legislative work to popular mobilizations in the streets. Núñez sees combining the struggles of the popular organizations, which represent different sectors of society (women, youth, neighborhood dwellers), with the defense of these new economic subjects as giving the revolution a nucleus around which a vision of alternative power can be constructed and organized.

Looking toward 1996, Núñez asserts that "If the FSLN wins the elections, it will institutionalize these reforms. If it loses, we will patiently and tenaciously continue the daily work of consolidating these new forms of property from below, just as the incipient [Western] European bourgeoisie did between the 16th century and the French Revolution in the 18th century."[19] What Núñez has done is to give substance to Daniel Ortega's promise at the time of the 1990 electoral loss that the FSLN would govern from below. No one quite understood what the revolutionary forces could do without control of the state. Work with the popular organizations did not appear to offer solutions to the grave economic problems that the great majority of Nicaraguans were facing. But here it is evident that even without control of the state, the struggle has a major economic component, economic subjects, and very possibly a viable economic solution. It is a development that was unanticipated in previous socialist analysis.

Núñez's framework in this most recent *Envío* article theoretically rounds out the work that he did on self-management in 1992. Since that year the reformed sectors have grown and developed and shown themselves worthy of being considered the new economic subjects of the revolutionary movement. Earlier, many Sandinistas had been doubtful about private property, even private associative property, as a revolutionary subject, while others urged caution with relation to the small producers, either rural or urban, who, it was thought, would not be able to compete for long in the present open local and world markets. But the small and medium-sized enterprises, without the coercion of government, have joined together to pool resources and to receive training and financing. They have come to cooperative and associative methods of work on their own without "stunning," as Marx said.

The great variety of these associative forms must be noted because Marxist economic thought has often been very suspicious of choice and variety in the economic sphere. Such variety makes control by the state difficult. And many forms chosen will not correspond with correct theory. It must be noted, however, that the ultimate goal of Marx himself was human emancipation and a society in which the free development of each was the condition for the free development of all. This was not put into practice in the economic planning of the socialist countries of Eastern Europe, Cuba, or elsewhere. The Sandinistas broke new ground with their idea of a mixed economy in the years they were in power. It would be appropriate that they would break new ground now as well. It is also logical that Núñez, as a Marxist political economist, would need an economic subject that would accompany his social subjects, the popular organizations—which he has called the new "democratic vanguard"—in a continuing struggle for economic, participatory and political democracy. This struggle will be political, but it may not be partisan. Both the popular organizations and the cooperative and associative enterprises declare themselves to be non-partisan. The FSLN as a party will have to be a political voice for their interests and earn their support. Given the Party's past record of verticalist management, it will not be able to count on that support.

## CONFRONTING THE NEW WORLD ORDER

One of the major controversies within the FSLN at the present moment is the question of how to confront the international economic situation. The disappearance of the Soviet Union and of the socialist bloc has meant the substantial lessening of financial support for an economic alternative to the reigning neo-liberal (or neo-classical) economic philosophy. This economic philosophy, which emphasizes private capitalism, is considered to be a revival of the thought of the classical liberal economists of the eighteenth and nineteenth centuries, including Adam Smith and David Ricardo. The Scandinavian countries and some large private voluntary organizations do continue to finance other kinds of projects, a fact Orlando Núñez remarks upon in his analysis cited above. However, the principal assistance for meeting governmental debt service obligations, supporting currency and balance of payments, and carrying out governmental development projects comes from the major international financial institutions (IFIs). In the case of Nicaragua, these institutions are the International Monetary Fund (IMF), the World Bank and the Inter-American Development Bank (IDB). In order to obtain these funds as well as bi-lateral assistance from the U.S. government, President Chamorro has adopted the stabilization and structural adjustment measures prescribed by them for the Nicaraguan economy.

The agreements the government has signed with the IFIs are secret but information about what they include often leaks out. Such arrangements have not been submitted to the National Assembly to be ratified, even when portions of them violate previously existing laws, international treaties, or even the constitution of Nicaragua. One of the amendments to the constitution passed in 1995 established that the National Assembly had to approve international financial agreements. It was opposed by the IFIs and it remains to be seen if it will be observed. A major World Bank structural adjustment loan package to Nicaragua in 1994 required a "Letter of Labor Policy" in which the Chamorro government, in effect, promised to deny internationally recognized labor rights which form part of International Labor Organization (ILO) treaties that Nicaragua has ratified.[20]

The use of such power by multilateral organizations has theoretical implications for democracy. A country cannot be considered to be democratic if the decisions governing its national life are made outside its borders. This situation, in fact, resembles colonialism.

The measures can also be criticized from a practical standpoint. Edmundo Jarquín, who served as minister of foreign cooperation under the Sandinista government and who is now an official at the Inter-American Development Bank, says that the structural adjustment in Nicaragua should have been more gradual. Nicaragua's productive capacity, which had been destroyed by the war, should have had some protection. In fact, a recent document from the Economic Commission on Latin America of the United Nations notes Nicaragua's special circumstances of triple transition, that is, emergence from war, transition to a market-oriented economy, and movement away from authoritarian government. It recommends that steps toward liberalization of markets should be reduced and more heterodox economic measures adopted, including some protection for infant industries and peasant production and restriction on credit for importing consumer goods, with those funds instead being allocated to small and medium-sized farmers.[21] Some members of the U.S. Congress agreed. In June of 1994 the Foreign Operations Subcommittee of the U.S. House of Representatives Appropriations Committee released a report stating that too little U.S. assistance was going to "small and medium-sized farmers, cooperatives and urban entrepreneurs, to reduce unemployment particularly among ex-combatants from both sides, to improve health and education and for environmental conservation."[22]

Edmundo Jarquín also points out that, in spite of all the errors that were made under the Sandinista government, the country has the most democratic land ownership profile of any nation in Latin America. Since land reform is necessary for economic development and ending poverty, this democratization of land ownership is Nicaragua's greatest resource and should be protected, Jarquín insists. The World Bank, the Food and Agricultural Organization, and the Inter-American Development Bank signed a document in March of 1992[23] recommending that agricultural land in Nicaragua remain in the hands of those who hold it and that those farmers should be given incentives to produce. Jarquín has some hope that new, more heterodox, ideas on development are taking hold in the IFIs and within the U.S. Agency for International Development[24] but most Sandinistas remain pessimistic.

For economist Adolfo Acevedo, the choice of economic model is at heart a question about how the problem of poverty is confronted. He says that there are basically two positions:

> The first maintains that poverty is a de facto situation resulting from social marginalization; sooner or later it will be absorbed by economic development and modernity through the mechanism of the market. It is caused not by the structure of the market itself, but by certain inefficiencies of the model. The second position argues . . . that it is the economic model that creates and reproduces poverty. It leads us to a search for alternatives for global development and to distance ourselves from policies . . . that try to humanize structural adjustment with measures of social compensation.[25]

But it is such development alternatives that have been so hard to find and even harder to put into place, given the power of the existing world system.

For Acevedo, governments which are more sensitive to the needs of their citizens than to their creditors can make better deals with the IMF. Democratic governments which have to respond to their citizenry can go into negotiations with the Fund with greater firmness, demand better terms, and have a better chance of being heard. But, he says, the Chamorro government has not used this advantage and instead has followed the prescriptions of the IMF almost to the letter. As a result, Acevedo asserts, the Fund has imposed a regimen that is closed, ironclad, and totally in keeping with the goal of asphyxiating the productive sectors which could offer real economic possibilities to the majority of the population which has been excluded from the market.[26] Acevedo may, however, be overestimating the negotiating power that even a democratic state of Nicaragua's tiny size can exert against the enormous economic strength of the IFIs and the U.S. government. But, in support of Acevedo's critique of the IMF's programs, one could cite the internal document of the Economic Commission on Latin America (ECLA) mentioned above, which states that "the specificities of Nicaragua make impossible or at least extremely risky at the present moment the attempt to achieve macroeconomic stability through recessive adjustment programs. Better combinations of goals should be tried—although it takes more time to achieve them—that put economic reactivation and expansive adjustment at the service of political stabilization and institutional rebuilding."[27]

Acevedo does not absolve the Sandinistas of blame for Nicaragua's economic situation, which has meant that the country has had to subject itself to the dictates of the international financial institutions. He criticizes the enormous growth of the state under the FSLN, which stemmed in part from each leader's seeming need to increase the power of the part of the bureaucracy which he led. He also deplores the financing of giant government projects through forced savings which took the form of inflation, and the subsidizing of urban consumption which eventually made it more sensible for the peasant farmer to buy subsidized (and often imported) food rather than produce it himself or herself. Finally, he criticizes the orthodox stabilization measures put in place by the Sandinistas in the late '80s without consultation with and input from the affected population.[28]

Acevedo sees two possibilities for the future. First, there could be an insistence that the present neo-liberal model be continued. This, he believes, will cause social turbulence and repressive responses from the government. The other possibility that he sees is a recomposition of interests and alliances leading to the economic and political inclusion of the majority without excluding any economic sector. Acevedo would try to create progressively the bases for a sustainable insertion into the world economy for Nicaragua, establishing clear priorities for those types of investment which would have the maximum multiplier effect on the whole economy. It is not enough to pursue equitable development, but the democratic decision-making apparatus must also be extended to include the new socio-political subjects created by the revolution. Solution of the nation's economic problems must pass through the development of political institutions that formalize negotiation so that those points of conflict growing out of the present structural adjustment measures can be isolated and addressed. A strategy of national and democratic development, he feels, can only arise from a broad national consensus and for this all parties have to come together in wide-ranging discourse.[29]

Xabier Gorostiaga, the economist and Catholic priest who is head of the Jesuit university in Managua, speaks of a "geoculture of despair . . . part of the nihilism of Nietzsche" that has overtaken even the political left, adding that "this may be the greatest achievement of neoliberalism." With so many forces abandoning the struggle, dominance of the global economic arena can be reserved for capital with little or no resistance; labor can be excluded.[30] Gorostiaga contends that the international financial institutions must be democratized. He calls for a democracy open to all the citizens of the planet and for national democratic projects that would be complemented internationally. In place of the forced opening to the international market that in the case of Nicaragua and other Third World countries has destroyed local industries, he proposes: "Insertion in the world market would be defined selectively according to the phases and the prerequisites of the project itself. . . . Neither the isolation of autarky, nor indiscriminate, asymmetric neo-liberal insertion, but rather the selective insertion that responds to one's own project."[31]

Gorostiaga would not do away with the market but rather reform it in those areas where "deformations in social and economic relations either block entrance or eliminate those subjects less capable of competing." He adds that "the 'economic Darwinism' prevailing today reduces markets," an argument that should carry weight with representatives of international capital.

Gorostiaga does not limit the power of the state in poor, dependent countries but believes rather that it has a necessary balancing and generating role which can give impetus to sustainable development. He emphasizes that "a new State that is democratic, efficient, participatory, and transparent [i.e., open] is a crucial element of the alternative proposals." On the international level, he proposes a network of common human values in order to build a new world community. He refuses to believe that "growth" and "capital" are the only concepts with the capacity to transcend differences among the earth's peoples. He wants those common human values to inspire and summon the world at large "to a more humane community project."[32] The unlikelihood of any prompt achievement of this goal should not lead us to criticize the call or diminish its urgency.

Thus, Adolfo Acevedo insists on further internal democratization in order that Nicaragua might address the international market from a position of greater strength. Xabier Gorostiaga asks for changes on an international scale in the international financial institutions and on the part of the nations of the north that will result in a more humane world. Although his writing in that area has not been examined, Gorostiaga was also an active leftist critic of Sandinista economic policy.

## SUMMARY

In the late 1980s and early 1990s, Nicaragua was subjected to rigorous stabilization and structural adjustment policies, first by the Sandinista government and then by that of Violeta Chamorro. The Sandinistas were accused of imposing their stabilization and adjustment measures without consulting with the different revolutionary mass organizations to obtain their input and perhaps soften the blows that they inevitably were to feel. The voting public did make its views known, however, on the 30,000 percent rate of inflation and the economic disintegration of the nation by voting the Sandinistas out of office in February of 1990. The implications of Mrs. Chamorro's stabilization and adjustment measures for democracy, however, are even more serious. Nicaragua's economic policies are being made in Washington, D.C., at the headquarters of the World Bank and the IMF, and not in Managua. Granted, in its early months Mrs. Chamorro's government appeared to be in entire agreement with the prescriptions of the international financial institutions but, later, consensus appeared among all sectors of the Nicaraguan population, including many government ministers, against the policies of the IFIs. Constitutional amendments that gave the National Assembly veto power over international economic agreements were opposed by these organizations.

Sandinista theorists present philosophical objections to the neo-liberal model but most sectors of the Nicaraguan population oppose the structural adjustment measures, not for theoretical reasons but because they see that they are not working. They have not brought recovery; in fact, the nation has lapsed into deep depression and is in danger of serious political and military disturbances. Rightly or wrongly, the depression is blamed on the structural adjustment policies. Because of this general opposition, the measures cannot be put in place democratically but rather have to be imposed. It appears that for practical as well as theoretical reasons the advice of some international observers such as those at the Economic Commission on Latin America of the U.N. in favor of more heterodox measures should be heeded.

Sandinistas are caught up in a debate about whether compromise has to be made with the "neo-liberal model" or whether the struggle must be continued against the model and in support of a yet to be defined "new economic model." It would seem that while the search must go on for a "new model" that could combine efficiency with justice, modifications in the model in vogue, namely the neo-liberal model, should be pursued vigorously. Orlando Núñez Soto's ideas on the new economic subject of the still-continuing revolution seem to be precisely that. Freedom and variety are the order of the day in Núñez's vision with no attempt being made to impose correct theory onto wriggly, unconforming reality. No one knows if worker ownership can survive in Nicaragua or, indeed, if small and medium-sized farmers have a future in the new economy of world trade. But economic democracy in Nicaragua will definitely be furthered if Núñez's ideas turn out to be correct and they do survive. Other countries in the South will be watching to see if this alternative model, partial as it is, is successful.

# 7

# Democracy in the FSLN Party

## HISTORICAL BACKGROUND: ORTHODOX VERSUS RENOVATIONIST

Chapter 1 examined briefly, insofar as it related to the question of electoral democracy, the image that many Sandinistas had of their party as a democratic vanguard. This image was one which retained the mystique of a vanguard party, a party that included as members only the best sons and daughters of the homeland, but a party which at the same time could win democratic elections because it represented the general will of the people, not in some mystical sense, but truly. However, from the beginning of the revolution, there coexisted within the party an altogether different element, one which opposed to the vanguardist aspect of Sandinista philosophy a social democratic vision. While these differences existed from the beginning, the dichotomy was papered over by the series of historical crises confronting the Sandinista state from 1979 to 1990. What added to the lack of clarity was that the FSLN tended to use the language of social democracy when it spoke of government policy and Leninist language when it spoke of party matters.[1]

The events taking place in Eastern Europe following the accession of Mikhail Gorbachev in the Soviet Union were watched closely in Nicaragua. The fall of the Berlin Wall reverberated in the meeting places of the Sandinistas. It may not always be clear precisely how the leadership was affected, to what extent radicals were sobered and moderates felt strengthened, but as everywhere else in the world where socialism had a foothold, the historical significance of the collapse of the Soviet state and its spheres of influence was clearly perceived. Many Nicaraguans supported the movement toward more openness begun by Gorbachev. Orlando Núñez, writing in 1988, included the process of "renovation, rectification and opening-up which is happening in the Soviet Union under the leadership of Gorbachev" as part of what he called the "democratic critique of socialism" in the face of "authoritarian and statist tendencies."[2]

In 1989, an international symposium was held in Managua to discuss "Democracy and Revolution." It included participants not only from Europe and Latin America, but also from the Soviet Union, Poland, and Cuba. The latter three discussed the changes taking place in their respective lands: "*perestroika*" in the USSR, a "revolution within the revolution" in Poland, and "rectification" in Cuba. Alejandro Bendaña, close advisor to Daniel Ortega, remarked a year later that without a doubt the collapse of the Eastern European regimes provoked reexamination and self-criticism of the fundamentals of their societies and their philosophy among the left in general. Could what happened in Eastern Europe take place in other countries as well? Bendaña said that the results of the ongoing reexamination were yet to be seen in socialist governments of the Third World such as Cuba, Vietnam, Mongolia, and Angola. If their political and economic model was a copy of or was tied to the old Soviet model these nations would likely have problems, caused in part by what Bendaña calls an "infantile intellectual effervescence that leads to a rejection of the past upon seeing paradise in the free market." What Bendaña means is that the people living in Soviet-model countries believed that the accounts of the evils of capitalism told them by their rulers were untrue and that the streets of the United States and other capitalist nations really were paved in gold. Bendaña maintains that those regimes, like Ethiopia, which adopted the orthodox model for geopolitical reasons, have their days numbered. On the other hand, those which based their revolutions on a nationalist struggle against a colonial or imperialist power, such as Mozambique, have a better chance, given peace and a modicum of popular support, of making the transition to a unipolar world. As for Nicaragua, he says that the Sandinistas were bad students of the Soviets and the Cubans. They would sell to anyone who would pay them in dollars and buy from anyone who would give them credit and, in the end, "Marxist-Leninist orthodoxy turned out to be incompatible with geopolitics, with the war, with the nature of the society and last, but not least, with ourselves, given the eclectic and basically anti-dogmatic nature of the Sandinista movement."[3]

There are Leninists, however, whose lament is, according to Núñez Soto, that if the Soviet Union had not stopped assisting Nicaragua, if the United States had not treated Nicaragua so badly, and if the Sandinista government had not agreed to the 1990 elections, then the FSLN would still be in power. For Núñez, this is confusing wishes with reality and the FSLN (as noted above) needs to develop with greater urgency the democratic features implicit in its break with what he calls the vanguard statist model.[4] In sum, therefore, the Sandinistas recognized the impact of the collapse of what they called *socialismo real,* or what is often called in English "actually existing socialism," but felt that, in general, its impact had been less for Nicaragua than for some other Third World countries.

When the FSLN lost the elections for the presidency and the National Assembly in February of 1990, the differences within the party suddenly came into the open and were discussed in all forums, written and spoken. The party's first congress in July of 1991 took some steps forward in democratization as well as a few steps back. The Sandinista Assembly, elected by the Congress, was made the highest decision-making body in the Party between congresses. Previously, the National Directorate had had a higher rank than the Assembly. However, the voting for members of the National Directorate was by slate and there was only one slate. But, the delegates decided that at the next party congress, the voting would be by individual selection. The two categories of membership, affiliate and militant, which had existed historically, were retained. The attempt to elect a woman to the National Directorate was unsuccessful. Daniel Ortega was made general secretary of the party, a post that had not existed previously. A step away from democratic centralism was taken when, after heated debate, the congress voted down a proviso that would have forbidden party members to speak out publicly against an official party decision already taken.

As economic conditions in the country worsened and the Chamorro government was able to roll back many of what Sandinistas called "the gains of the revolution," especially in the areas of health and education, many persons within the party began to question seriously the FSLN collaboration with Chamorro simply for the purpose of preserving the existing democratic constitutional order. Several other conflicts emerged as well. As time went by, the differences in the party became so grave that neither within the Sandinista Assembly nor the National Directorate could any consensus be reached, and therefore, at the end of 1993, Daniel Ortega called for an Extraordinary Party Congress to convene in May of 1994. Because this was to be an extraordinary congress, no new elections were to be held and the delegates that would be seated would be the same as those who had served at the first congress in 1991.

In early February of 1994, three months before the Extraordinary Party Congress, a group calling itself the Forum of the Democratic Sandinista Left—most of whom would attend the May congress—released a document expressing the views of those Sandinistas considered to be more orthodox and who were sometimes called Danielistas because of former president Daniel Ortega's association with the group. Later that month, a group of supporters of renovation in the party, who were mainly followers of former Sandinista vice-president Sergio Ramirez, considered to be a social democrat (and who had declared his interest in being the FSLN candidate for president in 1996), released a document that called for "A *Sandinismo* that Returns to the Majorities." These documents reflect the convergences and divergences of the thought of the two groups.

The documents contain pronouncements in favor of economic and social as well as representative and participatory democracy. But that of the Forum of the Democratic Left (*Danielistas*) states that its members want to reclaim the "revolutionary, humanist and democratic inspiration of sociaLism"[5] and, in fact, the document refers to socialism in four places. The document of the Sandinistas for the Majorities (*Sergistas*) does not refer to socialism at all, although it speaks of "keeping alive our revolutionary ideal of a just, fraternal, and democratic society."[6] Both strongly condemn imposed neo-liberal economic policies and call for a new international economic order. However, the members of the "Democratic Left" go on to identify themselves as "anti-imperialists" which the "Return to the Majorities" members do not.

Both Sandinista groups reject any further confiscation of private property in Nicaragua. They proclaim their support for different kinds of property ownership, private, cooperative, worker-owned, city-owned, with neither document referring to "state-owned property."

It is, however, in the statements on the party itself that the principal differences between the ideas of the two groups can be seen. The document of the renovationist "Return to the Majorities" group makes a strong criticism of the Sandinista years in power. It says: "We Sandinistas should remove from our minds and hearts all those mistaken forms of conduct that we practiced while in power, and that the people rejected, and never repeat them."[7]

The document of the more orthodox Democratic Left has no such self-criticism but rather proposes that in the new society it envisions, the rule of law would be combined with social justice and all popular classes and sectors would have real participation in political and economic power. It goes on to say: "The Sandinista commitment to socialism is not tied to dogmatism or orthodoxy or sectarianism. Efforts toward socialization would be combined with efforts in support of worker and popular self-management and efforts toward distribution would be combined with efforts to increase growth and production."[8] Thus, in a new Sandinista regime, socialization would not mean state socialism, and growth would be given equal importance with the distribution of wealth.

At the May 1994 Extraordinary Party Congress each democratic reform that was approved was counterbalanced by a decision that reinforced some aspect of vanguardism. On the democratic side, the Congress voted to grant autonomy to the FSLN in the Caribbean (Atlantic) Coast region of Nicaragua—an area which has some political and economic autonomy under the 1987 constitution. Delegates voted for three-year terms for members of the National Directorate and Sandinista Assembly and for recall of elected party officials. The congress also approved a quota of 30 percent for women and 10 percent for youth in all local, regional, and national leadership organs. At the same time, with an eye to preserving some aspects of vanguardism, party members voted again to maintain the two party-membership categories of affiliate and militant. They also retained the description of the party's character as "vanguard" and its anti-imperialist stance and voted against institutionalizing currents of opinion inside the party. Despite this, the two opposing groups which solidified within the party called themselves "currents." In the elections for a new 15-member National Directorate (which included five women) and a 135-member Sandinista Assembly, the social democratic wing or "current" of the party lost out as the more orthodox wing gained 53 percent of the seats in the National Directorate and 65 percent of seats in the Sandinista Assembly.[9] One of those who, despite his prestige, was not reelected to the National Directorate was Sergio Ramírez, the former vice-president of Nicaragua under the Sandinistas, and at the time leader of the Sandinista bench in the National Assembly.

In September of 1994, the Sandinista Assembly asked Daniel Ortega to take his seat in the National Assembly, which had been occupied since 1990 by Ramírez, his alternate. In October, the Sandinista Assembly voted to remove Carlos Fernando Chamorro from his position as editor of the Sandinista daily newspaper, *Barricada*. Top journalists such as Sofia Montenegro resigned from the paper in protest. Before the removal of Chamorro, the renovationists had dominated FSLN print media, leaving the majority, orthodox wing of the party without a newspaper outlet. *El Nuevo*, a private Sandinista paper, remained in the hands of renovation sympathizers. Each week brought new resignations from the FSLN party, including the well-known poet and priest Ernesto Cardenal.

One of the first editorials by the new editor of *Barricada*, William Grigsby, accused Sergio Ramírez of political treason. It was, however, a venomous personal attack on Ramírez and his family and on Dora María Téllez by Carlos Guadamúz, the director of the FSLN station, "Radio Ya," in January of 1995 that brought the resignation of Ramírez from the FSLN and of Téllez from the National Directorate (to which she had been elected only eight months before). Three weeks later, Téllez and two other members of the National Directorate, Luis Carrión and Dr. Mirna Cunningham, resigned from the FSLN Party. The statement released by the three said that the party "has abandoned all political principles and ethics, and has dedicated itself to crushing the dignity of all those who do not think as they do."[10] Others such as Enrique Picado and Omar Cabezas stayed in the party. Cabezas said: "I am staying with the FSLN with all its errors."[11] Major divisions developed within the Sandinista bench in the National Assembly, where the majority of the thirty-nine members sympathized with the renovationists but were not willing to leave the FSLN. The long-time leader of the Farmworkers Association, Edgardo García, was elected by the Sandinista Assembly to replace one of the members of the National Directorate who had resigned. On May 21, 1995, the Sandinista Renovation Movement (MRS) was formally founded as a political party.

In June of 1995, the Sandinista Assembly voted to hold an open primary to select FSLN nominees for all local and national races in the October 1996 elections. The Assembly also said that 30 percent of FSLN candidates for office should be women and 10 percent youth. The primaries were held on February 18, 1996. There were three candidates in the write-in straw-poll for the presidential nomination (candidates for other offices were listed): former president Daniel Ortega, the former Supreme Court justice and human rights leader Vilma Núñez, and former army colonel and vice-Foreign minister Alvaro Ramírez. Ortega won easily and, although there evidently were irregularities, the principle of competition within the party for candidacies for public office was established. Over 400,000 people took part, substantially more than the 335,000 who had registered as Sandinistas a year earlier. Vilma Nuñez said in a statement after the election results were announced: "The many limitations and inadequate procedures of the polling should not be an argument to delegitimize the process. . . . Rather, it should help us to do an objective diagnosis of the weaknesses and strengths which we have. . . . I ran not only to win but, above all, to contribute to the Party's internal democratization and reactivation and to rescue its credibility."[12] The FSLN party congress was held on May 4–5, 1996.

## FROM A THEORETICAL PERSPECTIVE

For some with knowledge of European history, the debates within the Sandinista movement will by now sound familiar. We might be looking at Bolsheviks versus Mensheviks, Lenin versus Martov, hards versus softs, the Third versus the Second International. There is definitely some of this same conflict present today in Nicaragua and it has existed since before the triumph of the Sandinista revolution in 1979: for example, the hardness of some of the rhetoric within the party versus the softness of the Sandinista collaboration with many different sectors and groups, a cooperation that was needed in order for the Sandinistas to take power in 1979. Edmundo Jarquín says that these conflicts are not connected with the old tactical divisions about the means for attaining state power that racked the party from 1975 to 1979. Rather, he says, the debate is the same debate that took place earlier in this century within socialist thought between the Leninist position and that of the social democrats. He says that he in particular never hid his social democratic views and feels that the most important achievements of the Sandinista revolution in Nicaragua were those that are at the heart of the social democratic tradition, namely democratization of property ownership and the establishment of political democracy.[13]

The need for unity to take power and then to hold onto that power against onslaughts unleashed by the United States kept this conflict under wraps for many years. But now, inevitably. it has reemerged. Interestingly enough, however, one cannot say that only the more orthodox of the FSLN are "hard." Some members of the social democratic supporters of renovation have reacted so strongly against the verticalism of the past (in which, needless to say, many of them participated and even believed), that they are totally uncompromising in their rejection of anything that even approaches vanguard party procedure or methodology. This blurring of factions has made it more difficult for the ordinary Sandinista, who is more interested in programs to combat unemployment, to understand the nature of the controversy. On matters of program, the two sides have seemed to differ little. The ordinary Sandinista could often be heard saying, "Stop arguing about these unimportant internal party matters, and come together around a party program to get us out of this economic mess!"

Long before the differing documents of the two currents were composed and, in fact, from the time of their electoral defeat in February of 1990, the Sandinistas were discussing the differences among themselves. There were some who thought that the party should not have accepted the electoral result and instead should have held on to power. These are likely to be found among the more orthodox group today. For Henry Ruíz, however, writing in 1990, the electoral defeat strengthened the anti-imperialist forces precisely because it brought to that fight legal and electoral methods of struggle that had in the past been viewed as illegitimate by contemporary revolutionary movements. With the addition of international observers to eliminate fraud—this was the case in the Nicaraguan elections of 1990—elections could be accepted by the left as valid. (Ruiz was writing before it was revealed that the CIA had violated both U.S. and Nicaraguan law and had indeed "intervened" to the tune of about five million dollars in the 1990 Nicaraguan elections.[14] Most observers, both North American and Nicaraguan agree, however, that without this intervention the results would not have been very much different.) Ruiz states that "In considering the electoral process as the method of renovation and of establishing political consensus, change becomes the permanent variable through the expression of the popular will in the exercising of power. It is now not enough to espouse the ideas of the conscious political vanguard that plans, carries out and leads based only on the perception that the content and actions of a particular political program will automatically bring to realization the historic desires and demands of the people."[15]

Ruíz adds that the electoral defeat makes it possible to rescue "the critical role of criticism" according to classical Marxist theory.[16] He refers to the fact that political discussion and criticism were stifled while the Sandinistas were in power both as a result of the war and of mistaken philosophy. In too many cases, orthodoxy took the place of analysis. Now, freed from the restrictions of state power, open analysis and criticism, such as that done by Marx, can begin. "A revolution is without a doubt the greatest historical enterprise that a people can undertake," Ruíz says. "Why not, then, include from the beginning as participants the people as a whole whom we want to convince and to commit to the struggle? Democratization of the party is the first task."[17]

According to Dora María Téllez, rigidity and verticalism in the FSLN have a concrete, structural cause stemming from the history of the party. She says that the Sandinista Front was a political-military organization at the time of its 1979 victory. The verticalist method of work that had been necessary during the clandestine struggle against the Somoza regime was still intact. But it was accentuated by the leadership structure set up at the time of the reintegration of the three tendencies in the late 1970s. She is referring to the fact that, in 1975, as was noted at the outset of this study, differences about strategy were dividing the Sandinistas. The Front split into three tendencies based on differences about how to attain state power. The first was the traditional Prolonged Popular Warfare Tendency, which insisted that the armed struggle is long and difficult and involves the establishment of support committees throughout the nation but mainly in the countryside. The second, the Proletarian Tendency, believed that organizing should center around the new agricultural and industrial proletariat. And, finally, within the Prolonged Popular Warfare Tendency, a group arose that called for mass multiclass insurrection in the cities, supported by the organization of a regular army to fight Somoza's National Guard. This last group was known as the Third or Insurrectional Tendency. In March of 1979, the three tendencies came together to achieve the final defeat of the dictatorship. Téllez explains further:

> The only organic unifying element that the Sandinista Front had after 1979 was the Joint National Directorate. There were three, plus three, plus three, nine individuals. There were three representatives of each Tendency; it was that simple. It was a federation, the round table of the three parliamentary kingdoms of the Sandinista movement. Each Tendency wanted its people there and wanted them there on equal terms. . . . There was no horizontal communication established between the Tendencies; and any that had existed before disappeared. The weight of the power of the National Directorate and its almost total decision-making power within the FSLN was enormous because it was the only element of unity among the Tendencies.[18]

Many analysts have referred to the collective leadership that was characteristic of the Sandinista party and government, assuming it to be less authoritarian than "one-man rule" in other revolutionary countries. The nine men on the National Directorate met (on Fridays, according to Nicaraguan lore), arrived at consensus on the issues and then sent down the orders. Victor Hugo Tinoco says that, in Nicaragua, the ideas of a vanguard party were combined with a cultural tendency toward *caudillismo,* or government by a strong authoritarian leader. He adds that Nicaraguans produced a variation in which "*caudillismo* of one person was replaced by a *caudillismo* of nine people. But in the end it was still *caudillismo,* if a collective one."[19]

Daniel Ortega, in an interview, confirms the collective nature of decision-making under the FSLN government. He says that as president, he never took decisions alone; his decisions were always consulted with the National Directorate. He goes on: "When I had some proposal, I took it to the Directorate, there we discussed it and it was approved or discarded. . . . There was never an attempt to centralize power on my part, my role was limited. I was a president with limited powers."[20]

With the 1990 electoral defeat, the FSLN party structures opened up. As was noted above, the First Party Congress in July of 1991 made the Sandinista Assembly the highest organ of the party between congresses. When the National Directorate decided on its own authority in 1993 to request membership in the Socialist International, members of the Sandinista Assembly immediately protested, called a meeting of the Assembly, chastised the National Directorate for taking on powers that did not now correspond to it, and then proceeded to vote just as the National Directorate had voted. (Full membership was denied then but granted in 1996.) The popular organizations no longer looked to the Sandinista leadership for guidance to the degree they had before the party left government. As I have noted, the National Directorate became divided on important issues with consensus harder to reach. For that reason, Daniel Ortega, as general secretary of the party took on more decision-making powers and, as we know, called for an extraordinary party congress to bring the party out of its stalemate. While the May 1994 congress did, in fact, end the stalemate, it ended it with one current of opinion defeating the other by majority vote rather than by compromise and negotiation between the two sides.

In some cases, the differences between the currents seemed to be based on the role in the party structure played by the individuals involved. Victor Hugo Tinoco says that at certain levels of the Sandinista movement or in certain institutional spaces such as the Sandinista bench of the National Assembly, it is natural, that, first, the comfortable economic situation of the member and, second, his or her role, which is to negotiate and reconcile differences, will be likely to make him or her flexible in attitude. This may lead that person to be a member of the renovation group. On the other hand, the local party leader whose personal economic situation is difficult and whose function is not to negotiate, but rather to demand and search for solutions to desperate economic and social problems, will likely have a more orthodox attitude. Tinoco adds to this that less-educated Sandinistas at the grassroots level of the party still demand that the leaders tell them what to do. He says that

> there is greater creativity at the middle levels, where women, youth, and nongovernmental groups are organized around their own issues while philosophically forming part of the Sandinista movement. But here we're talking about the middle sectors, to some degree the intelligentsia of this society. Below that level many people still are waiting for the leader to tell them what needs to be done. . . . While the middle sectors want a party that helps organize and articulate the needs of the different groups within society, below them the people want a party that tells them what to do. That's the truth.[21]

One device for understanding the philosophical differences and overlaps among the Sandinistas is the following diagram:[22]

democratic methods
of work

| popular | | multiclass |
|---------|---|-----------|
| classes | | compromise |

verticalist methods of work

The two cross-cutting cleavages are between commitment to the popular classes and openness to multiclass compromise and between more democratic versus more verticalist methods of work. Although these are only two of the issues that divide Sandinistas, the first can be seen to represent policy differences and the second differences on internal party matters. These are also the differences that appear to be the most important to the most committed members of the two sides. Orthodox Sandinistas accuse renovationists of having abandoned their commitment to the poor and oppressed while renovationists accuse orthodox Sandinistas of retaining the verticalist ideas of the old vanguard party. These accusations are, of course, only true in the most extreme cases, as may be seen if one places individuals from each group on the graph. Not all the orthodox FSLN members will end up in the bottom left hand corner nor all the renovation supporters in the top right corner. In fact, there will be a big overlap in the middle with many on both sides trying to move toward democratic methods within the party but retaining some verticalist residue; and both sides firmly committed to the popular classes while realizing that other sectors have to be taken into account when a party must govern a nation.

The extremes, however, have become important, as Henry Ruíz lamented after the May 1994 party congress: "The debate got divided into left vs. right. This is horrible. We are a Left party. Everyone is Left. Analyze the documents. There are not true differences. Understand that we've always had currents. We always tried to claim unity but it was a lie. We've always been able to discipline ourselves to unite around a single path. With the electoral defeat we had no idea what to do! We were ambushed while eating ice cream."[23] Ruíz; who attended Patrice Lumumba University in Moscow in the 1960s, has at times been associated with both currents and with those who wish to align themselves with no current, possibly the majority of Sandinistas.

## IN SEARCH OF MASS SUPPORT: TWO VIEWS

Sergio Ramírez, now principal leader of the Sandinista Renovation Movement, said in a 1994 interview that one of the reasons for the Sandinista electoral loss might have been that it was using a vanguard model which was not appropriate to an electoral situation in an immanently political electoral period. "We were using a key in a lock that it did not fit and could not open." He goes on to say that the FSLN has to convert itself into a civic political party, capable of competing in elections and winning them. Others, he says, within the FSLN think that a proposal from the radical left can win the elections in the face of the increasing poverty and unemployment of the citizens, that these conditions will inspire the imagination of the people to vote for a radical proposal. But, he insists, the problem is that even if this radical proposal were to succeed, which he does not think is very possible, this type of Sandinista government in power would only have problems. It would have no solutions because solutions have to be national and have to be negotiated.[24]

For renovationist Dora María Téllez (speaking before she left the FSLN National Directorate), the type of party the FSLN chooses to be depends on what is seen as the social base of the party, the "historical subject of our project." For her, that has to be the peasant agricultural sector, the small and medium-sized private farmers, and cooperative members, but she would also include the workers in the worker-owned businesses, the urban informal sector, and the people of the Atlantic coast region. The FSLN, she feels, has given too much importance to the salaried workers of the Pacific, who are a minority in Nicaragua. The economic subjects will also be the political subjects of the party's efforts, Téllez says. There have to be economic and political parts to the Sandinista project, she insists. If there is a return to concentration of land ownership in the hands of a few in Nicaragua, "democracy will die," she states.[25] Téllez repeats again and again the point that if the FSLN does not reconnect with the majorities of the Nicaraguan people, the party will become a small minority sect without the ability to effect change.[26] She sees the FSLN as having a role in providing daily support for the struggle of the population at all levels, in the streets, in city councils, and in the National Assembly, but she maintains that it also has to win elections.[27] Renovation supporters emphasize that the popular sectors of peasants, women, urban unemployed, and so forth, are not as radical as orthodox Sandinistas maintain and that they will not vote for a radical, left solution.

The emphasis of the orthodox Sandinistas is different. Support for the struggles of the popular sectors against the attempts of the Chamorro government and the international financial agencies to roll back the achievements of the Sandinista revolution is the most important thing; thought of winning elections comes in a distant second. Daniel Ortega says, "We have a moral obligation to support the people's struggles. We are not a party that just goes to the people at the time of elections to ask for their votes; we are a revolutionary party."[28]

Former foreign minister and Maryknoll priest Miguel D'Escoto, right-hand man to Daniel Ortega, has been one of the most vocal in expressing the views of the "Danielistas." He wants to represent those within the FSLN who sacrificed a great deal for the revolution. In D'Escoto's case it was his right to exercise his priesthood; for others, such as Daniel Ortega, it was his youth, spent in jail and in hiding; for many parents, it was a son or daughter who died in the fight against Somoza or against the contras. These Nicaraguans retain a love for the revolutionary cause and mystique, and do not want to see the Sandinista Front converted into just another political party for which it would be preposterous to fight and die. Although they are often accused of being Leninist, their inspiration in most cases comes much more directly from the examples of sacrifice of "Che" Guevara, who died in Bolivia at the hands of the CIA and the Bolivian army, and Padre Camilo Torres, the Colombian priest who died fighting with the guerrillas in his country. Writing in 1994, D'Escoto says:

> At the Extraordinary Party Congress we will have to express our definitive rejection of these leaders who, at any price, but while believing that it is for the best, want to change the nature of the FSLN. Although they do not want to admit it, the problem is ideological. They want to turn the Sandinista Front into something different. They want to have it become something for which it would not have been worthwhile that our heroes and martyrs and so many thousands of our citizens shed even one drop of blood.[29]

For D'Escoto, the principle obligation of the FSLN is to maintain its "authenticity" as the defender of justice and of the interests and rights of the poor. The other group, he says, wishes to lower this profile and make the principal obligation of the Sandinistas the winning of the 1996 elections. D'Escoto maintains that if the FSLN is to gain power again, it must be because of what it is, not because it has compromised in its support of justice. He laments that some comrades in the FSLN have fallen into the habits of the traditional parties of Nicaragua. "I personally," he says, "do not like the idea of the FSLN turning into a political party. I would have preferred that it be a front of popular organizations."[30] After the party congress, D'Escoto said, "The only reason for the FSLN to exist is to defend the rights of the poor. Being elected is not the highest goal."[31]

One might say that D'Escoto and those who agree with him are mistaken about the role of a political party. That would not be true, however. They seem to understand all too well the role of a political party and to be rejecting it. They seem to want the FSLN to be a social movement similar, perhaps, to the civil rights or anti-Vietnam war movements in the United States, whose role it was to present an uncompromising moral position. It is the political party, such as the Democratic Party in the United States, which has to make the compromises necessary to govern a nation. The social movement can remain pure; in fact, that is its role: to present in an unadulterated fashion the position of the people who belong to it. If a social movement were to be elected to office, it would either have to compromise or impose its views by force. This, of course, is what vanguard parties have done in the past.

By contrast to D'Escoto, Orlando Núñez Soto, who signed the "Democratic Left" documents and is loyal to the FSLN, does place importance on "being elected" in order to carry out the revolutionary program. To achieve this end, he presents a strategy that incorporates both party and popular organizations. Núñez says that, on the one hand, we hear talk about decentralization, about doing without a political party, of raising immediate concerns, of respecting the wishes of the majority, of autonomy, of self-management. But on the other hand, the need is recognized for coordination of the struggle, for overcoming simple activism, for carrying actions beyond mere social explosions, for finding an integral, global vision of things, for provoking ruptures in the alienated behavior of the great majorities of people, in their alcoholism, their ritualistic religiosity, *machista* behavior, and indolence.[32] He sees both party and mass organizations as necessary and therefore fits their roles together to make them complementary.

Núñez believes that the revolutionary opposition in Nicaragua should force the conservative government to the limit of its contradictions, while it accumulates strength so that the majority of the population will join its position. The role of the FSLN party is to coordinate the political space it has gained, in the National Assembly as well as in the streets. The popular organizations need to defend that space and cultivate the alternative forms of production and the alternative culture of the revolution. And, Núñez says, both party and popular organizations must try to achieve in all possible ways the inclusion of the majority of the Nicaraguan people in the revolutionary project.[33] Núñez accepts the fact that the majority of a population may not be revolutionary and may even at times be fascist. He states that some would say that decisions or actions can be said to favor the people if they objectively support their interests, independent of whether the people participate in the making of those decisions or actions. But this, he says, brings us to the question of who can say what represents the people's interests, if not the people themselves?[34]

Núñez incorporates Antonio Gramsci's concept of ideological hegemony into his defense of a democratic vanguard. Gramsci, writing in the late 1920s and early 1930s, says that the dominant group in a country exercises hegemony over civil society in the form of spontaneous consent given by the great masses of the population to its general direction. The same dominant group then exercises political power through its direct control of the state and the use of its coercive powers to enforce discipline on those groups which do not consent.[35] Núñez emphasizes that

> the [1990] electoral defeat showed the need to make revolutionary hegemony more profound and deep in the heart of civil society; and, based on that, the taking of the apparatus of state power by a vanguard will be the best complement and not the starting point of the social and economic transformations carried out by the revolution. In

the contrary case, the reconquest of the government would be no
more than the naive recovery of liberal democracy or the re-editing of
badly learned socialist history.[36]

Núñez, therefore, does not want to abandon the vanguard party
concept altogether. However, the question then becomes: Has he
changed its meaning so much that it no longer refers to a vanguard
party in any traditional sense? Writing with Roger Burbach in 1986,
Núñez says that in order to overcome the authoritarian, verticalist,
and undemocratic tendencies of the past, "the democratic principles enunciated by Marx and other revolutionary figures must be
incorporated into a new concept of the vanguard."[37] They go on to
say that the "new vanguard parties must be mass fronts in which the
base has a direct role in deciding the direction and program of the
party."[38] This does not sound like Lenin's "organization that will
consist of professional revolutionaries . . . led by the real political
leaders of the entire people"[39] nor "Che" Guevara's vanguard organization, which includes only the best workers proposed by their
comrades for membership and which would become a mass party
only when the masses attain "the "level of development of the vanguard, that is, when they are educated for communism."[40] If, however, Núñez wants to capture the mystique of a political leadership
devoted to the people that was intrinsic in the old vanguard idea
and combine it with democratic methods of internal decision-making, this could be a very potent combination. There is still a substantial segment of the Nicaraguan people that retains a devotion to
those who died for the revolution and even to some of those (although it may be misplaced) who led the revolution in government.
But they also demand from their leaders democratic methods of
work and of decision-making. It is likely that it was just this combination which the majority of Sandinistas voted to support at the
May 1994 party congress.

As to which individual could lead the party to victory in 1996,
Daniel Ortega, according to Orlando Núñez in 1994, would not be
the best choice for a presidential candidate. But Núñez believes that

"there are still radical tendencies in the revolution and perhaps Daniel is closer to those, and more moderate tendencies as well and perhaps Sergio is closer to them." He adds that while laws and the rule of law are important, the problems of Nicaragua's poor are not going to be resolved without the actions of the popular organizations. Sometimes the poor are vulgar, he says, sometimes violent, but only the organized actions of the poor masses are going to be able to confront the massive national and international machinery of the neo-liberal economic model, with its goal of re-concentration of capital in Nicaragua. So, he says that he is with the "popular group, the one with the connections to the unions and all . . . in spite of the costs."[41] For many this is the central issue.

The seeming repudiation of the state on the part of some Sandinistas brings to mind theories of anarcho-syndicalism which were dominant in some parts of Spain at the beginning of the twentieth century. The anarcho-syndicalists sought to smash the state because they recognized in its existence the negation of the people's interests. Although they sought to replace the state with large unions (syndicates), which would make treaties with one another, the total absence of any existing state in their theory reminds one of the debates currently taking place within the Sandinista movement. The Sandinistas could come to this point quite legitimately because their hero, Augusto Sandino, had been influenced by just such doctrines during his stay in Mexico in the 1920s.

## TO COLLABORATE OR NOT TO COLLABORATE

Another area in which renovation and orthodox Sandinistas differ is that of relations with the existing government of Violeta Chamorro and the attitude which should be taken in the face of the government's economic policy. Following its defeat in February of 1990, the FSLN signed a Transition Protocol with the victorious UNO coalition, setting up the mechanism of the transition, establishing which measures of the revolution the new government would respect, and also establishing the firm commitment of the Sandinistas to work to preserve the constitutional order that they themselves had set up during the period of revolutionary government. The government gained greater and greater success in rolling back the achievements of the revolutionary years, particularly in health and education, and imposed with ever greater rigor the economic stabilization and adjustment measures required by the IMF and the World Bank. The policies ended inflation but took the country into deep recession with unprecedented levels of unemployment and poverty. Many of the party's grassroots members began to question their party's collaboration in these policies, which at times amounted to what seemed to them like co-government. If the FSLN was collaborating out of concern for the whole nation, in the search for a truly national solution, then it was time to end the collaboration, because the nation was going steeply downhill. Many thought that the strategy was not working and the FSLN, in order to preserve its own credibility, should abandon it.

Orthodox Sandinistas tend to be those who are most critical of cooperating with the Chamorro government, even though Daniel Ortega himself has gone back and forth on the question, seeming at times to be promoting strife in the streets and at other times to be putting out as many fires as a government firefighter. The renovationists are more likely than orthodox Sandinistas to believe that the international economic order is a given (just as the IMF and the World Bank are givens) and that a realistic economic plan must make the best of the world capitalist market and the measures required by the predominant neo-liberal (or neo-classical) economic philosophy.

It was as a result of several newspaper articles by Victor Tirado, longstanding member of the FSLN National Directorate, in 1992, that an intense discussion got under way and continues to the present day about whether, in a post-Cold War, unipolar world, the FSLN and the left in Central America should abandon their position of anti-imperialism and try to set up a new, nonconfrontational relationship with the United States. For Tirado, this does not mean abandoning one's principles. It means being realistic and realizing that no country in Central America can apply its own economic theory no matter how positive because the international economic community will "gobble it up." "Nicaragua needs international assistance in the form of investment, especially from the U.S., in order to move forward." What the United States requires, he adds, is stability in order to invest. He goes on: "The United States must remember that it is not possible to have a common market in misery and if they desire Central America as a market under the Enterprise for the Americas Initiative, there must be a certain minimum standard of living in Central America. I do not think that United States policy could be so short-sighted not to see this because if the U.S. is going to have markets where the people live in misery, it is not going to be able to revive its own economy."[42] Tirado says that economic problems are not even on the table for discussion within the party and that it is high time the FSLN looked at the economic aspects, rather than only the political aspects, of privatization, economic adjustment, the market economy, and foreign investment. Tirado questions whether it is possible in the present period of a single capitalist world market, to continue to speak of imperialism as a world force in its traditional sense.

The reaction was to be expected. Many Sandinistas expressed shock and dismay that a Sandinista would bow down to the nefarious "neo-liberal economic model." Others maintained that Tirado was being unrealistic about any supposed opening by the United States, that it was the United States that was guided by political rather than economic considerations and could not be trusted to be dispassionate on the question of Nicaragua or, indeed, of Central America as a whole. Many Sandinistas maintained that imperialism was very much alive in the unequal economic relationships between nations. Anti-imperialism was seen as a necessary part of Sandinista philosophy, as expressed by Tomas Borge in these words: "The FSLN is a revolutionary organization and one cannot be a revolutionary without being anti-imperialist."[43]

A group of twenty-nine middle-level Sandinistas came together at about this time (October of 1992) to protest both the FSLN's close relationship to the government and any softness toward neo-liberal economics. As far as they could see, the relationship with the government was producing no benefits for the party but instead was damaging it. At the same time they protested the apparent rapprochement with capitalist economics, according to Victor Hugo Tinoco, "either because they believed that there was an alternative to neo-liberalism and capitalism or because they thought that there was no alternative but at any rate we should keep our distance."[44]

A middle-level FSLN leader, José González, Sandinista political coordinator for the Department of Matagalpa, describes why he was part of the Group of Twenty-Nine: "I signed the document of the Twenty-Nine because it called on the FSLN to rescue the true roots of the Sandinista movement. The true roots of the Sandinista movement do not include arrangements with any government in power at the moment. The true roots of the Sandinista movement do not include giving economic privilege to a few. . . . U.N. figures show 70 percent of the country living in poverty. . . . [T]his country is being converted into a banquet for the transnational corporations and for the old families of the oligarchy. That is why we wrote that document."[45] Other signers of the document include Orlando Núñez, Mónica Baltodano, and Victor Hugo Tinoco. None of the then-members of the National Directorate were consulted. (Baltodano and Tinoco were elected to the National Directorate at the May 1994 Congress.) The members of the group were conscious of the problem of wanting to support the democratic constitutional order but at the same time needing to make the strongest possible protest against what they saw as the "economic totalitarianism" of the Chamorro government. Political goals and economic necessities clashed in this case.[46] In spite of popular support from all sides within the FSLN for the position that the FSLN must present an alternative to the Chamorro government's economic policies, no economic policy paper was able to achieve wide support in the party before the May 1994 party congress. Both sides agreed that this was task number one in preparation for the 1996 elections.

A related issue deals with the question of the use of violence in actions opposing the government's economic policies. For Miguél D'Escoto, representative of the Danielistas, the powerful are fighting an unequal and violent war against the weak. They want the latter to refrain from defending themselves or from crying out, and simply die quietly. He says that the "Return to the Majorities" document condemns violence but does not speak of "the moral obligation to defend the lives of the unemployed and exploited with all the methods of civic struggle within our reach."[47] Orlando Núñez argues that the opposite of armed struggle is not just legislative work, "as the social democrats would have us believe." Revolutionary opposition, within a capitalist system and with a bourgeois government in power, means mass struggle and the exercise of alternative forms of power. He goes on: "Without the popular struggle in the street, without the strikes and stoppages in the workplaces, without the censure of the government by the Sandinista media, the FSLN would have been reduced to a precarious reformism in the best of cases and to a defeatist collaboration in the worst."[48]

But Sergio Ramírez sees things slightly differently. He says that there are strikes everywhere. In France, for example, transportation strikes close down the highways and isolate Paris. But, he says, these are labor strikes, not political strikes. The general secretary of the Communist Party does not lead them. If a political party puts itself at the head of a strike, it is because it wants to bring down the government. And he believes that it is important to the growth of democracy in Nicaragua that Mrs. Chamorro's government be allowed to serve out its term until 1996, although he says that he is not going to go out of his way to save it from falling, if that is what is going to happen. He states that the FSLN as a party should support the actions of the popular movements "that we believe are legitimate and clearly reject those tactics that are violent." Any vacillation when it comes to violent methods moves public support away from the Sandinistas, according to Ramirez.[49]

The disagreement in this case appears to be centered in the role which party officers, such as the general secretary, should play in

strikes and protests. Neither side is saying that union and movement leaders who are Sandinistas should not be leading such activities. But should the general secretary of the FSLN be leading them?
The best answer to this puzzle appears to be the solution proposed
by Orlando Núñez above, in which there is a division of labor. In
order to regain the lost hegemony for the revolutionary forces
among the people, the party and movements work together but in
separate spheres.

For the rest, the popular organizations need a political party to
campaign on a politically coherent platform which will include
their demands, win elections, and put at least some of those demands into law using the institutions of government. The organizations are not set up to do this themselves. What they are set up to do
is to bring together demands felt at the grassroots and to express
them forcefully. They need the political party to try to put the demands into law.

## INSIDE THE PARTY: FURTHER DISAGREEMENTS

The renovationist and orthodox Sandinistas disagree perhaps most
strongly of all on internal party matters. And on this subject the
principals themselves have made clear statements expressing their
views. With reference to the matter of different levels of membership, Sergio Ramírez says, writing in 1994, that the FSLN cannot
continue to be a party with selective entrance as if it were a Masonic
Lodge. He goes on:

> When I was in Diriomo a little while ago, I gave [FSLN] party cards to
> some new party militants. I gave out eight cards. My reflection at that
> point was that if this party is gaining support in Diriomo at the rate of
> eight militants per year, it is not prepared to win any election. Then I
> was told that these people had been waiting years to be awarded their
> party militancy! And I say, a party cannot be a sect, a closed club; it has
> to be open to everyone. The people we call "sympathizers" should
> have their party cards so that they will identify more with the Sandin-
> ista movement.[50]

Ramírez sees the FSLN as a political party similar to other political parties. Many Sandinistas, Father Miguél D'Escoto is one example, abhor the idea of the FSLN becoming just like any other political party and feel that they can prevent that by retaining categories of membership.

Daniel Ortega, in a radio interview shortly before the May 1994 party congress, took a slightly different position, saying that all human groupings have categories, and the FSLN is not different from the others: "There is no party, religious organization, social group, capitalist or socialist business enterprise, that does not have a minimum of discipline, that does not have categories, that does not have hierarchy. They all have this because that is the level of development which humanity has reached in these times, and which requires these mechanisms."[51]

But, of course, he is wrong. Democratic parties have elected leaders and thus hierarchy but they do not have different classes of members. And the same thing applies to the other types of organizations he mentions: they have elected or appointed officers but not moral categories of membership such as those found in a vanguard party.

Dora María Téllez explains that the two classes of members in the vanguard party had legitimate reason for existing when the FSLN was fighting to overthrow the Somoza dictatorship. At that time, militants were measured in concrete terms, for example, if they were ready to give their lives for the cause, or if they were ready to go underground or into the mountains. Téllez knows whereof she speaks. At great risk to her life, she was "Commander Two" of the Sandinista raid on the Nicaraguan National Palace in 1978, when the Chamber of Deputies in session was taken hostage for forty-five hours. She was in charge of the political negotiation with the representative of Somoza which resulted in the release of political prisoners, including party founder Tomás Borge. She was also the commander of Sandinista forces for the city of Leon during the final offensive of 1979. But, Téllez says, if she were to say now that she was ready to give her life, it is merely rhetorical, because reality is not asking that of her. The category became deformed and was applied out of context with the times. Now, she maintains, it serves only to reduce support for the FSLN and limit its relationship with the population.[52]

When Sergio Ramirez openly declared himself a candidate for president of Nicaragua, he said that "within the old conduct of the clandestine party, to speak of candidacies is almost a conspiracy."[53] He was right. A tremendous uproar resulted after his declaration. Daniel Ortega commented that he believed that

> from any point of view, it is not a good idea to permit the contamination of the atmosphere . . . with this type of speculations. At no time have I gone around promoting my candidacy, nor do I have presidential ambitions. I would like to remind you that when I was nominated as the candidate for the 1984 elections, it was a collective decision, made in a fraternal manner, in the heart of the Sandinista National Liberation Front. What I mean is that it was not a personal decision of mine.[54]

What he means is that it was a decision taken solely by the nine men of the National Directorate of the FSLN. But, obviously, if the rank and file were to decide on a candidate for the 1996 elections, they would have to know the identity of the persons running and something about their views. Ramirez, in declaring himself a candidate for president, adopted the procedure of a electoral party such as the Social Democrats at a time when, at least according to the general voting pattern of the May 1994 party congress, a majority of the members still cherished the ideals of personal modesty and self-denial that are part of the mystique of the vanguard party. The decision of the Sandinista Assembly in mid-1995 to hold a party primary election in February of 1996 to choose candidates for the October 1996 elections was a clear, and for many unexpected, break with vanguard tradition.

At the May 1994 party congress there was another example of this same kind of disagreement. Legendary guerrilla leader and National Directorate member Henry Ruíz allowed his candidacy to be presented to challenge Daniel Ortega for the post of general secretary of the party. Ruíz, whose nom de guerre was Modesto, and about whom people always say "Modesto is too modest," is the last person who could be accused of being egotistical or of violating the codes of personal modesty of the revolutionary leader. Considered one of the most trustworthy members of the National Directorate, he served as treasurer and as chair of the Ethics Commission of the party. Ruíz describes his thoughts: "I actually liked the idea. I thought my contribution could be to replace a General Secretary of a Left party, which never happens!"[55] When Daniel Ortega was asked about a poll showing a majority of Sandinistas supporting the idea that there should be at least two candidates disputing the post of general secretary, he said that he did not think this was healthy for a revolutionary party and that it could sow discord in the ranks.[56] Daniel Ortega won the election for general secretary (with 286 votes to 147 for Ruíz) but, in a break with tradition, there were indeed two candidates for the post.

## A LOOK AT THE FUTURE

What of the future of the FSLN as a party? Will it remain a revolutionary party, some sort of modified vanguard? Will the social democratic or renovationist ideas remain strong within the FSLN? Will more people with renovationist ideas join the Sandinista Renovation Movement (MRS)? It is important to note that FSLN leaders expressed a willingness to enter the elections of 1996 in coalition with other parties, presumably of the center and/or center-left. Thus, it would not be inevitable, as Dora María Téllez has predicted, that the FSLN would, upon losing the 1996 elections, become a minority leftist sect. A modified vanguard FSLN might win elections in coalition but this would necessarily be as a party which shows itself willing to make the compromises necessary to govern and thus one in which the renovationists have substantial influence.

It is important that revolutionaries in Nicaragua sort out the different roles that the party and the popular organizations will play in the struggle for social justice in that country. The confusion apparent in the statements of people like Miguél D'Escoto must be resolved. The FSLN will continue to be a political party, not a coalition of popular organizations, as D'Escoto would like. It will have to make compromises if it is to run for election in coalition with other parties and if it is to govern upon election to power. That does not mean that it necessarily has to lose its "identity" as many orthodox Sandinistas fear. But it is possible that some of the mystique of the uncompromising revolutionary commitment will be lost. That mystique can be assumed by the popular organizations. Most Sandinistas already wear two hats, that of their party membership and of their membership in a popular organization. Internal democracy must replace any residue of vanguardist verticalism within the party and in the relationship between the party and the organizations with which it sympathizes; further, a coherent party program must be written that can attack the dire economic situation Nicaragua faces at this point in its history.

These discussions within the FSLN are also taking place within a larger Latin American and world context. The Communist parties in Russia and in other Eastern European countries are still strong. In Latin America, broad-based leftist parties (not vanguard in nature) have not been able to win presidential elections as yet but continue to be viable political actors. Their continued existence (with all the problems that these parties are known to have) and longterm struggle for more just systems in their countries will give moral support to the Sandinistas to work for unity

Henry Ruíz says that aside from its failures, there were two successes of the May 1994 congress: first, putting women on the National Directorate of the party and, second, "we accept that it is not a crime to think!"[57] FSLN founder Tomás Borge expresses the same idea with some historical perspective: "What happened in the countries of actually existing socialism? The militants were obliged to think with unanimity. You used to shout in the plaza, "National Directorate, give us your orders!" That is to say, you thought exactly the same as the National Directorate. Now you begin to doubt, to question, and to agree. And this doubting, this questioning, this agreement, the real possibility of each one of us expressing our own ideas, this is democracy."[58]

# 8

## Concluding Thoughts

This work has examined the development of ideas within the Sandinista movement in Nicaragua around three essential elements of
democracy: 1) political, or representative democracy—that is, a republican form of government which is based on periodic elections
with universal suffrage; 2) participatory or mass democracy—a
regime which incorporates continuous citizen participation in popular organizations; and 3) economic democracy—under which
there is an equalization in the ownership of wealth and the people
exercise control over the use of the resources of the nation as well as
over the kind of economic system under which they live.

These could be called the three legs of the stool of Nicaraguan
revolutionary democracy. In the formation of the theoretical and
practical project for each leg, there have been conflicts and differences of opinion as well as changes and evolution in policy and
thought. In the chapter on political democracy (chapter 2) we examined the thought within the FSLN on the subject of elections as
it evolved from rejection of "bourgeois" elections, to acceptance of
elections as tactically useful, to a final recognition on the part of
most Sandinistas that elections were valid and necessary if government was to be accountable to the people. We saw how the FSLN, as
a self-described "vanguard party," set up a liberal electoral democ-

racy the outline of which was embodied in the constitution of 1987. Sandinista leaders (and the rank and file within the party) believed that the FSLN was a vanguard party that could win free and fair elections, as it had done in 1984, because it truly reflected the "general will" of the Nicaraguan people. This unique and possibly untenable combination of democratic and vanguard principles was gravely damaged by the electoral loss of 1990 and remains one of the major subjects of controversy in the party to this day.

In the chapters on participatory democracy (3 and 4), we considered the evolution in thought around the role of popular organizations from that of traditional Leninism, which mandates organizations under control of the party and state, through the "liberation" of those organizations so that they might more fully represent the needs of their members. The neighborhood and women's movements are good examples of this evolution in thought and practice. The changes in Nicaragua's popular organizations occurred at a time (in the late 1980s and early 1990s) when the organisms of "civil society" were flowering in all of Latin America, forming networks and working out mechanisms to influence policy in their nations. Sandinistas are prominently engaged in these efforts today.

It is the popular organizations, and most importantly, the women's movement, which in the view of Sofía Montenegro represent the force for true democratic change. Orlando Núñez terms the popular organizations "the new democratic vanguard" of the revolution which can bring egalitarian values to the workplace, the neighborhood, and even to the family.

In our examination of economic democracy in chapter 5, the modernistic, philosophically coherent, orthodox Marxist vision of economic development of Sandinista Agriculture Minister Jaime Wheelock was seen to be in sharp contrast with the ideas of the leaders of the grassroots organizations of peasant farmers. Wheelock emphasized the modern, large sector of the farming economy, which included state farms, agro-industrial complexes, large private producers and agricultural cooperatives. The smaller-scale vision of the peasant farmers, who demanded land, credit, and technical assistance for individual, small, and medium-sized farmers (as well as for cooperatives) was not adopted by the Agriculture Ministry in time to prevent thousands of peasants from joining the counterrevolution. But not only was the latter vision more democratic, because it was the choice of the peasant farmers themselves, but it proved economically more successful in the long run. It is this "reformed" sector of the economy, which since 1990 includes worker-owned industries and businesses, that is seen by Orlando Núñez as the new "economic subject" for the Sandinista movement. This is a major break with traditional Marxist thought and gives Sandinista economists a basis from which to propose alternatives to the reigning world order of neo-liberal economics.

The chapter on democracy in the FSLN party (chapter 7) scrutinized in some detail the controversies that developed since the electoral loss of 1990 between those who wished to retain aspects of vanguardism and those who believed that the party should abandon vanguardism in its entirety and adopt the policies and characteristics of a social democratic political party. In the end, Sandinistas must remember that it was they who set up the system of electoral democracy in Nicaragua and they now have to find the internal party structures and policies that will enable their party to function effectively within it.

How have the ideas of the Sandinista movement changed in the thirty-five years of its existence? We noted at the outset that some scholars maintain that the three strands formed by the ideas of Augusto Sandino, Marxist thought, and Christian Liberation Theology form the basis of Sandinista ideology. Certainly, the emphasis that Carlos Fonseca gave to the ideas and cause of Augusto Sandino remains constant within the FSLN and, indeed, within the Sandinista Renovation Movement as well. In fact, Sandinistas on both sides of the renovation/orthodox debate admit that there are now two parties with roots in the ideas of Sandino. To Sandino's nationalism and anti-imperialism and his use of an explicitly class-based analysis, an awareness of his use of a race analysis has now been added as well. Some of this awareness came to Sandinistas from their experience working with the indigenous groups on the Caribbean coast during the contra war. But it also came from an analysis of the non-European heritage of the mestizo peoples of the central and Pacific regions of Nicaragua by such people as Sofía Montenegro.

Many Nicaraguans still participate in the popular organizations because of a faith-based commitment that they acquired during the struggle against Somoza. Some of the Catholic priests who served in the Sandinista government, such as Ernesto Cardenal and his brother Fernando Cardenal, have left the FSLN party and are sympathetic to the MRS while others such as Miguél D'Escoto remain firmly within the FSLN. If the present Pope has succeeded in limiting the influence of Liberation Theology, there is a strong religious current in the international opposition to the structural adjustment measures being imposed by the IMF and World Bank that finds supporters in Nicaragua. And, while the emphasis of Sandinista Marxist thought has changed—no one is speaking of state-owned factories or farms these days—some of the basics of Marxist philosophy remain.

We have seen that the political thought of the Nicaraguan Sandinistas on democracy falls firmly within the tradition of western political thought. At the same time it offers several important aspects which have their origins in the South. In spite of early Leninist repudiation of "bourgeois democracy," European liberal thought is resurrected in the eventual acceptance of elections for president and representatives to a National Assembly in 1984 and 1990 and in the statement of Dr. Mariano Fiallos, former head of the Supreme Electoral Council, that liberal democracy is a part of the progressive heritage of all humanity and does not exist merely for bourgeois society or the bourgeoisie. Also, the insistence of the Nicaraguan feminist movement on the inalienable right of the freedom to decide what happens to their own bodies expands on the liberal tradition of John Locke and Mary Wollstonecraft. The assertion that national independence is a prerequisite for democracy has its roots in the radical liberalism of Sandino. But it is also reminiscent of the

Thomas Jefferson who demanded "the separate and equal station to which the laws of nature" entitle a nation, as well as to the fight of Simón Bolívar to achieve independence from Spain. It also reminds one of the post-World War II continental struggle of Africa and Asia for liberation from European colonialism.

The Sandinistas took from Marx several aspects of his most democratic thought. Of these, the primary one, from the *Communist Manifesto,* proclaims that the revolution must elevate the proletariat to the position of dominant class—that is, "win the battle for democracy." In Nicaragua, this translated itself into the struggle to place the majority (workers, peasants, artisans,) in the position of dominant class. The Sandinistas believed, as did Lenin, that they as a vanguard party truly represented the general will of the Nicaraguan people. But, unlike Lenin, they were willing to test that conviction twice in free elections. When in 1990 they lost the second election, they were willing, for the first time in Nicaraguan history, to peacefully turn the government over to the victors and go into opposition. Thus, the answer to the question that was laid out in the introduction of this work—What is the role of political or representative democracy in an agricultural society in which the working class is not in the majority—is now made clear. The role is an essential one. It means, however, accepting the possibility of losing elections, leaving government, and becoming an opposition party. The important achievement becomes the setting up of a democratic system, a republican form of government, seen by Marx as the first step toward socialism, which is democracy extended into the economic sphere as well as the political. This contribution of the Sandinistas to political theory and practice can be a useful example to other countries of the South.

If the Sandinistas were not able to achieve ideological hegemony among the Nicaraguan people during their years in power, it was not from ignorance of Gramsci, the great Italian Marxist thinker who is so well known in Nicaragua. Gramsci's ideas on hegemony and on civil society were studied extensively by the Sandinistas. At the present moment, however, Sandinista thought on civil society has gone beyond Gramsci and is an important part of the new concepts the South is now offering in political theory. If there were Stalinist aspects in the Sandinista practice toward the mass organizations during the Sandinista era in government, the practice in the years since then and the radical democratic ideas of such writers as Sofía Montenegro and Orlando Núñez Soto mark a change which places Nicaragua in the forefront of left democratic thought in Latin America.

Sandinista thought regarding traditional peasant and indigenous customs also reveals residues of that type of orthodox Marxism which disregarded them, but as a result of the pressure from the peasant and indigenous sectors themselves as well as the examination of the ideas of Sandino and of other Latin Americans, such as Peruvian José Carlos Mariátegui, those vestiges disappeared. Consequently, one sees today that the small and medium-sized peasant farmer and the peasant cooperative along with other economic groups of the reformed sector are regarded as the new economic subject in the thought of Orlando Núñez and others. Now, there is no single favored economic form which corresponds to the state farm of the Leninist past.

Montenegro's insistence that Nicaraguans reclaim their indigenous heritage and form a true *mestizaje* based on equality and respect for difference before they move forward together on a new national project is very important for the future of democracy in Nicaragua. In spite of her debt to western feminism, which she freely acknowledges, Montenegro rejects what she considers to be the immobilizing theories of postmodernism and in this she is joined by virtually all other Sandinista thinkers. The work of the critical theorists, especially of the Frankfurt School, has had greater influence in Nicaragua because, in their thought, the emancipatory aspects of socialism survive the rejection of the authoritarian aspects of Marxism-Leninism.

Sandinista economists like Acevedo and Gorostiaga are contributing to a growing literature from the South that is based on principles of radical democracy and seeks possible ways to parry the thrusts of a unipolar world and the universal imposition of neo-liberal economics.

But if democratic thought has developed dramatically with the incorporation of electoral forms, the discovery of a "new democratic vanguard" in the popular organizations, and of "new economic subjects" in the multitudinous variety of productive associative and cooperative enterprises, great confusion persists about the role of the democratic left party and indeed about what it means to be a party of the democratic left at the present moment. The party is not a mass organization or even a coalition of mass organizations. The popular organizations and producers' associations cannot turn demands into government policy. For this a political party is needed that can run for office and, if elected, form a government or form part of a governing coalition that will bargain, compromise, and negotiate with other political forces in the nation in order to make laws that will serve their own constituency and hopefully the rest of the nation as well. A vanguard party that will not compromise cannot govern democratically, and there are still residues of vanguardism among the Sandinistas. The theorists who have done such excellent work clarifying the roles of the actors in civil society and in the economic sphere must now turn their attention to a theoretical examination of how the Sandinista National Liberation Front itself can go forward as a truly democratic party.

# Postscript

The Sandinistas lost the October 20, 1996, elections to the Liberal Alliance headed by the right-wing, populist, former mayor of Managua, Arnoldo Alemán. In the presidential contest, Daniel Ortega, the FSLN candidate, received 38% of the vote to 51% for Alemán. In the 93-member National Assembly, the Liberal Alliance holds 42 seats (45%) while the FSLN holds 36 seats (39%) with smaller parties holding the remaining seats. The FSLN won mayoral elections in 52 municipalities, as against 13 in the previous elections of 1990, but far below the 91 mayorships taken by the Liberal Alliance.

The elections were fraught with irregularities. In January of 1996, the National Assembly passed amendments to the electoral law which politicized the formerly apolitical Supreme Electoral Council to the degree that the long-time head of that branch of the Nicaraguan government, Mariano Fiallos, resigned after energetically lobbying against them. The subjection of the Electoral Council's national and regional structures to the pressures of party politics along with the complexity of the electoral process [there were 24 political parties running for local, national and Central American offices on six separate paper ballots] presented the former supporters of the Somoza dictatorship with the opportunity to commit fraud. While there is little evidence of nationally-planned fraud, the Supreme Electoral Council was incapable of preventing or responding to local fraud.[1] For example, politically-appointed heads of precincts telegraphed or faxed results to the National Computing Center in Managua that did not correspond to official tallies signed by all poll-watchers at the time of the ballot count. Then, official documents and ballots were "lost" so that recounts were impossible. Some analysts believe that opinion polls immediately before the elections, which showed Daniel Ortega in a statistical dead heat with Arnoldo Aleman, frightened Liberal Alliance members into carrying out these actions. These same polls and the massive 300,000 person strong end-of-campaign rally of the FSLN also were believed to have frightened many who would have voted for smaller third parties into voting for Aleman and thus put him over the 45% threshold needed in order to avoid a run-off.

The FSLN challenged the results in two departments, Managua and Matagalpa, where the party said that irregularities were widespread. After examining the challenges, however, the Supreme Electoral Council declared that the "problems" were "not sufficient" to invalidate the elections in those two departments and that the elections were in general "free, fair and transparent."[2] The Council of Freely Elected Heads of Government Delegation, organized by the Carter Center, however, does not use the phrase "free, fair and transparent" anywhere in its report. The Delegation cites "irregularities . . . including the disappearance of ballots and tally sheets [which] caused the annulment of about 6% of the polling stations." [According to the electoral law, this means that more than 50% of the ballots in those precincts were invalid, a very high threshold.] The Carter Center Delegation "respectfully suggests" the creation of a commission to study changes in the electoral law before the next elections.[3] Highly placed Nicaraguan sources quoted former Costa Rican president Oscar Arias—who was a member of the Carter Center Delegation—as saying (in private only) that elections like these would not stand in Costa Rica or in Europe.[4] The truth, however, was that Nicaragua could not afford to hold another set of elections and even the Sandinistas accepted Aleman's victory, albeit, they said, with a lower total.

The implications of the flawed elections for the philosophical development of political, participatory and economic democracy in Nicaragua are varied. The implications for political (electoral) democracy are serious. Alejandro Bendaña called the elections "a disaster in terms of the democratic process." On a visit to Washington, DC, shortly after the elections, he said that the fact that over 80% of the population went to the polls showed that the Nicaraguan people had faith in electoral democracy. That faith could be lost now, he asserted. He called for changes in the electoral law to reestablish public trust.[5]

It is ironic that the FSLN, the "vanguard" party, was able to organize and carry out free and fair elections in Nicaragua in 1984 and 1990, but that the "bourgeois" parties, which are by definition associated with elections and all the other aspects of liberal democracy, were unable or unwilling to do the same. It is likely that those members of the FSLN who have always doubted the value of what they called "bourgeois elections," because they could readily be manipulated by powerful economic interests, feel vindicated and some of the battles within the FSLN about the acceptance of the principles of electoral democracy will have to be refought.

After generations of manipulation by the party in power (whether Liberal or Conservative) and by outside intervention forces (customarily those of the United States), free elections are something of a novelty in Nicaragua. If electoral democracy was one of the major achievements of the Sandinista revolution, and few would argue that it was not, then it is entirely appropriate that the FSLN continue to struggle for its preservation in Nicaragua today. On January 9, 1997, Vilma Núñez, President of the Nicaraguan Center for Human Rights (CENIDH), presented a petition before the Inter-American Commission on Human Rights of the Organization of American States in Washington, DC. It was based on articles in the Inter-American Convention of Human Rights which establish the right of citizens to freely elect their public representatives.[6] The petition declared that the flawed electoral law and the irregularities of the elections of October 1996 violated that right and Dr. Núñez called upon the Commission to issue a recommendation to the Nicaraguan government to make changes in its electoral law prior to the 1998 regional elections. The Commission has taken this step in previous cases brought before it. While this is an initiative of CENIDH, it should also be seen as part of the struggle by the most democratic Sandinista forces to preserve the gains of electoral democracy in Nicaragua.

The implications for the development of ideas on participatory democracy are of interest. The FSLN campaign focussed on bringing together a coalition of farmers, individual and cooperative, small and large, and on reconciliation between Sandinistas and former contras, 4,500 of whom joined the FSLN in an electoral alliance. Sandinista women were active in the Women's Coalition, a group of women of all political parties working to advance a women's agenda. However, the traditional "Sandinista popular organizations" did not participate in the campaign as such, maintaining the autonomy from the party that they had achieved after the 1990 electoral defeat. Most Sandinistas active in these organizations, however, did participate in the campaign as individuals. Benigna Mendiola relates how Daniel Núñez, President of the Union of Farmers and Ranchers (UNAG), had given strict orders that UNAG workers' time and UNAG jeeps were not to be used for the FSLN campaign. Then he heard reports of an Alemán speech in Miami promising Somocistas that their farms in Nicaragua would be returned to them if he were elected to the Presidency. At that point, Mendiola says, Núñez (who represents thousands of farmers who benefited from Sandinista agrarian reform) decided that perhaps, after all, the rules would not be so rigid![7] Thus, leaders of the popular organizations, careful to maintain their autonomy from the FSLN party, but at the same time mindful of the genuine interests of their constituencies, provided philosophical and practical support for the party in many cases.

Within the FSLN there remain controversies around economic policy. The party took a moderate line in the campaign in which the basic tenets of neo-liberal economics were modified only slightly. Daniel Ortega promised many times that if he were elected there would be neither evicted nor confiscated property holders.[8] During the campaign, the National Directorate of the FSLN approved an economic proposal entitled "Program 2002" which emphasized exports and gave no priority whatsoever to the reformed sector of the economy. In doing this, the National Directorate rejected an earlier economic plan that had emphasized strengthening the poor sectors of the economy. This earlier plan had been written by Orlando Núñez and others and then adopted by the Sandinista Assembly.

Some say that the "moderate" campaign line was a failure because neither those who supported the "old" FSLN nor those who opposed it believed the new economic rhetoric. The former voted for the FSLN while the latter voted against it. Orlando Núñez Soto, writing shortly after the elections, called on Sandinistas "within or outside the party" and all other progressives to join together to support a "popular economic option" based on agricultural production and in which the economic and social policies of the government would be complemented by the policies of the people themselves, organized in different ways in civil society.[9]

In terms of democracy within the party, the campaign and elections included steps forward and steps backward. Vilma Núñez (with Orlando Núñez Soto as her advisor) challenged Daniel Ortega for the presidential nomination in the party primary of February 1996 and at the May 1996 party congress. This challenge to the choice made by the leadership of a revolutionary party was extremely important and positive. What was negative was that the night before the congress vote, a member of the FSLN National Directorate, in true vanguard fashion, went from departmental delegation to delegation to tell members that the candidate had to be Daniel Ortega.[10] In other respects, women achieved an agreement at the party congress which gave them one half of the places on the slates (alternating with male candidates beginning at the top of the slate in what was called a "braid") for at-large deputies to the National Assembly and the Central American Parliament. As a result, seven out of the eight women in the new National Assembly are from the FSLN.

There are those who say that Daniel Ortega was not the right candidate for the party if it was ever to move beyond its base. But, at the same time, it is also true that the FSLN did conserve its base and it remains the largest and best organized political party in Nicaragua and one of the strongest parties of the left in all of Latin America. It was not reduced to a small sect on the left as some had predicted. In fact, it was the break-away Sandinista Renovation Movement (MRS), led by former Vice-President Sergio Ramírez, that was unable to gain popular support and achieved only one deputy in the National Assembly. The challenges for the FSLN in the years immediately ahead will be to continue its own internal democratization and to craft economic proposals that deal realistically with the question of Nicaragua's place in the global economy while addressing the plight of the 70% of Nicaraguans who now live in poverty.

# Notes

## INTRODUCTION

1. See especially Harry E. Vanden and Gary Prevost, *Democracy and Socialism in Sandinista Nicaragua* (Boulder: L. Rienner, 1993); David Close, *Nicaragua: Politics, Economics and Society* (London: Printer Publishers, 1988); Susanne Jonas and Nancy Stein, "The Construction of Democracy in Nicaragua," in Jonas and Stein, eds., *Democracy in Latin America: Visions and Realities* (New York, Bergin & Garvey, 1990); Jose Luis Coraggio, *Nicaragua: Revolution and Democracy* (Boston: Allen & Unwin, Inc., 1986); George Irvin and Jose Luis Coraggio, "Revolution and Democracy in Nicaragua," *Latin American Perspectives* (spring 1985); Giulio Girardi, "'Democracy' and Ideological Struggle in Nicaragua Today," *Crosscurrents* (spring 1989); John Booth, *The End and the Beginning: The Nicaraguan Revolution*, 2d ed., rev. (Boulder: Westview Press, 1985); Gary Ruchwarger, *People in Power: Forging a Grassroots Democracy in Nicaragua* (South Hadley, Mass.: Bergin & Garvey, 1987); Midge Quandt, *Unbinding the Ties: The Popular Organizations and the FSLN in Nicaragua* (Washington, D.C.: Nicaragua Network Education Fund, 1993); Dennis Gilbert, *Sandinistas: The Party and the Revolution* (New York: B. Blackwell, 1988); LASA Delegation to Observe the Nicaraguan General Election of November 4, 1984, *The Electoral Process in Nicaragua: Domestic and International Influences* (Pittsburgh: The Latin American Studies Assoc., 1984); Council of Freely-Elected Heads of Government, *Observing Nicaragua's Elections, 1989–1990* (Atlanta: Carter Center, 1990.

2. Orlando Núñez Soto, *Transición y lucha de clases en Nicaragua, 1979–1986* (Mexico: Siglo Veintiuno Editores, 1987), 95. Unless otherwise indicated, translations from the Spanish are by the author of this work.

## 1. THE SETTING

1. For further information on Nicaraguan history see the following primary and secondary sources. Primary Sources: Gonzalo Fernandes de Oviedo y Valdés, *Centroamérica en los cronistas de Indias* (1559, rpt. Managua: Banco

de Anérica, 1977); Ephraim Squier, *Nicaragua: Its People, Scenery, Monuments, Resources, Conditions and Proposed Canal* (New York: Harper, 1860); William Walker, *The War in Nicaragua* (Mobile, Ala.: S. H. Goetzel, 1860); Sergio Ramírez and Robert Edgar Conrad, eds., *Sandino: The Testimony of a Nicaraguan Patriot, 1921–1934* (Princeton, N.J.: Princeton Univ. Press, 1990); Henry Lewis Stimson, *American Policy in Nicaragua* (1927, rpt. New York: AMS Press, 1971); Pedro Joaquin Chamorro, *Estirpe sangrienta: los Somoza* (Buenos Aires: Editorial Triangulo, 1959). Secondary Sources: Linda A. Newson, *Indian Survival in Colonial Nicaragua* (Norman: Univ. of Oklahoma Press, 1987); William O. Scroggs, *Filibusters and Financiers: The Story of William Walker and His Associates* (New York: Russell and Russell, 1916); Jose Coronel Urtecho, *Reflecciones sobre la historia de Nicaragua, de Gainza a Somoza* (León, Nicaragua: Editorial Hospiciom, 1962); Gregorio Selser, *Sandino*, trans. Cedric Belfrage (New York: Monthly Review Press, 1981); Thomas Walker, *Nicaragua: The Land of Sandino*, 3rd. ed., rev. (Boulder: Westview Press, 1991); Walter Knut, *The Regime of Anastasio Somoza, 1936–1956* (Chapel Hill: Univ. of North Carolina Press, 1993); Richard Millet, *Guardians of the Dynasty* (Maryknoll, N.Y.: Orbis Books, 1977); Jaime Wheelock, *Imperialismo y dictadura*, 2d ed. (Mexico: Siglo Veintiuno, 1978); John Booth, *The End and the Beginning: The Nicaraguan Revolution*, 2d ed. (Boulder: Westview Press, 1985).

2. E. Bradford Burns, in his book *Patriarch and Folk: The Emergence of Nicaragua, 1798–1858* (Cambridge, Mass.: Harvard Univ. Press, 1991), maintains that Nicaraguan political conflicts of this period were rather between the elite of both parties and the common folk.

3. Augusto C. Sandino, *El pensamiento vivo de Sandino*, ed. Sergio Ramírez (San José, Costa Rica: EDUCA, 1976), 90.

4. Quoted in José Román, *Maldito País* (Managua: El Pez y la Serpiente, 1979), 146. This book was written in 1934, but Román vowed not to puiblish it until his country was free.

5. Quoted and tanslated in Neil Macaulay, *The Sandino Affair* (Chicago: Quadrangle Books, 1967), 109.

6. For more information, see Rodolfo Cerda, *Sandino, el APRA y la Internacional Comunista* (Lima: EDIMSSA, 1983), 91–103, and John M. Baines, *Revolution in Peru: Mariátegui and the Myth* (University, Ala.: Univ. of Alabama Press, 1972), 135–36.

7. Sandino, 214.

8. Carleton Beals, *Banana Gold* (Philadelphia: Lippincott, 1932), 242.

9. Thomas John Bossert, "Health Care in Revolutionary Nicaragua," *Nicaragua in Revolution*, ed. Thomas Walker (New York: Praeger, 1982), 261.

10. Jaime Wheelock, interview by Marta Harnecker in *Nicaragua: el papel de la vanguardia* (Buenos Aires: Editorial Contrapunto, 1986), 67.

11. O. Núñez, *Transición y lucha de clases,* 64.

12. Carlos Núñez, *Un pueblo en armas,* 2d ed. (Managua: Editorial Vanguardia, 1986), 20.

13. Humberto Ortega, *Cincuenta años de lucha sandinista* (Havana: Editorial de Ciencias Sociales, 1980), 49.

14. Daniel Ortega, "Democracia y Revolución en Nicaragua," in *Democracia y Revolucíon* (Managua: Centro de Documentación y Ediciones Latinoamericas, 1989), 19.

15. Alejandroi Bendaña, interview by the author, Managua, Jan. 28, 1994.

16. Sergio Ramírez, "Nicaragua: Primera Frontera," *Pensamiento Propio* (July/Aug. 1983): n.p.

17. V. I. Lenin, "The Right of Nations to Self-Determination," in *The Lenin Anthology,* ed. Robert C. Tucker (New York: W. W. Norton & Co., 1975), 154.


## 2. POLITICAL DEMOCRACY?

1. See for example, Harry E. Vanden, *Latin American Marxism: A Bibliography* (New York: Garland Publishing, Inc., 1991); Sheldon B. Liss, *Marxist Thought in Latin America* (Berkeley: Univ. of California Press, 1984); Sheldon B. Liss, *Radical Thought in Central America* (Boulder: Westview Press, 1991); Richard L. Harris, "Marxism and the Transition to Socialism in Latin America," *Latin American Perspectives* 15.1 (winter 1988); and on the present-day left in Latin America, Jorge G. Castañeda, *Utopia Unarmed: The Latin American Left after the Cold War* (New York: Vintage Books, 1993).

2. Carlos Fonseca, *Obras, Tomo 1: Bajo la bandera del Sandinismo* (Managua: Editorial Nueva Nicaragua, 1982), 350.

3. Pedro Joaquín Chamorro, "Speech on Unity," in *The Central American Crisis Reader,* ed. Robert Leiken and Barry Rubin (New York: Summit Books, 1987), 173–74.

4. D. Ortega, "Democracia," 35.

5. FSLN, "Statement on the Electoral Process," in *The Central American Crisis Reader,* ed. Robert Leiken and Barry Rubin (New York: Summit Books, 1987), 227.

6. Ibid.

7. Bayardo Arce, interview by Gabriele Invernizzi, Francis Pisani, and Jesús Ceberio, in *Sandinistas: Entrevistas con Humberto Ortega Saavedra, Jaime Wheelock y Bayardo Arce Castaño* (Managua: Editorial Vanguardia, 1986), 81.

8. FSLN, "Statement in the Electoral Process," 228–29.

9. Sergio Ramírez, interview by the author, Managua, Feb. 3, 1994.

10. Luis Carrión, interview by the author, Managua, Feb. 3, 1994.

11. Conversation between the author and Henry Ruiz, which took place in Washington, D.C., Jan. 29, 1992.

12. Dr. Mariano Fiallos, interview in *Monéxico: Revista del concejo de Estado*, No. 3.

13. Angela Rosa Acevedo, interview by the author, Managua, Jan. 28, 1994.

14. Dora María Téllez, interview by the author, Managua, Feb. 8, 1994.

15. Humberto Ortega, interview by Invernizzi, Pisani, and Ceberio, in *Sandinistas*, 17–18.

16. Arce, interview by Invernizzi, Pisani, and Ceberio, 93.

17. Bayardo Arce, "Secret Speech on Strategy and Tactics," in *The Central American Crisis Reader*, ed. Robert Leiken and Barry Rubin (New York: Summit Books, 1987), 292–93.

18. Ibid., 294–96.

19. Arce, interview by Invernizzi, Pisani, and Ceberio, 94.

20. Victor Hugo Tinoco, interview by the author, Managua, Jan. 28, 1994.

21. Orlando Núñez, interview by the author, Managua, Feb. 3, 1994.

22. Bendaña, interview by the author.

23. Rafael Solís, interview, "Elecciones y participación popular," *Pensamiento Propio* (Jan. 1984): 22–23.

24. Rafael Solis, interview, "Habrá negociación y reconciliación nacional," *Pensamiento Propio* (Jan.–Feb., 1990): 18–19.

25. Dr. Constantion Periera, quoted in "El debate constitucional," *Amanecer* 44 (Sept./Oct. 1986): 5.

26. Carlos Núñez, "Acto de Promulgación de la Constitución de la República de Nicaragua," *Monéxico: Revista de la Asamblea Nacional* (12): 282.

27. Dora María Téllez, interview by Octavio Corea, Managua, October 29, 1992, photocopy.

28. O. Núñez, interview by the author.

29. O. Núñez, *Transición y lucha de clases*, 21–22.

30. Orlando Núñez, *La insurrección de la conciencia* (Managua: Editorial Escuela de Sociología de la Universidad Centroamericana, 1988), 54.

31. Daniel Ortega, "Declaración del Presidente Ortega," *Amanecer* 66 (Mar./Apr. 1990): 18.

32. Dora María Téllez, "El socialismo pasa por la solución del problema nacional," *L'Avispa* (Apr./May 1991): 13.

33. Carlos Núñez, "Las puertas del FSLN sólo se abren a los mejores ele-

mentos de la sociodad," in *Habla la Dirección de la Vanguardia* (Managua: Departamento de Propaganda y Educación Política del FSLN, 1981), 71.

34. V. I. Lenin, "Two Tactics of Social Democracy," in *The Lenin Anthology*, ed. Robert C. Tucker (New York: W. W. Norton & Company, 1975), 141.

35. Orlando Núñez, *En busca de la revolución perdida* (Managua: CIPRES, 1992), 106.

## 3. PARTICIPATORY DEMOCRACY IN ACTION

1. For readers who wish to examine the general literature on participatory democracy, the following may be consulted: Peter Bachrach and Aryeh Botwinick, *Power and Empowerment: A Radical Theory of Participatory Democracy* (Philadelphia: Temple Univ. Press, 1991); Benjamin Barber, *Strong Democracy* (Berkeley: Univ. of California Press, 1984); Samuel Barnes, Max Kaase, and Klause R. Allerbeck, *Political Action: Mass Participation in Five Western Democracies* (Beverley Hills, Calif.: Sage Publications, 1979); Jane S. Jaquette, *The Women's Movement in Latin America: Participation and Democracy* (Boulder: Westview Press, 1994); Thomas Jefferson, "Letter to John Adams, October 1813," "Letter to Joseph Cahill, February 2, 1816," and "Letter to John Taylor, May 28, 1816," in Thomas Jefferson, *Writings*, ed. Merrill D. Peterson (New York: Library of America, 1984); Carol Pateman, *Participation and Democratic Theory* (Cambridge: Cambridge Univ. Press, 1970).

2. Gary Richwarger, *People in Power: Forging a Grassroots Democracy in Nicaragua* (South Hadley, Mass.: Bergin & Garvey, 1987), 5.

3. Téllez, interview by the author.

4. Joaquín Cuadra, interview by Marta Harnecker, in *Pueblos en Armas* (Managua: Editorial Nueva Nicaragua, 1985), 54–55.

5. Jaime Wheelock, interview by Marta Harnecker, 105–6.

6. Humberto Ortega, interview by Marta Harnecker, in *50 Años de Lucha Sandinista*, by Humberta Ortega (Havana: Editorial de Ciuencias Sociales, 1980), 40.

7. Dora María Téllez, interview by Marta Harnecker, in *Pueblos en Armas* (Managua: Editorial Nueva Nicaragua, 1985), 94–95.

8. Téllez, interview by Harnecker, 98–99.

9. René Mendoza, "We Erred to Win," *Envio* (Oct. 1990).

10. Carlos Núñez, "El papel de las organizaciones de masas en el proceso revolucionario," in *Sandinistas: Key Documents*, ed. Dennis Gilbert and David Block (Ithaca, N.Y.: Cornell Univ. Latin American Studies Program, 1990), 213.

11. For similar expressions, see Lenin's April 1918 article "The Immediate Tasks of the Soviet Government," included in *The Lenin Anthology*, ed. Robert C. Tucker (New York: W. W. Norton, 1975), 448.

12. C. Núñez, "El papel."

13. Carlos Fonseca, *Obras, Tomo I*, 109–10.

14. FSLN, "'Seventy-Two Hours' Document (September 1979)," in T*he Central American Crisis Reader*, eds. Robert Leiken and Barry Rubin (New York: Summit Books, 1987), 224.

15. Ibid., 226–27.

16. Joseph Stalin, *Problems of Leninism*, 11th ed. (Moscow: Foreign Languages Publishing House, 1940), 135; quoted in Merle Fainsod, *How Russia Is Ruled*, rev. ed. (Cambridge, Mass.: Harvard Univ. Press, 1963), 137.

17. Luis Carrión, in Tomás Borge, Luis Carrión, et al., *Nicaragua: La Batalla por el Poder Ideologico* (Buenos Aires: Editorial Cartago, 1986), 84.

18. Sergio Ramírez, "El logro principal: nuestra patria ha consolidado su estabilidad interna," *Barricada*, May 5, 1980.

19. Republican Party, "Platform (1980)," in *The Central American Crisis Reader*, ed. Robert Leiken and Barry Rubin (New York: Summit Books, 1987), 515.

20. Edward Boland, "The Boland Amendment: May 1983," in *The Central American Crisis Reader*, ed. Robert Leiken and Barry Rubin (New York: Summit Books, 1987), 577.

21. Dora María Téllez, interview by Corea.

22. Angela Saballos, quoted in Midge Quandt, *Unbinding the Ties: The Popular Organizations and the FSLN in Nicaragua*, monograph, (Washignton, D.C.: Nicaragua Network Education Fund, 1993), 51.

23. Tomás Borge, "El nuestro es un proyecto enredado," *Pensamiento Propio* 24 (June–July 1985): 8.

24. Téllez, interview by the author.

25. Enrique Picado, interview by the author, Managua, Nicaragua, Feb. 8, 1994.

26. Carríon, interview by the author.

27. Téllez, Corea interview, 12.

28. Mónica Baltodano, interview by the author, Managua, Feb. 8, 1994.

29. Enrique Picado, interview by the author.

30. Omar Cabezas, "Organícense como quieran y para lo que quieran," interview by Mariúca Lomba, *Pensamiento Propio* 21 (July–Aug. 1988): 46.

31. Ibid., 45–46.

32. Ibid., 48.

33. Ibid., 47.

34. Ibid., 48.

35. Picado, interview by the author.

36. Ibid.

37. Quoted in Quandt, 48.

38. Oficina Central de Promoción y Desarrollo Comunal, Movimiento Comunal Nicaragüense, *Memoria 1991* (Managua: DISA-Editores, 1991), 2–3.

39. Quoted in Quandt, 47–48.

40. Ibid.

41. Ibid, 48.

42. Picado, "El FSLN está jugando un papel dual," *L'Avispa* 12 (Jan.–Feb.–Mar. 1993): 20–21.

43. Picado, interview by the author.

44. Ibid.

45. Victoria González, "La historia del feminismo en Nicaragua: 1837–1956," *La Boletina* 22 (July–Aug. 1995): 11. See also Margarita López Miranda, *Una chontaleña en la educación: Biographia de Josefa Toledo de Aguerri* (Juigalpa, Nicaragua: ASOGACHO, 1988) and Richard Whisnant, *Rascally Signs in Sacred Places: The Politics of Culture in Nicaragua* (Chapel Hill: Univ. of North Carolina Press, 1995), 407–13.

46. Mónica Baltodano, "Las Mujeres Sandinistas," interview by Rosario Murrillo, *Ventana* (June 3, 1991): 18.

47. Ileana Rodríguez, *Registradas en la Historia: 10 años del quehacer feminista en Nicaragua* (Managua: Centro de Investigación y Acción para la Promoción de los Derechos de la Mujer, 1990), 85–86.

48. Ibid, 88.

49. Magda Enríquez, "Letter to Solidarity: FSLN Women Prepare for Congress," *Nicaragua Monitor* (Feb. 1994): 3.

50. María Teresa Blandón, Lillian Levi, and Sofía Montenegro (Comisión de Contenido), *La Situación Nacional desde la Perspectiva Feminista* (Managua: Primer Encuentro Nacional Feminista, 1993), 8.

51. Ibid.

52. Ibid.

53. AMNLAE, Estrategia Nacional, booklet, Aprobada en la I Asamblea Nacional Extraordinaria, Aug. 1993, 5.

54. Enríquez, 3.

55. Baltodano, Murillo interview, 18.

56. Ibid., 18–19.

57. Blandón, Levi, and Montenegro, 7.

58. Benigna Mendiola, interview by the author, Managua, Nicaragua, Jan. 20, 1994.

59. Benigna Mendiola, "We Have More Serious Problems," *Barricada Internacional* (English edition, Mar. 1992): 25–26.

60. Benigna Mendiola, interview by the author, Washington D.C., May 1993.

61. Rodríguez, 96.

62. Blandón, Levi, and Montenegro, 2.

63. Ibid., 10.

64. Ibid., 4.

65. Ibid., 4–5.

66. Dora María Téllez, "El socialismo pasa por la solucíon del problema nacional," *L'Avispa* (Apr./May 1991): 21.

67. Blandón, Levi, and Montenegro, 9.

68. Sofía Montenegro, interview by the author, Managua, Nicaragua, Jan. 17, 1994.

69. Comisión de Divulgación del Primer Encuentro, "Diversas pero unidas," *Barricada* (Mar. 8, 1992): 4.

70. Sofía Montenegro, *Identidad y colonialismo: El retorno de la Malinche,* (Santo Domingo: Fundación Friedrich Ebert, 1993), 27.

## 4. NEW RADICAL THOUGHT IN PARTICIPATORY DEMOCRACY

1. Xabier Gorostiaga, "Is the Answer in the South?" (paper presented at the First World Ethics and Third World Economics: Christian Responsibility in a World of Plenty and Poverty seminar, Sept. 20–23, 1993), 12.

2. Ibid., 12–14.

3. Nelly Miranda, *La sociedad civil en un contexto teórico* (Managua: Centro de Estudios Internacionales, February 1993), 5.

4. Ibid., 7–9.

5. Ibid., 10.

6. Alejandro Serrano Caldera, *La unidad en la diversidad: Hacía la cultura del consenso* (Managua: Editorial San Rafael, 1993), 6.

7. Ibid., 137.

8. Montenegro, *Identidad y colonialismo,* 25.

9. Montenegro, interview by the author.

10. Ibid.

11. Ibid.

12. See Katherine Hoyt Gonzalez, "Democracy, National Tradition and the Sandinista Experience," *CrossRoads* (Mar. 1992).

13. Montenegro, *Identidad,* 24.

14. Montenegro, interview by the author.

15. Ibid.

16. Ibid.

17. Montenegro, "Un proyecto nuevo para nueves sujectos," *L'Avispa* 12 (Jan.–Mar. 1993): 14.

18. Orlando Núñez, *La insurreción de la conciencia* (Managua: Editorial Escuela de Sociología de la Universidad Centroamericana, 1988), 40, 41, 64.

19. Ibid., 29.

20. Ibid., 52–54.

21. Ibid., 29.

22. Ernesto Guevara, *Che: Selected Works of Ernesto Guevara,* ed. and trans. by Rolando E. Bonachea and Nelson P. Valdes (Cambridge, Mass.: The MIT Press, 1969), 113.

23. O. Núñez, *La insurrección,* 76–77.

24. Ibid., 81–85.

25. Karl Marx and Frederick Engels, *The Marx-Engels Reader,* ed. Robert C. Tucker (New York: W. W. Norton & Company, 1978), 490.

26. Orlando Nuñez and Roger Burbach, *Fire in the Americas: Forging a Revolutionary Agenda* (London: Verso, 1987), 7.

27. Ibid., 66–68.

28. O. Núñez, *La insurrección,* 143.

29. O Núñez, interview by the author.

30. Ibid.

31. O. Núñez, *La insurrección,* 199.

32. O. Núñez, *En busca,* 83.

33. Karl Marx, *The Marx-Engels Reader,* 143.

34. O. Núñez, *La insurrección,* 19–20.

35. Ibid., 197.

36. O. Núñez, *En busca,* 91.

37. Ibid., 191.

38. Ibid., 99.

39. O. Núñez, interview by the author.

40. O. Núñez, *En busca,* 89.

41. Jean-Jacques Rousseau, *The Social Contract* (London: Penguin Books, 1968), 73–74.

## 5. ECONOMIC DEMOCRACY: THE REVOLUTIONARY YEARS

1. Téllez, Corea interview.

2. Bendaña, interview by the author.

3. For analyses of Nicaragua's recent economic history by outside scholars,

the following books are useful: Victor Bulmer-Thomas, *The Political Economy of Central America Since 1920* (Cambridge: Cambridge Univ. Press, 1987); Richard E. Feinberg and Bruce M. Bagley, *Development Postponed: The Political Economy of Central America in the 1980's* (Boulder: Westview Press, 1986); Rose Spalding, ed., *The Political Economy of Revolutionary Nicaragua* (Boston: Allen & Unwin, Inc., 1987); Forrest D. Colburn, *Post-Revolutionary Nicaragua: State, Class, and the Dilemmas of Agrarian Policy* (Berkeley: Univ. of California Press, 1986); Forrest D. Colburn, *Managing the Commanding Heights: Nicaragua's State Enterprises* (Berkeley: Univ. of California Press, 1990); Laura J. Enriquez, *Harvesting Change: Labor and Agrarian Reform in Nicaragua, 1979–1990* (Chapel Hill: Univ. of North Carolina Press, 1991); Geske Dijkstra, *Industrialization in Sandinista Nicaragua: Policy and Practice in a Mixed Economy* (Boulder: Westview Press, 1992); Rose Spalding, *Capitalists and Revolution in Nicaragua: Opposition and Accommodation, 1979–1993* (Chapel Hill: Univ. of North Carolina Press, 1994); and Carlos M. Vilas, *Between Earthquakes and Volcanos: Markets, State, and Revolution in Central America* (New York: Monthly Review Press, 1994).

4. Wheelock, Harnecker interview, Nicaragua: *El papel,* 42–43.

5. FSLN, "The Historic Program of the FSLN," *Sandinistas Speak* (New York: Pathfinder Press, 1982), 13–22.

6. Jaime Wheelock, in Invernizzi, Pisani, and Ceberio, 221.

7. Jaime Wheelock, *Entre la crisis y la agresión: La Reforma Agraria Sandinista* (Managua: Editorial Nueva Nicaragua, 1986), 35.

8. Edmundo Jarquín, interview by the author, Washington, D.C., May 4, 1994.

9. O. Núñez, *Transición,* 97.

10. Jarquín, interview by the author.

11. Wheelock, *Entre la crisis,* 74–75, 88.

12. Wheelock in Invernizzi, Pisani, and Ceberio, 206–7.

13. O. Núñez, *Transición,* 193.

14. Alejandro Martínez Cuenca, *Sandinista Economics in Practice: An Insider's Critical Reflection* (Boston: South End Press, 1992), 44.

15. Wheelock, *Entre la crisis,* 35.

16. O. Núñez, *Transición,* 99, 156.

17. Wheelock in Invernizzi, Pisani, and Ceberio, 198.

18. Wheelock, *Entre la crisis,* 39.

19. Noel Sánchez, interview by the author, Managua, Nicaragua, Jan. 17, 1994.

20. O. Núñez, *Transición,* 187.

21. Wheelock in Invernizzi, Pisani, and Ceberio, 197.

22. Wheelock, *Entre la crisis,* 82–85.

23. Wheelock in Invernizzi, Pisani, and Ceberio, 224–25.

24. Núñez and Burbach, 58.

25. For example, Paul Rice, lecture at Princeton University, Princeton, N.J., April 24, 1989.

26. Rice lecture at Princeton.

27. Alejandro Bendaña, *Una Tragedia Campesina: Testimonios de la Resistencia* (Managua: Editora de Arte, S.A., 1991), 257.

28. The book is Jaime Wheelock, *Imperialismo y dictadura: crisis de una formación social* (México: Siglo Veintuno Editores, 1975).

29. Jaime Wheelock,. *Entre la crisis,* 22–23.

30. Ibid., 233.

31. Ibid., 29.

32. Wheelock in Invernizzi, Pisani, and Ceberio, 238, 256.

33. Wheelock, *Entre la crisis,* 68.

34. Wheelock in Invernizzi, Pisani, and Ceberio, 219–20.

35. Wheelock, *Entre la crisis,* 46.

36. Ibid., 58, 61.

37. Ibid., 62, 64.

38. For the socialist argument, see Karl Marx, "The Eighteenth Brumaire of Louis Bonaparte," in *The Marx-Engels Reader,* 594–617, and for a contemporary discussion within capitalist thought, see James C. Scott, *The Moral Economy of the Peasant* (New Haven: Yale Univ. Press, 1976), and Samuel L. Popkin, *The Rational Peasant* (Berkeley: Univ. of California Press, 1979).

39. Wheelock in Invernizzi, Pisani, and Ceberio, 179.

40. Wheelock, *Entre la crisis,* 25.

41. Wheelock in Invernizzi, Pisani, and Ceberio, 247.

42. O. Núñez, *La insurreccion,* 47–49, 51.

43. Ibid., 69.

44. O. Núñez, *Transición y,* 131.

45. Ibid., 162.

46. O. Núñez, interview by the author.

47. O. Núñez, *Transición y,* 133–34.

48. O. Núñez, interview by the author.

49. Mendiola, interview by the author, Jan. 20, 1994.

50. Ibid.

51. Daniel Núñez, "Talar los grandes arboles: Reforma Agraria en Nicaragua," *Pensamiento Propio* (1986): 32.

52. Ibid., 33.

53. Henry Ruiz, conversation with the author, Washington, D.C., Jan. 29, 1992. For a discussion of Lenin's later ideas on peasants, to which Ruiz refers, see Lenin's report on March 21, 1921, to the Tenth Party Congress in which he introduces the New Economic Policy, in "Introducing the New Economic Policy," *The Lenin Anthology*, 503–510.

54. Carrión, interview by the author.

## 6. ECONOMIC DEMOCRACY

1. "A Year of UNO Economic Policies: The Rich Get Richer . . . ," *Envio*, Vol. 10, No. 116 (March 1991): 38.

2. "TELCOR Privatization and Property Laws Pass; Strikes Continue," *Nicaragua News Service*, Nov. 26–Dec. 2, 1995, Vol. 3, No. 48, 2.

3. For more detail on the Nicaraguan debt, see Paul Lostritto and Marie Dennis, "External Debt of Nicaragua," Washington, D.C.: Maryknoll Justice and Peace Office, 1994, photocopy; and Sharon Hostetler, et al, "Bitter Medicine: Structural Adjustment in Nicaragua," Washington, D.C.: Witness for Peace, 1994.

4. Quoted in Comisión Económica para América Latina y el Caribe (CEPAL), "Nicaragua: Una Economia en Transición" (internal document, Dec. 7, 1993): 7.

5. Ronald Membreño, interview by Octavio Corea, Managua, 1992, photocopy.

6. René Núñez, "The Views of René Núñez," *Envio* (July 1992): 32.

7. See Karl Marx, "Manifesto of the Communist Party," in *The Marx-Engels Reader*, 469–500.

8. Membreño, Corea interview.

9. See, for example, the publication of the Inter-American Foundation, *grassroots development*, especially vol. 17, no. 2, 1994.

10. O. Núñez, *En busca*, 6, 142.

11. Ibid., 75–77, 181.

12. O. Núñez, interview by the author.

13. See Karl Marx, "Contribution to the Critique of Hegel's *Philosophy of Right*: Introduction," in *The Marx-Engels Reader*, 53–65.

14. Orlando Núñez, "The New Sandinista Utopia," *Envio* (July 1994), reprinted in *Nicaragua Monitor* (Sept. 1994): 8–11.

15. Ibid., 9. A great deal has been written about worker ownership in different parts of the world in recent years. A sampling might include the fol-

lowing: Sherri DeWitt, *Worker Participation and the Crisis of Liberal Democracy* (Boulder: Westview Press, 1981); David P. Ellerman, *The Democratic Worker-Owned Firm: A New Model for the East and West* (Boston: Unwin Hyman, 1990); Mark Holmstrom, *Spain's New Social Economy: Workers' Self-Management in Catalonia* (Providence, R.I.: Berg, 1993); Helen Isiganou, *Workers' Participative Schemes: The Experience of Capitalist and Plan-Based Societies* (New York: Greenwood Press, 1991); Francisco Iturraspe, ed., *Participación y autogestión en America Latina*, 2 vols. (Caracas: Editorial Nueva Sociedad, 1986); Louis O. Kelso, *Democracy and Economic Power: Extending the ESOP Revolution* (Cambridge, Mass.: Bailinger, 1986); Janez Prasnikan, *Worker Participation and Self-Management in Developing Countries* (Boulder: Westview Press, 1991); Jaroslav Vanek, *The Participatory Economy: An Evolutionary Hypothesis and a Strategy for Development* (Ithaca: Cornell Univ. Press, 1971); Peter Winn, *Weavers of Revolution: The Yarur Workers and the Chilean Road to Socialism* (New York: Oxford Univ. Press, 1986).

16. O. Núñez, "The New Sandinista," 10.

17. Ibid., 9–10.

18. Ibid., 10.

19. Ibid., 11.

20. See Chapter 9 of World Bank, "Nicaragua: Country Economic Memorandum" (WB Report No. 12066-NI, Oct. 1993) and Pharis Harvey, Jerome I. Levinson, Lisa Haugaard, and Lance Compa, "Potential Labor Rights Violations in Nicaragua Labor Code Proposals: A Memorandum to Nancy Katz, Interim Executive Director to the World Bank," June 16, 1994.

21. Comisión Económica para América Latina, "Nicaragua: Una Economía en Transición," 8.

22. U.S. House Committee on Appropriations, *Report 103–287*, to accompany H.R. 4426 Foreign Operations, Export Financing, and Related Programs Appropriations Bill, 1995, House Committee on Appropriations, 103d Cong., 2d Sess., 29.

23. The writer has been told that this document is confidential.

24. Jarquín, interview by the author.

25. Adolfo Acevedo, *Nicaragua y el FMI: El pozo sin fondo del ajuste* (Managua: CRIES, 1993), 146–47.

26. Ibid., 31, 37.

27. Comision Económica para América Latina, "Nicaragua: Una Economía en Transición," 8.

28. Adolfo Acevedo, interview by the author, Managua, Nicaragua, Jan. 17, 1994.

29. Acevedo, *Nicaragua y el FMI*, 145–49.

30. Gorostiaga, "Is the Answer," 9.

31. Ibid., 17.

32. Ibid., 17–19.

## 7. DEMOCRACY IN THE FSLN PARTY

1. Jarquín, interview by the author.

2. O. Núñez, *La insurrección*, 52–54.

3. Alejandro Bendaña, "El problema del colapso del comunismo a nivel internacional," *Amanecer* (Sept.–Oct. 1990): 13.

4. O. Núñez, *En busca*, 106.

5. Foro de Izquierda Democrática Sandinista, "Por la Unidad Revolucionaria del FSLN," Managua, Feb. 1994, 1.

6. Sergio Ramírez, et al., "Por un Sandinismo que Vuelva a las Mayorías," Managua, Feb. 1994, 4, photocopy.

7. Ibid., 1–2.

8. Foro de Izquierda, 1–2.

9. "FSLN: Congress Voted for the 'Left,'" *Barricuda Internacional* (English edition) 374 (June 1994): 18–19; Chuck Kaufman, "The FSLN Party Congress: Report to Staff and Friends of the Nicaragua Network" (June 1994), photocopy; several articles in *Barricada* daily newspaper, May 20–23, 1994.

10. Quoted in Coleen Littlejohn, "Three Members of the National Directorate Resign from the FSLN," *Nicaraguan News Service* 3.6 (Jan. 30–Feb. 4, 1995): 1.

11. Quoted in Ibid.

12. Vilma Núñez, "Carta Abierta," March 8, 1996, faxed statement.

13. Jarquín, interview by the author.

14. "Secret Help," *Newsweek* (Sept. 25, 1989): 4; "Money Isn't Everything," *Newsweek* (Oct. 9, 1989): 47; "The CIA on the Stump," *Newsweek* (Oct. 21, 1991): 46–47.

15. Henry Ruiz, "Democratización del Frente Sandinista de Liberación Nacional," *Amanecer* 69 (Sept.–Oct. 1990): 16.

16. Ibid.

17. Ibid.

18. Téllez, Corea interview, 13.

19. Victor Hugo Tinoco, interview by the author.

20. Daniel Ortega, "60 Preguntas a un Sandinista," transcript of an interview on the Revista Sin Frontera radio program, Radio La Primerísma station, Managua, Nicaragua, May 6, 1994.

21. Tinoco, interview by the author.

22. Both Judy Butler and Michele Costa contributed to the first formulation of this device.

23. Ruiz is quoted in Kaufman, "FSLN Party Congress."

24. Ramírez, interview by the author.

25. Téllez, interview by the author.

26. Most recently in Kaufman.

27. Téllez, interview by the author.

28. Ortega, "60 Preguntas."

29. Miguél D'Escoto, "El divisionismo de Sergio," (pamphlet) Managua, Ediciones Esperanza, No. 1, Marzo 1994, 24.

30. Ibid., 19–20, 11.

31. D'Escoto is quoted in Kaufman.

32. O. Núñez, *En busca*, 101.

33. Ibid., 141.

34. Ibid., 111.

35. Gramsci, *Selections from the Prison Notebooks*, ed. Quintin Hoare and Geoffrey N. Smith (New York: International Publishers, 1974), 11.

36. O. Núñez, *En busca*, 106–7.

37. Núñez and Burbach, 49.

38. Ibid., 50.

39. V. I. Lenin, "What Is to Be Done?" in *The Lenin Anthology*, 66.

40. Ernesto Guevara, "Socialism and Man in Cuba," in *Che: Selcted Works of Ernesto Guevara*, 166–67.

41. O. Núñez, interview by the author.

42. Victor Tirado, "Aportes para el debate: Sandinismo y año 2000," *Barricada* (Sept. 19, 1992).

43. Tomás Borge, "No se puede ser revolucionario sin ser antiimperialista," interview by Sergio Ferrari, *Critica* 13 (Aug. 1990): 14.

44. Victor Hugo Tinoco, interview by the author.

45. José González, interview by the author, Matagalpa, Nicaragua, Jan. 24, 1994.

46. Bendaña, interview by the author.

47. D'Escoto, "El diversionismo," 19, 10.

48. O. Núñez, *En busca*, 119–21.

49. Sergio Ramírez, "Tengo aspiraciones presidenciales," interview by Helena Ramos, *El Pais* (1994): 63.

50. Ibid., 62.

51. D. Ortega, *60 preguntas*.

52. Téllez, interview by the author.

53. Ramírez, "Tengo aspiraciones," 65.

54. D. Ortega, *60 preguntas.*

55. Ruiz quoted in Kaufman.

56. D. Ortega, *60 preguntas.*

57. Ruiz quoted in Kaufman.

58. Tomás Borge, "Coincidencias y diferencias en el FSLN," *Barricada,* Feb. 8, 1994.

## POSTSCRIPT

1. Vilma Núñez, "Morning Newsmakers" press conference, National Press Club, Washington, DC, January 10, 1997.

2. "Election Results Released, Fraud Ignored," *Nicaragua Monitor,* 1.

3. Council of Freely Elected Heads of Government International Delegation to Observe the Nicaraguan Elections, Jimmy Carter, James Baker III, Oscar Arias, Osvaldo Hurtado, and Luis Alberto Lacalle, "Final Statement," Atlanta, GA, Dec. 6, 1996, faxed copy.

4. One of these was Alejandro Bendaña in a talk at the Institute for Policy Studies in Washington, DC, on November 18, 1996, (handwritten notes).

5. Ibid.

6. Vilma Núñez, press conference.

7. Benigna Mendiola, conversation with the author, Managua, Nicaragua, May 3, 1996.

8. One example was in his acceptance speech at the FSLN Party Congress, May 4, 1996.

9. Orlando Núñez, "Speaking of liberalism and neo-liberalism: popular economy and national development," NY Transfer News Collective [internet news service], translated by Toby Mailman from an article in *Barricada,* Dec. 9, 1996.

10. Vilma Núñez, conversation with the author. A delegate to the congress from the Department of Río San Juan confirmed this. Neither Dr. Núñez nor the Río San Juan delegate would name the National Directorate member involved.

# Bibliography

## BOOKS

Acevedo, Adolfo. *Nicaragua y el FMI: El pozo sin fondo del ajuste.* Managua: CRIES, 1993.

AMNLAE. *Estrategia Nacional.* (pamphlet) Approved at the First National Extraordinary Assembly, August 1993.

Arce, Bayardo. Interview by Gabriele Invernizzi, Francis Pisani and Jesús Ceberio. In *Sandinistas: Entrevistas a Humberto Ortega Saavedra, Jaime Wheelock y Bayardo Arce Castaño.* Managua: Editorial Vanguardia, 1986.

———. "Secret Speech on Strategy and Tactics." In *The Central American Crisis Reader,* edited by Robert Leiken and Barry Rubin, 289–97. New York: Summit Books, 1987.

Beals, Carleton. *Banana Gold.* Philadelphia: Lippincott, 1932.

Bendaña, Alejandro. *Una Tragedia Campesina: Testimonios de la Resistencia.* Managua: Editora de Arte, S.A., 1991.

Blandón, María Teresa, Lillian Levi, and Sofía Montenegro (Content Commision). *La Situación Nacional desde la Perspectiva Feminista.* Managua: First National Feminist Encounter, 1993.

Boland, Edward. "The Boland Amendment: May 1983." In *The Central American Crisis Reader,* edited by Robert Leiken and Barry Rubin, 577. New York: Summit Books, 1987.

Borge, Tomás. "Social Classes and Political Power." In *The Central American Crisis Reader,* edited by Robert Leiken and Barry Rubin, 230–35. New York: Summit Books, 1987.

Borge, Tomás, Carlos Núñez, Bayardo Arce, Henry Ruiz, Victor Tirado and Luis Carrión. *Nicaragua: La Batalla por el Poder Ideológico.* Buenos Aires: Editorial Cartago, 1986.

Bossert, Thomas John. "Health Care in Revolutionary Nicaragua." In *Nicaragua in Revolution,* edited by Thomas Walker, 259–72. New York: Praeger, 1982.

Chamorro, Pedro Joaquín. "Speech on Unity." *In The Central American Crisis Reader,* edited by Robert Leikin and Barry Rubin, 173–75. New York: Summit Books, 1987.

Cuadra, Joaquín. Interview by Marta Harnecker. In *Pueblos en Armas*. Managua: Editorial Nueva Nicaragua, 1985.

D'Escoto, Miguél. *El divisionismo de Sergio*. Pamphlet. Managua: Ediciones Esperanza, No. 1 (Mar. 1994).

Fonseca, Carlos. *Obras, Tomo 1: Bajo la bandera del Sandinismo*. Managua: Editorial Nueva Nicaragua, 1982.

FSLN. "The Historic Program of the FSLN." In *Sandinistas Speak*. New York: Pathfinder Press, 1982.

————. "'Seventy-Two Hours' Document (September 1979)." In *The Central American Crisis Reader*, edited by Robert Leiken and Barry Rubin, 218–27. New York: Summit Books, 1987.

————. "Statement on the Electoral Process." In *The Central American Crisis Reader*, edited by Robert Leiken and Barry Rubin, 227–29. New York: Summit Books, 1987.

Gramsci, Antonio. *Selections from the Prison Notebooks*. edited by Quintin Hoare and Geoffrey N. Smith. New York: International Publishers, 1974.

Guevara, Ernesto. *Che: Selected Works of Ernesto Guevara*, edited and translated by Rolando E. Bonachea and Nelson P. Valdes. Cambridge, Mass.: The MIT Press, 1969.

Hostetler, Sharon, et al. *Bitter Medicine: Structural Adjustment in Nicaragua*. Pamphlet. Washinqton. D.C.: Witness for Peace, 1994.

Lenin, V.I. *The Lenin Anthology*, edited by Robert C. Tucker. New York: W.W. Norton & Company, 1975.

Macaulay, Neil. *The Sandino Affair*. Chicago: Quadrangle Books, 1967.

Martínez Cuenca, Alejandro. *Sandinista Economics in Practice: An Insider's Critical Reflection*. Boston: South End Press, 1992.

Marx, Karl, and Frederick Engels. *The Marx-Engels Reader*, edited by Robert C. Tucker. New York: W.W. Norton & Company, 1978.

Miranda, Nelly. *La sociedad civil en un contexto teórico*. Managua: Centro de Estudios Internacionales, February 1993.

Montenegro, Sofía. *Identidad y colonialismo: El retorno de la Malinche*. Santo Domingo: Fundación Friedrich Ebert, 1993.

Núñez, Carlos. "El papel de las organizaciones de masas en el proceso revolucionario." In *Sandinistas: Key Documents*, edited by Dennis Gilbert and David Block. Ithaca, N.Y.: Cornell Univ. Latin American Studies Program, 1990.

————. *Un pueblo en armas*, 2d ed. Managua: Editorial Vanguardia, 1986.

————. "Las puertas del FSLN sólo se abren a los mejores elementos de la sociedad." In *Habla la Dirección de la Vanguardia*, 67–73. Managua: Departamento de Propaganda y Educación del FSLN, 1981.

Núñez Soto, Orlando. *En busca de la revolución perdida.* Managua: CIPRES, 1992.

———. *La insurrección de la conciencia.* Managua: Editorial Escuela de Sociología de la Universidad Centroamericana, 1988.

———. *Transición y lucha de clases en Nicaragua 1979–1986.* Mexico: Siglo Veintiuno Editores, 1987.

Orlando Núñez Soto and Roger Burbach. *Fire in the Americas: Forging a Revolutionary Agenda.* London: Verso, 1987.

Oficina Central de Promoción y Desarrollo Comunal, Movimiento Comunal Nicaragüense. *Memoria 1991.* Managua: DISA-Editores, 1991.

Ortega, Daniel. "Democracia y Revolución en Nicaragua." In *Democracia y Revolución.* Managua: Centro de Documentación y Ediciones Latinoamericanas, 1989.

Ortega, Humberto. *Cincuenta años de lucha sandinista.* Havana: Editorial de Ciencias Sociales, 1980.

Quandt, Midge. *Unbinding the Ties: The Popular Organizations and the FSLN in Nicaragua.* Monograph. Washington, D.C.: Nicaragua Network Education Fund, 1993.

Republican Party. "Platform (1980)." In *The Central American Crisis Reader,* edited by Robert Leiken and Barry Rubin, 515. New York: Summit Books, 1987.

Rodríguez, Ileana. *Registradas en la Historia: 10 años del quehacer feminista en Nicaragua.* Managua: Centro de Investigacion y Acción para la Promoción de los Derechos de la Mujer, 1990.

Román, José. *Maldito País.* Managua: El Pez y la Serpiente, 1979.

Rousseau, Jean-Jacques. *The Social Contract.* London: Penguin Books, 1968.

Ruchwarger, Gary. *People in Power: Forging a Grassroots Democracy in Nicaragua.* South Hadley, Mass.: Bergin & Garvey, 1987.

Sandino, Augusto C. *El pensamiento vivo de Sandino,* edited by Sergio Ramírez. San Jose, Costa Rica: EDUCA, 1976.

Serrano Caldera, Alejandro. *La unidad en la diversidad: Hacía la cultura del consenso.* Managua: Editorial San Rafael, 1993.

Scruton, Roger. *A Dictionary of Political Thought.* London: MacMillan Press, 1982.

Téllez, Dora María. Interview by Marta Harnecker. In *Pueblos en Armas.* Managua: Editorial Nueva Nicaragua, 1985.

Wheelock, Jaime. Interview by Marta Harnecker. In *Nicaragua: el papel de la vanguardia.* Buenos Aires: Editorial Contrapunto, 1986.

———. *Entre la crisis y la agresión: La Reforma Agraria Sandinista.* Managua: Editorial Nueva Nicaragua, 1986.

PERIODICALS

Baltodano, Mónica. "Las Mujeres Sandinistas." Interview by Rosario Murillo. *Ventana.* June 3, 1991. 16–20.

———. "El partido revolucionario: instrumento revolucionario del pueblo." *Barricada.* January 25, 1994.

Bendeña, Alejandro. "El problema del colapso del comunismo a nivel internacional." *Amanecer* (Sept.–Oct. 1990): 12–15

Borge, Tomás. "Coincidencias y diferencias en el FSLN." *Barricada.* February 8, 1994.

———. "El nuestro es un proyecto enredado." *Pensamiento Propio.* 24 (June–July 1985): 7–15.

———. "No se puede ser revolucionario sin ser anti-imperialista." Interview by Sergio Ferrari. *Crítica* (Aug. 1990): 14.

Cabezas, Omar. "Organícense como quieran y para lo que quieran." *Pensamiento Propio.* 52 (July–Aug. 1988): 45–48.

Comisión de Divulgación del Primer Encuentro. "Diversas pero unidas." *Barricada* Mar. 8, 1992, 4.

"El debate constitutional." *Amanecer* 44 (Sept./Oct. 1986).

Enríquez, Magda. "Letter to Solidarity: FSLN Women Prepare for Congress." *Nicaragua Monitor.* (Feb. 1994): 3.

Fiallos, Mariano. "Entrevista." *Monéxico: Revista del Consejo de Estado* 3 (June 1983): 77–82.

"FSLN: Congress Voted for the 'Left.'" *Barricada Internacional* (English edition) 374 (June 1994): 18–19.

González, Katherine Hoyt. "Democracy, National Tradition and the Sandinista Experience." *CrossRoads* (Mar. 1992), 2–6.

González, Victoria. "La historia del feminismo en Nicaragua: 1837–1956." *La Boletina.* (July/August 1995): 7–15.

Littlejohn, Coleen. "Three Members of the National Directorate Resign from the FSLN." *Nicaragua News Service* 3. 6 (Jan. 30–Feb. 4, 1995).

Mendiola, Benigna. "We have More Serious Problems." *Barricada Internacional* (English edition, March 1992): 25–26.

Mendoza, René. "We Erred to Win." *Envío.* (October 1990): 23–50.

Montenegro, Sofía. "Un proyecto nuevo para nuevos sujetos." *L'Avispa* 12 (Jan.–Mar. 1993): 13–15.

Núñez, Carlos. "Acto de Promulgación de la Constitución de la República de Nicaragua." *Monéxico: Revista de la Asamblea Nacional* 12 (1987): 277–84.

Núñez, Daniel. "Talar los grandes arboles: Reforma Agraria en Nicaragua." *Pensamiento Propio* (1986): 31–36.

Núñez, René. "The Views of René Núñez." *Envío* (July 1992): 31–36.

Núñez Soto, Orlando. "The New Sandinista Utopia." *Envío* (July 1994). Reprinted in *Nicaragua Monitor* (Sept. 1994): 8–11.

Ortega, Daniel. "Declaración del Presidente Ortega." *Amanecer* 66 (Mar./Apr. 1990): 17–18.

Picado, Enrique. "El FSLN está jugando un papel dual." *L'Avispa* 12 (Jan.–Mar. 1993): 20–22.

Ramírez, Sergio. "El logro principal: nuestra patria ha consolidado su estabilidad interna." *Barricada* (May 5 1980).

———. "Nicaragua: Primera Frontera." *Pensamiento Propio* 6–7 (July/Aug. 1983): n/p.

———. "Tengo aspiraciones presidenciales." Interview by Helena Ramos. *El País* (1994): 57–67.

Ruiz, Henry. "Democratización del Frente Sandinista de Liberación Nacional." *Amanecer* 69 (Sept./Oct. 1990): 15–17.

Solís, Rafael. "Elecciones y participación popular." Interview. *Pensamiento Propio* (Jan. 1984): 22–23.

———. "Habrá negociación y reconciliación nacional." Interview. *Pensamiento Propio* (Jan.–Feb. 1990): 18–19.

Téllez, Dora María. "Hacia un socialismo genuíno, democrático y nacional." Interview by Linde Rivera. *Amanecer* (June 1991): 38–43.

———. "El socialismo pasa por la solución del problema nacional." *L'Avispa* (Apr./May 1991): 8–23.

"Testimonies from the Congress." *Barricada Internacional* (English edition) (June 1994): 23.

Tirado, Victor. "Aportes para el debate: Sandinismo y año 2000." *Barricada* (Sept. 19, 1992).

U.S. House Committee on Appropriations. *Report 103–287*, to accompany H.R. 4426 Foreign Operations, Export Financing, and Related Programs Appropriations Bill, 103d Congress, 2d Session, 1994.

World Bank. "Nicaragua: Country Economic Memorandum." WB Report No. 12066–NI, Oct. 1993.

"A Year of UNO Economic Policies: The Rich Get Richer." *Envío* 116 (Mar. 1991): 30–49.

## UNPUBLISHED DOCUMENTS

Comisión Económica para América Latina y el Caribe (CEPAL). "Nicaragua: Una Economía en Transición." Internal document. December 7, 1993.

Foro de Izquierda Democrática Sandinista. "Por la Unidad Revolucionario del FSLN." Managua, Feb. 1994. Photocopy.

Gorostiaga, Xabier, "Is the Answer in the South?" Paper presented at the First

World Ethics and Third World Economics: Christian Responsibility in a World of Plenty and Poverty Seminar, Sweden, September 20–23, 1993. Photocopy.

Harvey, Pharis, Jerome I. Levinson, Lisa Haugaard, and Lance Compa. "Potential Labor Rights Violations in Nicaragua Labor Proposals: A Memorandum to Nancy Katz, Interim Executive Director to the World Bank," June 16, 1994. Photocopy.

Kaufman, Chuck. "The FSLN Party Congress: Report to Staff and Friends of the Nicaragua Network." June 1994. Photocopy.

Lostritto, Paul, and Marie Dennis. "External Debt of Nicaragua." Washington, D.C.: Maryknoll Justice and Peace Office, 1994. Photocopy.

Membreño, Ronaldo. Interview by Octavio Corea. Managua, 1992. Photocopy.

Núñez, Vilma. "Carta Abierta." Managua, Nicaragua, Mar. 1996. Faxed statement.

Ortega, Daniel. "60 Preguntas a un Sandinista." Transcript of an interview on the Revista Sin Frontera radio program. Radio La Primerísima station. Managua, May 6, 1994.

Ramírez, Sergio, et al. "Por un Sandinismo que Vuelva a las Mayorías." Managua, Feb. 1994. Photocopy.

Rice, Paul. Lecture at Princeton University, Princeton, N.J. April 24, 1989. Handwritten notes.

Ruiz, Henry. Conversation with the author. Washington, D.C., Jan. 29, 1992. Handwritten notes.

Téllez, Dora María. Interview by Octavio Corea. Managua, Oct. 29, 1992. Photocopy.

## INTERVIEWS BY THE AUTHOR

Acevedo, Adolfo. Managua, Jan. 17, 1994.

Acevedo, Angela Rosa. Managua, Jan. 28, 1994.

Baéz, Gladys. Managua, Feb. 8, 1994.

Baltodano, Moníca. Managua, Feb. 8, 1994.

Bendaña, Alejandro. Managua, Jan. 28, 1994.

Borge, Tomás. Managua, Feb. 7, 1994.

Carrión, Luis. Managua, Feb. 3, 1994.

Fiallos, Mariano. Managua, Feb. 3, 1994.

González, Jose. Matagalpa, Jan. 24, 1994.

Gorostiaga, Xabier. Managua, Jan. 28, 1994.

Guevara, Onofre. Managua, Feb. 4, 1994.

Jarquín, Edmundo. Washington, D.C., May 4, 1994.

Mejía, Hugo. Managua, Jan. 28, 1994.

Mendiola, Benigna. Managua, Jan. 20, 1994; Washington, D.C., May 1993.

Montenegro, Sofía. Managua, Jan. 17, 1994.

Núñez, Daniel. Managua, Jan. 25, 1994.

Núñez Soto, Orlando. Managua, Feb. 3, 1994.

Picado, Enrique. Managua, Feb. 8, 1994.

Ramírez, Sergio. Managua, Feb. 3, 1994.

Samper, Jorge. Managua, Jan. 28, 1994.

Sánchez, Noel. Managua, Jan. 17, 1994.

Solís, Rafael. Managua, Feb. 1, 1994.

Téllez, Dora Maria. Managua, Feb. 8, 1994.

Tinoco, Victor Hugo. Managua. Jan. 28, 1994.

Wheelock, Jaime. Boston, May 7, 1994.

# Index

agriculture and, 103, 126
  dependent, 114
  socialism and, 62
Captaincy General of Guatemala, 5
Carazo, Rodrigo, 14
Cardenal, Ernesto, 154, 180
Cardenal, Fernando, 180
Carrión, Luis, 15, 154
  agro-industrial complexes and, 125
  on political democracy, 24
  on popular organizations, 54–55
  on resignation from FSLN, 154
  on working class unity, 47
Carter, Jimmy, 14
Castro, Fidel, 14
Catholic Church, 97
  influence of, 12
  population control and, 70
*Caudillismo*, 158
CDCs. *See* Civil Defense Committees
CDSs. *See* Sandinista Defense Committees
Center for the Study of Agrarian Reform (CIERA), 89, 120
Central American Common Market, 11, 103–104
Central American Federation, 5
Central American Peace Accord, 51, 65
Chamber of Deputies, hostage taking at, 173
Chamorro, Carlos Fernando, 83, 153
Chamorro, Pedro Joaquín, 21, 35
  assassination of, 13, 41
Chamorro, Violeta Barrios de, 13, 71, 136, 143
  Catholic Church and, 70
  economic policies of, 61, 132, 140, 146, 170
  election of, 129–30
  FSLN relations with, 151, 167, 168
  popular participation and, 56
  privatization and, 131
  UNO and, 35
Chibcha, 5
Chiltepe dairy farm, 119
Christians
  democracy and, 25
  FSLN and, 12
  Marxists and, 94
CIERA. *See* Center for the Study of Agrarian Reform

CIPRES, 89
Civil Defense Committees (CDCs), 40, 42
Civil society, 80–81, 89, 95, 96, 134, 178
  Hegelian model of, 81
  hegemony over, 165
  organizations of, 99–100
  Sandinistas and, 181–182, 183
Clean-up operations, 42
Collaboration, FSLN and Chamorro govt., 167–172
Collectivization, 120, 121
Colonialism, 16, 141, 181
Columbus, Christopher, 5
Communist International (Comintern), Sandino and, 9
*Communist Manifesto* (Marx and Engels), 92, 93, 181
Communist Party of the Soviet Union (CPSU), armed struggle and, 10
Community Movement, 77, 134
  CDSs and, 57–62
  defense and, 54
  FSLN and, 60, 61
*Comunidades de base*, 94
Conservatives, 6, 20
Constitution (1987), 31–32, 178
  democracy and, 38
  participation and, 53
  writing of, 32
Constitutional Advisory Commission, 33
Contras, 65, 71, 85, 163
  demobilization of, 129
  peasants and, 123, 126
  U.S. support for, 51
Contra war, 76, 130, 180
  economic costs of, 110–111
  verticalism and, 50–53
  women and, 64, 74
Cooperatives, 111, 122, 123, 136, 137, 178, 182
  goals of, 121
  organization of, 104
  production problems at, 121
Córdoba, Francisco de, 5
Corruption, 20, 80
Council of State, 25, 26
  functions of, 48–50
Counterrevolution, 30, 118, 122, 124
  FSLN and, 24

Farmers and Ranchers Association. *See*
Union of Farmers and Ranchers
Farmworkers' Association (ATC), 40,
111, 124, 129, 154
women's issues and, 74
women's section of, 65
Feminism, 63–76
FSLN and, 68–69
problems for, 73–74
Feminists, 75, 97
AMNLAE and, 71–72
democracy and, 72–73
issues for, 69–70
peasants and, 73
population control and, 70
traditional left women and, 74
women's organizations and, 74, 77
*See also* Eco-feminists; Traditional
left women
Festival of the 52%, 66
Fiallos, Mariano, 27
on liberal democracy, 180
on Political Parties Bill, 26
First National Assembly of Cadres, 46
First National Women's Encounter, 66
Fiscal adjustment program, 112
FNT. *See* National Federation of Work-
ers
Fonseca, Carlos, 10, 179
democratic centralism and, 46
on electoral farce, 21
on democracy in the party, 45–46
Food and Agricultural Organization,
142
*Foquismo*, 10
Foreign debt, 115, 132, 140
Formal democracy. *See* Political
democracy
Forum of São Paulo, 100
Forum of the Democratic Left
(Danielistas), 151, 152, 163, 171
FPN. *See* National Patriotic Front
Frankfurt School, 34, 90, 91, 182
Franklin (contra leader), on sandin-
ismo, 54
French Revolution, 81, 87, 138
FSLN. *See* Sandinista National Libera-
tion Front

García, Edgardo, 154
Gender issues, 64, 68–69, 94
democracy and, 83–89

*Gente*, Montenegro and, 83
Geoculture of despair, 144
Girardi, Giulio, 3
González, José, 170
Gorbachev, Mikhail, 34, 91, 148, 149
democracy and, 3
Gorostiaga, Xabier, 80, 98
on civil society, 79
criticism by, 145
on economic relations, 145
geoculture of despair and, 144
IFIs and, 144
participatory democracy and, 100
on popular organizations, 101
radical democracy and, 182–83
Gramsci, Antonio, 3, 19, 90, 99, 135
civil society and, 81
on hegemony, 165, 181–82
Grigsby, William: Ramírez and, 154
Group of Twenty-Nine, 170
*Grundrisse, The* (Marx), 84
Guadamúz, Carlos, 154
Guevara, Ernesto "Che," 10, 20, 90,
91–92, 98, 163
vanguard party and, 166

Habermas, Jürgen: civil society and,
81–82
Hands off Nicaragua Committee,
Sandino and, 9
Haya de la Torre, Victor, 8
Health campaigns, 52, 55
Hegel, Friedrich: civil society and, 81
Hegemony
ideological, 181–82
revolutionary, 165–66
Helms, Jesse: obstructionism of, 130
Henry, Patrick, 17
Historic Program (FSLN), 104–105
Hodges, Donald, 3
Humanism, 91, 95
Human rights, 14, 70, 131

IDB. *See* Inter-American Development
Bank
IFIs. *See* International financial institu-
tions
ILO treaties. *See* International Labor
Organization treaties
IMF. *See* International Monetary Fund
Imperialism, 29, 52, 124, 135
revolution against, 150

# Monographs in International Studies

*Titles Available from Ohio University Press, 1997*

## SOUTHEAST ASIA SERIES

No. 56    **Duiker, William J.** Vietnam Since the Fall of Saigon. 1989. Updated ed. 401 pp. Paper 0-89680-162-4 $20.00.

No. 64    **Dardjowidjojo, Soenjono.** Vocabulary Building in Indonesian: An Advanced Reader. 1984. 664 pp. Paper 0-89680-118-7 $30.00.

No. 65    **Errington, J. Joseph.** Language and Social Change in Java: Linguistic Reflexes of Modernization in a Traditional Royal Polity. 1985. 210 pp. Paper 0-89680-120-9 $25.00.

No. 66    **Binh, Tran Tu.** The Red Earth: A Vietnamese Memoir of Life on a Colonial Rubber Plantation. Tr. by John Spragens. 1984. 102 pp. (SEAT*, V. 5) Paper 0-89680-119-5 $11.00.

No. 68    **Syukri, Ibrahim.** History of the Malay Kingdom of Patani. 1985. 135 pp. Paper 0-89680-123-3 $15.00.

No. 69    **Keeler, Ward.** Javanese: A Cultural Approach. 1984. 559 pp. Paper 0-89680-121-7 $25.00.

No. 70    **Wilson, Constance M. and Lucien M. Hanks.** Burma-Thailand Frontier Over Sixteen Decades: Three Descriptive Documents. 1985. 128 pp. Paper 0-89680-124-1 $11.00.

No. 71    **Thomas, Lynn L. and Franz von Benda-Beckmann,** eds. Change and Continuity in Minangkabau: Local, Regional, and Historical Perspectives on West Sumatra. 1985. 353 pp. Paper 0-89680-127-6 $16.00.

No. 72    **Reid, Anthony and Oki Akira,** eds. The Japanese Experience in Indonesia: Selected Memoirs of 1942–1945. 1986. 424 pp. 20 illus. (SEAT, V. 6) Paper 0-89680-132-2 $20.00.

No. 74    **McArthur M. S. H.** Report on Brunei in 1904. Introduced and Annotated by A. V. M. Horton. 1987. 297 pp. Paper 0-89680-135-7 $15.00.

No. 75    **Lockard, Craig A.** From Kampung to City: A Social History of Kuching, Malaysia, 1820–1970. 1987. 325 pp. Paper 0-89680-136-5 $20.00.

* Southeast Asia Translation Project Group

No. 76   McGinn, Richard, ed. Studies in Austronesian Linguistics. 1986. 516 pp. Paper 0-89680-137-3 $20.00.

No. 77   Muego, Benjamin N. Spectator Society: The Philippines Under Martial Rule. 1986. 232 pp. Paper 0-89680-138-1 $17.00.

No 79   Walton, Susan Pratt. Mode in Javanese Music. 1987. 278 pp. Paper 0-89680-144-6 $15.00.

No. 80   Nguyen Anh Tuan. South Vietnam: Trial and Experience. 1987. 477 pp. Tables. Paper 0-89680-141-1 $18.00.

No. 82   Spores, John C. Running Amok: An Historical Inquiry. 1988. 190 pp. Paper 0-89680-140-3 $13.00.

No. 83   Malaka, Tan. From Jail to Jail. Tr. by Helen Jarvis. 1911. 1209 pp., three volumes. (SEAT V. 8) Paper 0-89680-150-0 $55.00.

No. 84   Devas, Nick, with Brian Binder, Anne Booth, Kenneth Davey, and Roy Kelly. Financing Local Government in Indonesia. 1989. 360 pp. Paper 0-89680-153-5 $20.00.

No. 85   Suryadinata, Leo. Military Ascendancy and Political Culture: A Study of Indonesia's Golkar. 1989. 235 pp. Illus., glossary, append., index, bibliog. Paper 0-89680-154-3 $18.00.

No. 86   Williams, Michael. Communism, Religion, and Revolt in Banten in the Early Twentieth Century. 1990. 390 pp. Paper 0-89680-155-1 $14.00.

No. 87   Hudak, Thomas. The Indigenization of Pali Meters in Thai Poetry. 1990. 247 pp. Paper 0-89680-159-4 $15.00.

No. 88   Lay, Ma Ma. Not Out of Hate: A Novel of Burma. Tr. by Margaret Aung-Thwin. Ed. by William Frederick. 1991. 260 pp. (SEAT V. 9) Paper 0-89680-167-5 $20.00.

No. 89   Anwar, Chairil. The Voice of the Night: Complete Poetry and Prose of Chairil Anwar. 1992. Revised Edition. Tr. by Burton Raffel. 196 pp. Paper 0-89680-170-5 $20.00.

No. 90   Hudak, Thomas John, tr., The Tale of Prince Samuttakote: A Buddhist Epic from Thailand. 1993. 230 pp. Paper 0-89680-174-8 $20.00.

No. 91   Roskies, D. M., ed. Text/Politics in Island Southeast Asia: Essays in Interpretation. 1993. 330 pp. Paper 0-89680-175-6 $25.00.

No. 92   Schenkhuizen, Marguérite, translated by Lizelot Stout van Balgooy. Memoirs of an Indo Woman: Twentieth-Century Life in the East Indies and Abroad. 1993. 312 pp. Paper 0-89680-178-0 $25.00.

No. 93   Salleh, Muhammad Haji. Beyond the Archipelago: Selected Poems. 1995. 247 pp. Paper 0-89680-181-0 $20.00.

No. 94   Federspiel, Howard M. A Dictionary of Indonesian Islam. 1995. 327 pp. Bibliog. Paper 0-89680-182-9 $25.00.

No. 95    **Leary, John.** Violence and the Dream People: The Orang Asli in the Malayan Emergency 1948–1960. 1995. 275 pp. Maps, illus., tables, appendices, bibliog., index. Paper 0-89680-186-1 $22.00.

No. 96    **Lewis, Dianne.** *Jan Compagnie* in the Straits of Malacca 1641–1795. 1995. 176 pp. Map, appendices, bibliog., index. Paper 0-89680-187-x. $18.00.

No. 97    **Schiller, Jim and Martin-Schiller, Barbara.** Imagining Indonesia: Cultural Politics and Political Culture. 1996. 384 pp. Notes, glossary, bibliog. Paper 0-89680-190-x. $30.00.

No. 98    **Bonga, Dieuwke Wendelaar.** Eight Prison Camps: A Dutch Family in Japanese Java. 1996. 233 pp. Illus., map, glossary. Paper 0-89680-191-8. $18.00.

No. 99    **Gunn, Geoffrey C.** Language, Ideology, and Power in Brunei Darussalam. 1996. 328 pp. Glossary, notes, bibliog., index. Paper 0-89680-192-6. $24.00.

No. 100   **Martin, Peter W., Conrad Ozog, and Gloria R. Poedjosoedarmo, eds.** Language Use and Language Change in Brunei Darussalam. 1996. 390 pp. Maps, notes, bibliog. Paper 0-89680-193-x. $26.00.


AFRICA SERIES

No. 43    **Harik, Elsa M. and Donald G. Schilling.** The Politics of Education in Colonial Algeria and Kenya. 1984. 102 pp. Paper 0-89680-117-9 $12.50.

No. 45    **Keto, C. Tsehloane.** American-South African Relations 1784–1980: Review and Select Bibliography. 1985. 169 pp. Paper 0-89680-128-4 $11.00.

No. 46    **Burness, Don,** ed. Wanasema: Conversations with African Writers. 1985. 103 pp. Paper 0-89680-129-2 $11.00.

No. 47    **Switzer, Les.** Media and Dependency in South Africa: A Case Study of the Press and the Ciskei "Homeland." 1985. 97 pp. Paper 0-89680-130-6 $10.00.

No. 51    **Clayton, Anthony and David Killingray.** Khaki and Blue: Military and Police in British Colonial Africa. 1989. 347 pp. Paper 0-89680-147-0 $20.00.

No. 52    **Northrup, David.** Beyond the Bend in the River: African Labor in Eastern Zaire, 1865–1940. 1988. 282 pp. Paper 0-89680-151-9 $15.00.

No. 53    **Makinde, M. Akin.** African Philosophy, Culture, and Traditional Medicine. 1988. 172 pp. Paper 0-89680-152-7 $16.00.

No. 54    **Parson, Jack,** ed. Succession to High Office in Botswana: Three Case Studies. 1990. 455 pp. Paper 0-89680-157-8 $20.00.

No. 56    **Staudinger, Paul.** In the Heart of the Hausa States. Tr. by Johanna E. Moody. Foreword by Paul Lovejoy. 1990. In two volumes., 469 + 224 pp. Maps, apps. Paper 0-89680-160-8 (2 vols.) $35.00.

No. 57    **Sikainga, Ahmad Alawad.** The Western Bahr Al-Ghazal under British Rule, 1898–1956. 1991. 195 pp. Paper 0-89680-161-6 $15.00.

No. 58    **Wilson, Louis E.** The Krobo People of Ghana to 1892: A Political and Social History. 1991. 285 pp. Paper 0-89680-164-0 $20.00.

No. 59    **du Toit, Brian M.** Cannabis, Alcohol, and the South African Student: Adolescent Drug Use, 1974–1985. 1991. 176 pp. Notes, tables. Paper 0-89680-166-7 $17.00.

No. 60    **Falola, Toyin and Dennis Itavyar,** eds. The Political Economy of Health in Africa. 1992. 258 pp. Notes, tables. Paper 0-89680-166-7 $20.00.

No. 61    **Kiros, Tedros.** Moral Philosophy and Development: The Human Condition in Africa. 1992. 199 pp. Notes. Paper 0-89680-171-3 $20.00.

No. 62    **Burness, Don.** Echoes of the Sunbird: An Anthology of Contemporary African Poetry. 1993. 198 pp. Paper 0-89680-173-x $17.00.

No. 64    **Nelson, Samuel H.** Colonialism in the Congo Basin 1880–1940. 1994. 290 pp. Index. Paper 0-89680-180-2 $23.00.

No. 66    **Ilesanmi, Simeon Olusegon.** Religious Pluralism and the Nigerian State. 1996. 336 pp. Maps, notes, bibliog., index. Paper 0-89680-194-2 $26.00.

No. 67    **Steeves, H. Leslie.** Gender Violence and the Press: The St. Kizito Story. 1997. 176 pp. Illus., notes, bibliog., index. Paper 0-89680-195-0 $17.95.


LATIN AMERICA SERIES

No. 9     **Tata, Robert J.** Structural Changes in Puerto Rico's Economy: 1947–1976. 1981. 118 pp. Paper 0-89680-107-1 $12.00.

No. 13    **Henderson, James D.** Conservative Thought in Latin America: The Ideas of Laureano Gomez. 1988. 229 pp. Paper 0-89680-148-9 $16.00.

No. 17    **Mijeski, Kenneth J.,** ed. The Nicaraguan Constitution of 1987: English Translation and Commentary. 1991. 355 pp. Paper 0-89680-165-9 $25.00.

No. 18   **Finnegan, Pamela.** The Tension of Paradox: José Donoso's *The Obscene Bird of Night* as Spiritual Exercises. 1992. 204 pp. Paper 0-89680-169-1 $15.00.

No. 19   **Kim, Sung Ho and Thomas W. Walker,** eds. Perspectives on War and Peace in Central America. 1992. 155 pp. Notes, bibliog. Paper 0-89680-172-1 $17.00.

No. 20   **Becker, Marc.** Mariátegui and Latin American Marxist Theory. 1993. 239 pp. Paper 0-89680-177-2 $20.00.

No. 21   **Boschetto-Sandoval, Sandra M. and Marcia Phillips McGowan,** eds. Claribel Alegría and Central American Literature. 1994. 233 pp. Illus. Paper 0-89680-179-9 $20.00.

No. 22   **Zimmerman, Marc.** Literature and Resistance in Guatemala: Textual Modes and Cultural Politics from El Señor Presidente to Rigoberta Menchú. 1995. 2 volume set 320 + 370 pp. Notes, bibliog. Paper 0-89680-183-7 $50.00.

No. 23   **Hey, Jeanne A. K.** Theories of Dependent Foreign Policy: The Case of Ecuador in the 1980s. 1995. 280 pp. Map, tables, notes, bibliog., index. paper 0-89680-184-5 $22.00.

No. 24   **Wright, Bruce E.** Theory in the Practice of the Nicaraguan Revolution. 1995. 320 pp. Notes, illus., bibliog., index. Paper 0-89680-185-3. $23.00.

No. 25   **Mann, Carlos Guevara.** Panamanian Militarism: A Historical Interpretation. 1996. 243 pp. Illus., map, notes, bibliog., index. Paper 0-89680-189-6. $23.00.

No. 26   **Armony, Ariel.** Argentina, the United States, and the Anti-Communist Crusade in Central America, 1977–1984. 1997. 312 pp. Illus., maps, notes, bibliog., index. Paper 0-89680-196-9. $26.00.

## ORDERING INFORMATION

Individuals are encouraged to patronize local bookstores wherever possible. Orders for titles in the Monographs in International Studies may be placed directly through the Ohio University Press, Scott Quadrangle, Athens, Ohio 45701-2979. Individuals should remit payment by check, VISA, or Master-Card.* Those ordering from the United Kingdom, Continental Europe, the Middle East,. and Africa should order through Academic and University Publishers Group, 1 Gower Street, London WC1E, England. Orders from the Pacific Region, Asia, Australia, and New Zealand should be sent to East-West Export Books, c/o the University of Hawaii Press, 2840 Kolowalu Street, Honolulu, Hawaii 96822, USA.

Individuals ordering from outside of the U.S. should remit in U.S. funds to Ohio University Press either by International Money Order or by a check drawn on a U.S. bank.** Most out-of-print titles may be ordered from University Microfilms, Inc., 300 North Zeeb Road, Ann Arbor, Michigan 48106, USA.

Prices are subject to change.

\* Please add $3.50 for the first book and $.75 for each additional book for shipping and handling.

\*\* Outside the U.S. please add $4.50 for the first book and $.75 for each additional book.

# Ohio University
# Center for International Studies

The Ohio University Center for International Studies was established to help create within the university and local communities a greater awareness of the world beyond the United States. Comprising programs in African, Latin American, Southeast Asian, Development and Administrative studies, the Center supports scholarly research, sponsors lectures and colloquia, encourages course development within the university curriculum, and publishes the Monographs in International Studies series with the Ohio University Press. The Center and its programs also offer an interdisciplinary Master of Arts degree in which students may focus on one of the regional or topical concentrations, and may also combine academics with training in career fields such as journalism, business, and language teaching. For undergraduates, major and certificate programs are also available.

For more information, contact the Vice Provost for International Studies, Burson House, Ohio University, Athens, Ohio 45701.